# Kent Finlay, Dreamer

JOHN AND ROBIN DICKSON SERIES IN TEXAS MUSIC

Sponsored by the Center for Texas Music History
Texas State University–San Marcos
Gary Hartman, General Editor

Kent Finlay illustration by Sean P. Tracey, Mosquito Studios, Denver, Colorado. Based on a photo of Kent Finlay at Cheatham Street Warehouse by Brian T. Atkinson

# KENT FINLAY, DREAMER

The Musical Legacy behind
Cheatham Street Warehouse

Brian T. Atkinson and Jenni Finlay

FOREWORD BY GEORGE STRAIT

TEXAS A&M UNIVERSITY PRESS    COLLEGE STATION

This paper meets the requirements
of ANSI/NISO Z39.48–1992 (Permanence of Paper).
Binding materials have been chosen for durability.
Manufactured in the United States of America

Cover photo by Brian T. Atkinson
Frontispiece illustration by Sean P. Tracey
Back cover photo by Diana Finlay Hendricks

LIBRARY OF CONGRESS CATALOGING-IN-PUBLICATION DATA

Names: Atkinson, Brian T., author. | Finlay, Jenni, 1979– author.
Title: Kent Finlay, dreamer : the musical legacy behind Cheatham Street
    Warehouse / Brian T. Atkinson and Jenni Finlay ; foreword by George Strait.
Other titles: John and Robin Dickson series in Texas music.
Description: First edition. | College Station : Texas A&M University Press,
    [2016] | Series: John and Robin Dickson series in Texas music | Includes
    index. | Includes bibliographical references.
Identifiers: LCCN 2015038740|
ISBN 9781623493783 (cloth : alk. paper) |
ISBN 9781623493790 (ebook)
Subjects: LCSH: Finlay, Kent, 1938–2015. | Composers—Texas—Biography. |
    Honky-tonk musicians—Texas—Biography. | Talent scouts—Texas—Biography.
    | Finlay, Kent, 1938–2015—Influence. | Country musicians—Texas—20th
    century—Interviews. | Country music—United States—History and
    criticism. | Blues (Music)—United States—History and criticism. |
    Cheatham Street Warehouse (Music-hall)—Biography. | Texas—Intellectual
    life—20th century.
Classification: LCC ML429.F565 A75  2016 | DDC 780.92—dc23 LC record available
    at http://lccn.loc.gov/2015038740

Dedicated to our mentors,

James McMurtry & Tamara Saviano

My dreams are all daydreams. Usually it's something about music, something related to songs I'm writing, songs someone else wrote. Every once in a while I think about the past, but I really try to focus on tomorrow instead of yesterday.

—Kent Finlay, 2014

## "Cheatham Street Warehouse"

Waking up late in the afternoon
An old piano playing just out of tune
To the buzz of the heat through the telephone line
Some kind of song about a bottle of wine
And I knew it was you by the sound of your feet
Pushing the pedals and keeping the beat
We're a million miles away from those days now

But you can't get away from me
You can't get me wrong
I know how to keep you here
Where you know you belong
In a song

A Cheatham Street Warehouse honky-tonk song
The kind Billy Joe just can't get wrong
I'm gonna carve my name in the bar
And hope that you can hear it wherever you are
And wherever you are I'll be hoping you know
Wherever I am I'm missing you so
No longer a million miles away from anything

But you can't get away from me
You can't get me wrong
I know how to keep you here
Where you know you belong
In a song

Working on the last few lines last night
Trying to find a way to make it end all right
The telephone rang, it was you

You asked if I was working on anything new
I didn't have the heart to tell you about
The one I think I'm finishing up right now
No longer a million miles away from anything

But you can't get away from me
You can't get me wrong
I know how to keep you here
Where you know you belong
In a song

—Todd Snider, *Peace, Love and Anarchy*
(*Rarities, B-Sides and Demos, Vol. 1*), 2007.
Lyrics by Todd Snider / Shad N Froyd A Music (BMI)

# Contents

Finlay and George Strait, 1982. Photo by Rick Henson; courtesy Finlay family archives

# Foreword

I hope you enjoy reading the story of my friend Kent Finlay. He was a huge part of my early career, and I'm sure it was destiny that we met. We played together, tried to write together, had more than a few beers together, and just plain had a lot of fun together. His part in Texas music history is huge. He and his great little honky-tonk with indoor toilets gave me and a whole host of others a place to learn our craft and to learn how to be, sing, and play music on stage. Thanks, Kent, for believing in the up-and-coming Ace in the Hole Band, with a totally unknown singer who had big dreams—and for helping make those dreams a reality. I'll never forget those days. Thank you, my friend. You are The Man.

—George Strait
July 2014[1]

[1] George Strait, email interview with Brian T. Atkinson, July 10, 2014. For Strait's early years performing at Cheatham Street Warehouse, see Gregg Andrews, "It's the Music: Kent Finlay's Cheatham Street Warehouse in San Marcos Texas," *Journal of Texas Music History* 5, no. 1 (Spring 2005): 13–15. For Strait's first trip to Nashville with Kent Finlay, see Peter Cooper, "George Strait's Career Has Endured Like No Other," *Tennessean*, March 21, 2014, www.tennessean.com/ (accessed January 25, 2015). For the yellow 1976 Dodge cargo van that Kent Finlay and Darrell Staedtler used to drive Strait to Nashville for the first time, see Craig Hlavaty, "The Story of the Van That Took George Strait to Country Stardom," *Houston Chronicle*, February 16, 2015, www. chron.com/ (accessed February 16, 2015). For more on Strait's gratitude toward Kent Finlay and Cheatham Street Warehouse, see "George Strait: The Cowboy Rides Away, 2014: The Last Concert," YouTube, www.youtube.com/ (accessed January 25, 2015).

Jenni and Kent Finlay, San Marcos, Texas, 1989. Photo by Diana
Finlay Hendricks; courtesy Finlay family archives

# Preface

The quiet worries me.

We've been wiggling through Texas all week and are finally heading back from some fairground's flatbed trailer stage. My hair still smells like funnel cakes and cotton candy. Dad chooses a back road that winds through his old stomping ground, Fife, Texas, the place he feels most at home. We stop at the Finlay family cemetery and wander through our generations: Finlays, Shorts, Mitchells. I walk around aimlessly for a while and then look back. Dad's stopped. He's staring at his father's headstone. His head nods softly toward the ground. I think about the first time my dad described the grandfather I was too young to meet, James Finlay Jr.: "He was the strongest man that ever lived," Dad says. "Daddy was strong in every way. He did things well. He didn't do them half-ass. He was a great mechanic and a great farmer and a great shot. He could shoot a jackrabbit in the head at two hundred yards with a twenty-two."

My father stands at his father's headstone. Seconds turn into minutes as he shakes his head over and over. As if a timer goes off in his head, Dad looks up and signals toward our old orange Chevy van. We walk over together, climb in, and start the five-hour trip home. We don't speak. I tuck my legs under myself and curl up in the overstuffed front-seat captain's chair, resting my head against the threadbare arm. My father weeps gently. I listen to air and gravel out the window and cautiously eye my father. He coughs and tries to shake it off, noticing that I'm watching him. I'm nine years old, unsure and uncomfortable.

So, I sing:

"Talking to myself again, wondering if this traveling is good."

Dad loves singing in the van. We learned this John Sebastian song off an Everly Brothers cassette, and it's one of his favorites. Not mine. I know we're not working this one up for a gig, and we don't have time to sing for fun. We have plenty to learn for work already. Dad's still softly choking back tears, though, and I have to do something. This is what I do. I humor Dad on long drives. I sing the Sebastian song. This the only way I know to say, "It'll be okay, Dad."

I sing: "Is there something better you and I'd be doing if we could."

I wait while Dad stares straight ahead. I can't read him like usual. I realize I'm holding my breath unintentionally, but I can't let myself breathe yet.

Then he sings:

"But oh the stories we could tell / and if this all blows up and goes to hell."

I sing harmony, and Dad's tears turn to a smile. We sing the song together, and we sing another and then another, all the way home. Our harmonies fill the air the entire trip.

"Thank you for that," Dad says hours later when we climb out of the van and unload the instruments. "Thank you."

Dad and I performed together for a decade. We drove thousands of miles playing fairs and festivals, bars and honky-tonks. Our last gig was my Roots and Wings farewell concert, May 7, 1997, in San Marcos's Yancy P. Yarbrough Auditorium. We were backed by all-star sidemen—Jimmy Day (Hank Williams, Ray Price, Ernest Tubb), David Henry (Asleep at the Wheel), and Ernie Durawa (Texas Tornadoes, Delbert McClinton). It was a magical night. As I looked around the room at the amber-lit kaleidoscope of family, fans, and longtime friends, I realized how music and our crazy gypsy life on the road had shaped me, the lessons we learned, and the stories we could tell. Soon after, I moved to Nashville and got my music business degree from Belmont University. I haven't picked up the fiddle since.

Right after college, I worked at major publishing companies, independent record labels, and music history and preservation institutes. With the tools and experiences gathered from both my professional and personal life, I embarked on a new adventure, launching Jenni Finlay Promotions in August 2006. Since then, I've expanded into marketing and management with James McMurtry, dedicated to connecting an artist's music with those who need to hear it.

Dad reopened Cheatham Street Warehouse in 2000, where he continued to hone careers and cultivate the music scene around him. His story is that of a man who truly and freely gave his life to others. And those others, in turn, now carry his spirit with them wherever they go.

The stories surrounding Kent Finlay swirl and surge across Texas and beyond, told by the artists and writers and others whose lives and careers he inspired, encouraged, and motivated. "The harder you work, the luckier you get" is a point he always drove home. And whenever I am unsure about the road I've taken, lines from a certain song run through my head: "I can still see us sitting on a bed in some motel / Listening to the stories we could tell."

—Jenni Finlay
Austin, Texas

# Acknowledgments

Special thanks to our families for their ongoing encouragement and support as we wrote this book: Clay McNeill, Ted and Ruthanne Atkinson, Mark and Diana Hendricks, Sterling Finlay, HalleyAnna Finlay, Annie Finlay, Jack McNeill, Angela Williams, and Susanna Clark Atkinson.

We also owe endless thanks to our great friends Tamara Saviano, James McMurtry, Curtis McMurtry, Nathan and Ashley Brown, Harold Eggers, Sean Tracey, Gregg Andrews, Richard Skanse and everyone at Lone Star Music, and Jim Jacobs, Tony Magee, and all the fine and generous folks at Lagunitas Brewing Company. Adam and Chris Carroll, Terri Hendrix, Walt and Tina Wilkins, Sage Allen and Briannon O'Neil Allen, and the entire Cheatham Street Choir were particularly supportive as we wrapped up the book and companion album. Thanks also to Billy Abel, Abbey Road, Karina Salinas, and Cynthia White for help transcribing select interviews.

Additionally, many thanks to John and Robin Dickson Series in Texas Music editor Gary Hartman for offering this opportunity, Joe Specht for additional editorial guidance, and Thom Lemmons and Texas A&M University Press for making this book a reality.

Needless to say, this book would not exist without the songwriters who generously offered their time to talk about Kent Finlay, Cheatham Street Warehouse, and the venue's legendary songwriters' night. A few songwriters we wished to interview remained unavailable despite numerous requests but most effectively jumped when called upon.

Jenni especially would like to thank Brian T. Atkinson for the grind and the grins and for making the story better. Likewise, Brian thanks Jenni for the unforgettable journey and for opening doors to a story otherwise untold.

Most importantly, thank you, Kent, for creating such a strong and sustaining songwriting community. We hope this book honors your legacy.

Kent Finlay, Dreamer

*Todd Snider and Finlay at Finlay's home in Martindale, Texas, November 6, 2014. Photo by Brian T. Atkinson*

# Introduction

"You working on anything new?"

Cheatham Street Warehouse owner Kent Finlay asked the question almost daily for decades. Most songwriters immediately responded with their latest tune. They sang and hoped while Finlay listened closely. He heard every word. Considered every angle. Then he reviewed thoughtfully: "Work on the third line." "The chorus could be stronger." "Maybe add more detail in the second verse." Sometimes songwriters would simply receive the nod they were shooting for: "That's a nice little song."[1]

Finlay, a sharp songwriter in his own right and arguably the most respected lyrical editor in Texas, made no bones. Cheatham Street Warehouse, the legendary San Marcos, Texas, music venue that he opened in October 1974, exists for creation. Songs begin on Cheatham's stage. They grow. Breathe. Live. Earn more miles. Finally, they mature into shape. Finlay's songwriters' night, an open mike for original songs, which he hosted nearly every Wednesday night at the venue for more than forty years, nurtures singular songwriters and storytellers. Clearest evidence: the Class of 1987. "That was the most exciting year," Finlay said. "The regulars at songwriters' night were me and a bunch of nobodies: Todd Snider, James McMurtry, Terri Hendrix, Bruce Robison, Hal Ketchum, john Arthur martinez, and sometimes Tish Hinojosa, who would come with James from San Antonio. Those were the basic regulars, and nobody had ever heard of them." However, those young writers understood the gig's value. "Cheatham Street would let me play my songs," McMurtry says today. "That took balls back then."[2]

By 1987, Finlay was well seasoned at giving breaks. After all, he'd already helped launch blues guitarist Stevie Ray Vaughan, incendiary punk rockers the Skunks, and several other familiar names, including country music icon George Strait, who played his first show with the Ace in the Hole Band at Cheatham Street on October 13, 1975. In fact, Finlay effectively changed country music history—all music history, really—the day he drove the King of Broken Hearts to Nashville to record his very first demo tapes shortly thereafter. "George, Darrell Staedtler, and me went to Nashville in 1977, when George's grandfather had given him a thousand dollars to do demos," Finlay recalled. "We stayed at the Hall of Fame Motor Inn, and George even sang downstairs with the band. George recorded a bunch of songs during his demo sessions the next day. He did '80 Proof Bottle of Tear Stopper' and a song that never came out that was really country that Darrell wrote, a Merle Haggard–type thing called 'This Morning I'm Hung Over over You.'"[3]

Bucketsful more—including celebrated guitarists Eric Johnson and Monte Montgomery, deep-browed songwriters Adam Carroll and Walt Wilkins, fiery live acts Joe "King" Carrasco and Charlie and Will Sexton—have emerged from Finlay's honky-tonk stage. Additionally, legendary singer-songwriters such as Marcia Ball, Guy Clark, Ray Wylie Hubbard, Willie Nelson, Billy Joe Shaver, Ernest Tubb, Townes Van Zandt, and dozens upon dozens more regularly stepped on the Cheatham stage throughout the 1970s Cosmic Cowboy heyday. "I knew Kent Finlay, and I saw several shows [at Cheatham Street] and played there once or twice," says iconic singer-songwriter Steve Earle, who credits Clark and Van Zandt as his primary mentors. "I grew up in Schertz, Texas, and there was really only one place to play in San Antonio, a bar called The Beauregard. Cheatham Street, a hot-as-fuck tin-roof building, was a contemporary club [with] Liberty Lunch in Austin and about as far south as original music got in Texas."[4]

Several music historians acknowledge Finlay and his venue's indisputable importance in shaping modern Texas music as well. "When the annals of Texas music are finally written, I have no doubt that Cheatham Street Warehouse will be compared to Washington-on-the-Brazos," says Joe Nick Patoski, noted biographer of Willie Nelson and Stevie Ray Vaughan. "A humble little shed by the railroad tracks, it has nurtured, raised and showcased the greatest musicians this state has had to offer for the past [four] decades." "I'm proud of the great writers that have come out of there," Finlay himself said. "Tom Russell and Doug Sahm played there in the 1970s, right up through Randy Rogers in the 1990s. So many . . . cut their teeth here."[5]

Russell fondly frames his tenure. "I recall funky wood floors and cheap sweet wine in Mason jars and great music at Cheatham Street," the El Paso, Texas, resident says. "Laid back. Down-home. For me, the seventies were the highpoint of great music in Texas, and Kent was on the front lines. He knew songs and loved songwriters, and he had that old Texas drawl, a warm, big-hearted guy. Cheatham Street ranks with [Austin's] Armadillo World Headquarters and the old Split Rail on Lamar. It had the soul and the vibe: casual and crucial. They don't make venues like that anymore. You can't invent it."[6] Undoubtedly, the infamous railroad tracks behind the venue add atmosphere. "It's so unique when you're in the middle of a song and a train comes roaring by," Strait recalls. "Since

Finlay at his childhood
home in Fife, Texas, 1952.
Photo by Tommy Finlay;
courtesy Finlay family
archives

Cheatham Street Warehouse sits right beside a railroad track, that's what
you get. You just start playing louder."[7]

Kent Finlay was born on February 9, 1938, in Fife, and proof of the
same unique soul and vibe that Cheatham Street has emerges in his
songs. His finest narratives—earthy vignettes such as "They Call It the
Hill Country," "I've Written Some Life," "Plastic Girl," "Reaching for
the Stars," and "Comfort's Just a Rifle Shot Away"—measure proudly
against the songwriters he consistently championed over the years.
Additionally, he's cowritten album cuts with several artists, including
Slaid Cleaves ("Don't Tell Me," "Lost"), William Clark Green ("Hangin'
Around"), the Randy Rogers Band ("You Coulda Left Me"), Todd Snider
("Statistician's Blues," "24 Hours a Day"), and Walt Wilkins ("Blanco
River Meditation #2"). Plus, Rogers has recorded both Finlay's "Hill
Country" and "Plastic Girl." Finlay would kick off songwriters' night

every Wednesday with his own high-water mark, "I'll Sing You a Story (I'll Tell You a Song)."

The following are Jenni Finlay's selected interviews with her father, as well as my conversations with more than forty followers and friends telling the story of a man who has created an unparalleled songwriting community. "Kent's been something else," Asleep at the Wheel bandleader Ray Benson says. "He booked us at Cheatham Street Warehouse in 1974. It was packed, and we had a brand new lineup in the band. I was telling someone the other day about when I talked to George Strait and said, 'Yeah, man, when we played Cheatham Street we thought we hit the big time.' Kent has incredible staying power. He gave everybody a start. . . . [And now] the trains keep rolling."[8] As the interviews reveal, Finlay maintained a singular focus his entire life. Writing songs. Discovering and mentoring promising songwriters. Creating art every way possible. Constantly lifting his thoughts above and through the clouds. Fittingly, a swift glance across his business card immediately shows the hand held behind his eyes. The words simply read: *Kent Finlay, Dreamer.*

—Brian T. Atkinson
Austin, Texas

---

[1] Brian T. Atkinson, "Cheatham Street Warehouse Nurtures 40 Years of Talent," www.cmtedge .com/, February 5, 2014. For more information on Cheatham Street Warehouse, see Gregg Andrews, "It's the Music: Kent Finlay's Cheatham Street Warehouse in San Marcos Texas," *Journal of Texas Music History* 5, no. 1 (Spring 2005): 8–25. For more about Kent Finlay and his role in shaping the Central Texas songwriting community, see Richard Skanse, "The Storyteller: Cheatham Street's Kent Finlay on George Strait, Todd Snider, Randy Rogers and the Ongoing Legacy of His Beloved Shrine to Songwriters and Texas Music," *Lone Star Music*, March/April 2013, 40–43. For more on Cheatham Street Warehouse and the venue's role in the Central Texas songwriting community, see Lynne Margolis, "In It for the Long Haul," *Lone Star Music*, March/April 2013, 28–35; Andrew Dansby, "I'm Gonna Carve My Name in the Bar: Todd Snider on Cheatham Street," *Lone Star Music*, March/April 2013, 44. For more on Cheatham Street Warehouse's history as a music venue, see Diana Hendricks, "Cheatham Street Warehouse: A Behind-the-Scenes Look at the Storied History of San Marcos' Most Iconic Music Venue," *Lone Star Music*, March/ April 2013, 36–39.

[2] Kent Finlay, interview with Jenni Finlay, March 26, 2014; James McMurtry, interview with Brian T. Atkinson and Jenni Finlay, April 30, 2014.

[3] Kent Finlay, interview with Jenni Finlay, March 26, 2014.

[4] Steve Earle, interview with Brian T. Atkinson, January 15, 2015; for more on Steve Earle, see Lauren St. John, *Hardcore Troubadour: The Life and Near Death of Steve Earle*, (New York: Fourth Estate, 2003); for more on Steve Earle's diversity as a songwriter and performer, see Brian T. Atkinson, "Steve Earle Sings the Blues, Not Zip-a-Dee-Doo-Dah," www.cmtedge.com/2015/02/25/steve-earle-sings-the-blues-not-zip-a-dee-doo-dah/ (accessed March 1, 2015), Brian T. Atkinson, "Steve Earle Examines the Road to Recovery on The Low Highway," www.cmtedge.com/2013/05/13/steve-earle-examines-road-to-recovery-on-the-low-highway/ (accessed March 1, 2015), and Brian T. Atkinson, "Steve Earle: Boulder Theater (Boulder, CO), January 20, 2004," http://archives.nodepression.com/2004/03/steve-earle-boulder-theater-boulder-co/ (accessed March 1, 2015).

[5] "What Folks Are Saying about Cheatham Street Warehouse," Cheatham Street Warehouse, www.cheathamstreet.com/quotes (accessed June 2, 2015); Kent Finlay, interview with Jenni Finlay, March 26, 2014.

[6] Tom Russell, email interview with Brian T. Atkinson, June 6, 2014.

[7] George Strait, email interview with Brian T. Atkinson and Jenni Finlay, July 10, 2014.

[8] Ray Benson, interview with Brian T. Atkinson, March 30, 2014.

# PART I

The Story

# 1 | My Favorite Singer

*"I've written some life, I've lived some songs" ("I've Written Some Life")*

Johnny Horton was real big when I was in high school. He had songs like "The Electrified Donkey" about this donkey that backed into an electric fence and took off, a real fun song. He'd be doing Slaid Cleaves songs today. He did some really sweet things like "All for the Love of a Girl," which I loved, and some nature songs. You could tell he loved hunting and the outdoors. He ended up married to Hank Williams's widow, the daughter of the police chief in Bossier City [Louisiana], Billie Jean Jones. Then Hank died, and she was his widow, kind of fighting it out with [Williams's first wife] Audrey [Mae Sheppard]. Audrey won out, getting all the money, but then Billie Jean married Johnny Horton, so I guess it worked out for everybody. I got to go to a Johnny Horton concert at Brady High School Auditorium, which held about fifty or sixty people. I got Johnny to sign an autograph on a piece of blue paper at the end of the show, and I got to shake his hand. I treasured it until I lost it one day. Mother probably saw it as trash and threw it away.

I saw Johnny Horton a number of other times. I saw him in San Angelo by the time Tillman Franks was his manager. Tillman Franks managed Elvis a little while. He managed Claude King, and that fiddle player [Shoji Tabuchi], who's in Branson now. He managed some really big acts. Johnny Horton drifted along being really, really good. He was writing his own songs, and he did Leon Payne songs I thought were Hank Williams songs.

On the stage there at the San Angelo Municipal Auditorium, Tillman Franks said, "Hey, this guy's the most prolific songwriter I've ever met in my life. I can just give him a title and he can write a song about it. It can be anything. Excuse me, Johnny, would y'all like to hear that?" Everybody said, "Yeah." "Okay, Johnny, here's the title: 'When It's Springtime in Alaska, It's 40 Below.'" Johnny Horton went, "Well, I'm gonna hesitate some, but here goes." He started into that whole song [and performed it] pretty much in tact the way it ended up. I was pretty sure it was just a show business thing. I'm still pretty sure about that, but two weeks later Johnny Horton was on the *Louisiana Hayride*, and he said, "Here's a song I wrote on the stage in San Angelo Municipal Auditorium the other night, and it goes just like this." He did "Springtime in Alaska," and then he recorded it—had a big, big hit.

He had spent time in Alaska being a game warden. He was known as the singing fisherman. Johnny Horton started doing a Jimmy Driftwood song, "The Battle of New Orleans." It was a huge, huge hit. There was some controversy over whether he ought to do that song. The original producer thought, *No, put that out*, because it was different. But that song really changed his career. He started recording "Sink the Bismarck" and other historical songs.

He played the Skyline in Austin, and he was headed back on US 79 to Shreveport toward the Milano [Texas] bridge. He was driving a Cadillac limousine, and Tillman Franks was riding shotgun. On this bridge between Milano and Rockdale, my friend James Davis, from Brady, Texas, ran into him head-on, killing Johnny Horton instantly and beating up Tillman Franks pretty bad. Didn't hurt James. [Producer Tommy Tomlinson, a back-seat passenger, sustained injuries that resulted in his left leg being amputated.] James was going to A&M at the time, but three or four years before, in high school, he started having a terrible, terrible drinking and driving problem. He had several wrecks. He was a big fan of mine and [of] Charles Marshall [who had a band with Finlay in high school]. He loved country music, and then he ran into Johnny Horton and killed him. He showed up on Sunday back at the dorm where our mutual friend Philip Bloomer was one of his suite mates. Philip told me that he walked in and said, "Well, boys, I killed my favorite singer."[1]

[1] Kent Finlay, interview with Jenni Finlay, February 1, 2014. For more on Johnny Horton, see Paul Kingsbury, Michael McCall, John W. Rumble, *The Encyclopedia of Country Music* (New York: Oxford University Press, 2012), 229–30; Alan Cackett, *The Harmony Illustrated Encyclopedia of Country Music* (New York: Salamander Books, 1994), 80. For more on Johnny Horton's death, see "About Johnny Horton," CMT, www.cmt.com/artists/johnny-horton/biography (accessed January 27, 2015).

# 2 | McCulloch County

*"They call it the Hill Country, I call it beautiful" ("Hill Country")*

Driving from Brady to the Lohn Valley you go through Cow Gap, which is kind of a gateway, coming the other way to the Hill Country. Here are the Brady Mountains and a gap in the mountains, Cow Gap. There are eleven hundred springs, bobtail deer, so wonderful. When the Chisholm Trail was in business, one of the routes was through Cow Gap. There's a historical marker there, and that is what started the Hill Country. The government decided to repave the road there, and they just scrape off all the oak trees and build something ugly that could be in Houston or Chicago. They destroy instead of building a house around the tree or maybe not have any more shopping centers. You can't drive through the Hill Country anywhere and not see destruction. They decided to haul off the gateposts and the road. Then they put up a monument to commemorate what used to be there. It just broke my heart. Chisholm Trail was the last little bit of history. They call it progress. I call it home.

The Finlays came from Scotland. My great-grandfather, Robert Kaye Finlay, came over first. His father, James Finlay, came later. They first settled in Bee Cave [Texas] and worked cutting railroad ties by hand out of cedar. The Bradleys and Finlays saved enough money and bought that whole end of the county. My great-grandmother nominated "Fife," the name of the Scottish town they came from, as the name for the post office and [as the] town name. The family split [the land] up and built the schools. Robert Kaye was a county commissioner in McCulloch County, and they built the Waldrip Bridge over the Colorado River. He lived to be ninety-three. I was born James Kent Finlay a few months before Robert Kaye died.

My Texas heritage has always been so important to me. I'm so proud of my roots. Go back any number of generations and you'll find history-makers. One of the first poems I ever wrote had something in there about how smart my ancestors were to go just as far into Texas as you can go. Marshall Henry Short was on my mother's side, Mother's father's father. His father, George Washington Cottle, died in the Alamo. Marshall Henry Short joined the Texas Revolution—[in] Sam Houston's army—soon after and fought at San Jacinto. He was one of Sam Houston's officers. They fought and won the battle against Santa Anna. Everybody got paid in land, and he got several sections of land in Ector County, out there by Odessa [today the county seat] and Midland, so he didn't even go claim it. Thought it was sorry land you couldn't grow anything on. He went back to Bastrop and farming. Later on, he fought in the Civil War. He didn't have slaves or anything, but most of the people who fought from here didn't have slaves. Anyway, he's a definite hero. Granddad Finlay was a state representative. When Daddy and Uncle Bob were kids, they asked for roller skates for Christmas one year because they had sidewalks at the Capitol. So they would roller-skate there at the Capitol grounds. We didn't have sidewalks in Fife. It's hard to roller-skate in a herd of cattle.

We had one of the first telephones in the county, one of those that mounts on the wall. Our ring was two longs and a short. Everyone had their own ring then, and you just picked up when you heard yours, unless you were Myrtle Hickman, who picked up and listened in on everyone else's call. Grandmother and Granddad didn't have a telephone, but we did. Granddad would come over to our house to make any calls he needed to make. He'd come up and get his messages every now and again and have to call the operator, whose ring was one long, and holler, "Yes, Lohn? This is James Senior. Put me through to Chicago," and the operator in Lohn, Texas, would say, "You folks get any rain? Oh, that line's busy right now." Granddad would say, "Well, just ring me back when you get through." He'd hang around until his call came through. When we got our first dial phone, you could only talk on the phone for about eight minutes at a time, so the womenfolk wouldn't be yapping all day. I remember being on the phone with my girlfriend, Ann Fulliger, having to watch the clock and say, "Oops, call me right back," right before we got disconnected so she wouldn't think I hung up on her.

Kent's father, James
Finlay Jr., with Kent
seated on tractor, Fife,
Texas, 1941. Courtesy
Finlay family archives

Granddad taught me how to work. All Finlays are hard workers, and Granddad would pay me a dollar a day to do a job after school. We grew up on a farm digging holes, building fence, hauling hay. It was hard, hard work. If you do not get to it, you may lose it to storms. We'd go out and plant grass seeds back there at the Smith place in the back section, working on the fence and poisoning the mesquite trees, whatever there was to do.

I went to the school in the one-room schoolhouse for three years. It was one big room and educated first through sixth grades. Ms. Rice was the teacher. I'd walk to school through the pasture to get there. I learned a whole lot walking back and forth to school and catching minnows in the creek. I was on the last lap with the one teacher and one-room school, and then everyone went to a regular school in Lohn.

Daddy was the strongest man that ever lived, strong in every way. He worked hard, and he worked all the time. He whistled when he worked, which meant he enjoyed what he did even when it was dirty work. He always did things right and did things well. He didn't do them half-ass. He was a great mechanic, a great farmer, and a great shot. He could shoot a jackrabbit in the head at two hundred yards with a twenty-two. He just didn't shy away from work. One of his sayings was, "An idle mind is the devil's workshop." It's true. We worked all the time. If we didn't have something to do, we'd find something. You never run out of work to do. "Okay, we got all the cotton planted. All right, let's go fix that fence up there. We need to tighten that up." Sometimes we'd go hunting. That was work too. We would whistle when we did that too. I have a picture of me and Daddy at the house when I was a year and a half, two years old. He has me sitting on a big old tractor tire. You can see the proud all over his face. I'm sure that some of the songs, the music I did, made him proud in a way, but he couldn't say anything. That would just encourage me.[1]

[1] Kent Finlay, interview with Jenni Finlay, February 28, 2014. For more on the Texas Hill Country, see www.texashillcountry.com/ (accessed January 28, 2015) and "Road Trip: Hill Country Texas," *National Geographic*, http://travel.nationalgeographic.com/travel/road-trips/hill-country-texas-road-trip (accessed January 28, 2015).

# 3 | West Texas

*"The bright lights of Brady shine brighter than diamonds"*
*("Bright Lights of Brady")*

In my high school, the only arguments we had were who was best: Slim Whitman or Webb Pierce. Every once in a while, someone would like Eddy Arnold, but that was just the one guy. Everybody else liked more edgy stuff like Slim and Webb. Back in the day, nobody knew who wrote the songs except the publishers. People thought songs were written by the person who sang them. Until recently, I didn't know Johnny Cash borrowed some of the melody ideas for "Folsom Prison Blues" and put it all together. He wrote some of "Folsom Prison Blues" and did write "Hey, Porter," "Cry, Cry, Cry," and "I Walk the Line" and a lot of that early stuff. I think I was aware that he had written those, but before that it was just "a Webb Pierce song" or it was "a Slim Whitman song." Webb and Slim didn't write anything. At the time, we thought "Back Street Affair" was a Webb Pierce song.

Actually, I knew Hank Williams was a writer, but then I gave him credit for some Leon Payne stuff [such as "Lost Highway" and "They'll Never Take Her Love from Me"] and other stuff he did not write but I assumed he did. I didn't even know about Fred Rose at that time. Everything Hank did was going through Fred Rose's mind and editing pen. I didn't know that Fred Rose had written songs like "Roly Poly" and a bunch of Gene Autry songs when Autry was inventing the singing cowboy. He was following Jimmie Rodgers, and I knew Jimmie Rodgers wrote "T for Texas" ["Blue Yodel No. 1"] and "Waiting for a Train."

I bought my first guitar at a pawnshop in San Angelo. To get guitar strings in Brady, you went to the drug store and bought Black Diamonds. In San Angelo, they had a real music store, but they also had pawnshops.

I think that guitar cost under fifteen dollars. It wasn't much of a deal, but I played it all the way to Big Bend and back—played it and played it and played it until my fingers got big old calluses on the end. They're still there. I was able to buy another used Silvertone that I was so proud of. I probably bought that at a pawnshop too. I couldn't afford a new one, but I got a deal on that. I wish I had that guitar today, just because it was a Silvertone.

I remember going in the music store in San Angelo. Several of us went, but I was the most interested. Lohn was a pretty small school. There were twelve people and I was in the biggest class. The next class down had four people. We all did everything en masse. When I was in high school, they ran out of girls to get the government money to have home economics. I was a freshman, and they walked in and said, "Boys, y'all are gonna be taking home economics this year." Of course, we didn't question it. All the other big boys made fun of us. We got in there and started getting to cook every day. We'd make brownies and pies and all kinds of things. We all learned how to sew a hem, sew on buttons. We learned how to wash and iron. I use those things today. Nelda Moore, who [had] recently graduated from Lohn High School and had gone on to college to get her teaching certificate, was our teacher. It was so much fun.

When we would take the FFA trip, we took everybody. We went into the music store in San Angelo, and there was this real pretty girl, maybe a little older. She had a Gibson guitar, and she sang and played the guitar in a way that I hadn't heard before. She did a Webb Pierce song: "If I was free from you, my darling, I could start my life anew / We've been tied down so long, dear, I can no longer be true / Well, I know that I should tell you it would be the thing to do / But I haven't got the heart to say I'm not in love with you." I learned that song [Pierce's "I Haven't Got the Heart," a 1953 single that reached number five on the charts] that day just hearing it. She made a lifelong impression. I'm still impressed. I almost want to cry because it's an emotional moment in my life. I never saw her again that I know. I might've seen her on the Grand Ole Opry. I didn't know her name or anything, just how great she was. That was an influence on my life and probably still is in the back of my mind.

After that, I was always singing and writing songs. Singing on the tractor. Singing in the truck. Out there, the rows are pretty long. I'd get to the end of the row, run over, write down a line, jump back on the tractor, drive a mile and see if I could write another line to go with it. I remember one time we were planting cotton up to a certain point, and then we were gonna do something with the other land up there. We had a line where I was supposed to stop and turn around. I remember being way off over there in the middle of the place where I was not supposed to be, lost in a song. Daddy was running across about a half mile away, waving his hat. I thought, "Oh, man. Oh, no." I had planted all this cotton in the land and I couldn't undo it. Daddy came over and said, "Son, you have to think." Same thing I've said many times to a certain young man I know.

People could hear me for miles away. All the neighbors would say, "We've been listening to you sing." I was always so embarrassed. I was totally bashful as a kid. I wanted so much to sing in front of people, but I was scared. I was real strait-laced and wanted to do what's right. Mother and Daddy didn't know quite what to think. I think they thought it'd be a good hobby. It's not like they wanted me to hang out in honky-tonks, and I wasn't good enough to be a choir director at church. So I would sing at home, but I didn't want anyone to know it. Finally I started learning how to get out there a little bit, but I didn't sing very well at all. I sang loud, though.

We could get the *Louisiana Hayride* [Shreveport's 1130 AM KWKH program] all over Texas growing up. It came in loud and clear. We could pull in WSM too [Nashville's 650 AM] and listen to the Grand Ole Opry, but the *Louisiana Hayride* was where all the new stuff was. Elvis [Presley], Hank Williams, Johnny Cash, Jim Reeves, and Rusty and Doug Kershaw started at the *Louisiana Hayride*. I think they ended there too. The *Big D Jamboree* [on Dallas's KRLD] was similar, but it didn't have the clout. The *Louisiana Hayride* started off with Johnnie [Wright] and Jack [Anglin] before Kitty Wells. Kitty Wells owes a lot of her success and vice versa to the *Louisiana Hayride*. When Hank Williams got fired at the Opry, he came back to the *Louisiana Hayride*. I have a tape of that first night back and he's singing "Jambalaya."

KNEL [1490 AM] in Brady had a one-hour hillbilly roundup. They'd have Al Dexter singing, "Lay that pistol down / Pistol packing mama, lay that pistol down," songs like that. Mother was ironing—seems like she was always ironing—and listening to the *Louisiana Hayride*, such great music. Then they'd come on with that other stuff from New York. I don't know why they didn't play that good music all day. At that time, there weren't any full-time country stations that I know of, maybe WSM. So I started listening, and I was into music and Webb Pierce, Slim Whitman and Ernest Tubb, and every once in a while they'd play a Jimmie Rodgers tune. I remember one time hearing "In the Jailhouse Now" quite a bit.

Slim Willet, from over in Abilene, wrote this great song. He had a band and they had an hour show on [KRBC] TV. This is when we first got TV, and we had an antenna that went all the way up to the clouds. You could turn it around and zero it right in on Abilene or San Angelo. We had two different stations and we knew when Slim Willet was gonna be coming on with his band. Slim Willet didn't play an instrument, but he had a good band. He wrote this hit song called "Don't Let the Stars Get in Your Eyes": "Don't let the stars get in your eyes / Don't let the moon break your heart." I was in junior high school. I knew he was a songwriter because he was writing songs about the West Texas oil patches, like "Hadacol Corners," the name of a town out in West Texas.

Then "Don't Let the Stars Get in Your Eyes" got picked up by Perry Como, who was the top dog at the time, and he just had a huge pop hit. It was very unusual, like a Mexican song in that the line would go on and on. I loved the song, and I learned how to play it on the piano. Maybe I bought sheet music, but I played by ear. I know Ms. Youtsee that lived a mile away used to listen to me from her house because I was playing so loud. I'd bang the keys. I learned how to play a lot, how to keep the rhythm going with my left hand. My cousin Betty's first cousin, Bea Faye Watkins, right up the road, was an incredible piano player. They had an upright piano player. Mother and I used to go over and see Aunt Maude, Mary Francis, and Bea Faye. They all played a little, but Bea Faye could really play the "Darktown Strutters' Ball" and everything else by ear. She was an influence on me. I learned how to play the piano pretty good in C and G and F. Those are still my favorite chords.

After he got his check from Perry Como [for recording Willet's "Don't Let the Stars Get in Your Eyes" in 1952], Slim Willet was in the money. He bought a new Cadillac and an ice cream stand. He had both sides covered there. He has the ritzy side showing off, driving the Cadillac, but he also had the practical. If he didn't ever write another song, he had a living right there in the ice cream stand in Abilene, Texas. The first time I heard Jimmie Rodgers was on this one-hour show. Jay Skaggs was the DJ on the one-thousand-watt Coleman station. We would all listen to Jay Skaggs after school every day. He would play the hits and Dean Beard, who was a local guy who had a big following at the Big D Jamboree. I met Dean Beard one day swimming in the Colorado River at Chaffin Crossing, that's where we went after work, plowing and hauling hay and whatever it was. We'd go to Chaffin Crossing and jump in. That's where everybody would gather. Someone might take a couple watermelons.

Meeting Dean Beard was such a big day in my life. James Stewart [a member of Beard's band the Crew Cats] was my neighbor from just across the river in Rockwood. He was a great guitar player. He had a three-quarter-size Gibson cutaway electric guitar, and he could play "Boot Heel Drag" so good. We got [the Crew Cats] to come and play a dance at the gymnasium for the junior-senior prom that we sponsored. There were lots of problems in the community because it was a dance. The Baptists and the Church of Christ didn't believe in dancing, and those were the only two churches in town. We had to slide it in there. It was just wonderful. I bought this red sport coat, and I had black pants and a red sport coat, and I was so honored because Dean Beard wanted to wear my coat that night. He wore my coat, and I got to see it up there onstage. Dean Beard went on and had a full music career, but he never had any hits. He was doing rock music when everybody was still doing the Webb Pierce country stuff.

*Charles Marshall (left) and Kent Finlay. Courtesy Finlay family archives*

When Elvis came out, Dean Beard was right in there behind him with a three-piece band, and, boy, they played great music. [The Crew Cats] were a big influence on me. It was the first time I realized: you can play music for a living. Charles Marshall, who was a year younger than me, and I got together. We started doing some Johnny Cash and Elvis tunes and some regular country tunes. I had a guitar that I bought when we were on a Future Farmers of America trip. I was in junior high or first year of high school, and we were going to Big Bend. We went to San Angelo, the only town within any distance. I think you could buy guitars in Brownwood, but we didn't usually go that way. I bought this Regal guitar and practiced it and practiced it. Then I got this used Silvertone electric. Let me tell you, it was cool, a brown, cutaway, arch-top with a single pickup. Instead of plugging it in, you screwed it in on the end.

The first amp I got was a homemade one made by a fellow up there in Lohn. He worked on radios and he built amplifiers. He had two amplifiers, and I bought the cheaper one. Later on, I ordered a professional amplifier from Montgomery Ward in the mail. Wow, you talk about good. I had that Silvertone, and I sold or gave that other guitar to Charles Marshall. He was a great harmonica player but never had had a guitar. He learned overnight. He was very musical. We had a two-piece band. We entered the FFA talent show at home and, of course, won. Then we went to San Marcos to Evans Auditorium, where Elvis had recently appeared [on October 6, 1955]. We won regional. Charles had to be in the Freeport area all the rest of that summer to work so he could have enough money to go to high school, so we met in Dallas the night before we were gonna be in the finals for the state championship.

We hadn't had a chance to learn any new songs, but we learned [the 1956 Elvis Presley hit "Don't Be Cruel," written by Otis Blackwell]. It had just come out that week. We had picked that as the hit song of those two, but we picked the wrong one. We did "Folsom Prison Blues." I learned it the wrong way, but I had learned how to make that Luther Perkins sound: Boom-bop-ba-dum-dum. I was muting it with the wrong hand, but I was muting it. We did a good job and got in the finals of the finals. Then we got beat out by this pantomime group. It couldn't happen today, but it was these white boys who were black-faced, and they were pantomiming Little Richard songs. It was probably quite distasteful even then, but they were the winners. So we got beat out by a pantomime group and you can take that for whatever. We were either pretty bad or the judging was pretty stupid.[1]

[1] Kent Finlay, conversation with Jenni Finlay, December 28, 2013, and interview with Brian T. Atkinson, April 3, 2013. For more on Gene Autry, Johnny Cash, Jimmie Rodgers, Slim Whitman, Slim Willet, and Hank Williams, see Paul Kingsbury, Michael McCall, John W. Rumble, The Encyclopedia of Country Music (New York: Oxford University Press, 2012). For more on Dean Beard, see Joe W. Specht, "Beard, Dean," in The Handbook of Texas, Texas State Historical Association, www.tshaonline.org/handbook/online/articles/fbebr (accessed January 28, 2015). For more on the Louisiana Hayride and Elvis Presley and his impact on modern country and roots music, see Peter Doggett, Are You Ready for the Country (New York, Penguin Books, 2000).

# 4 | Music in the Blood

*"Laughter ringin,' pickin' and singin'" ("Going Home for Christmas")*

My parents didn't play music. Actually, Mother played piano a little bit. Her main song was "Moonlight on the Colorado." She'd do gospel songs like "In the Garden," which was her favorite song, I think. She thought playing by notes was better than playing by ear, so she would sometimes play by the sheet music instead of what she was feeling. I don't play that way. My mother's brother, Uncle T. J., and mother's cousins had a band they called the Short Brothers Band, and they would play house dances around . . . Lohn Valley. A house dance is where someone takes all of the furniture out of the living room so everyone could dance in there. They'd set the fiddle and guitar players up in the corner. I got to go to some house dances in Fife. Every once in a while someone would sing.

*Fife, Texas. Sketch by A. Shemroske, December 1975. Courtesy Finlay family archives*

The Short Brothers Band would play and Uncle T. J. would play the saxophone. He was really, really good. He played the alto sax and had great tone. He believed in harmonies and doing it old-style. He didn't play by note; he played by ear. They all played by ear. There were two cousins who were Uncle Henry's kids who were in the band. Uncle Jim's son, Clarence Short—his professional name was Sleepy—was in the band. Sleepy was an incredible fiddle player. I didn't say "good." I said "incredible." He was so good. He would show up back home once in a while. Uncle Woody would get him to come. Sleepy was probably the first real musician I knew.

Sleepy would come, and we would play second to him playing all these great fiddle tunes. He was in the Texas Top Hands, a great band based out of San Antonio. Their leader was [O. B.] Easy Adams. Easy Adams wrote "Bandera Waltz." It was a serious band, and they were one of the top Bob Wills–like bands of the time. Most bands were doing a lot of western swing at the time, Texas music people dance to. They were big enough to play with the biggest guy going then.

Everybody doesn't understand musicians, especially in a real conservative area like Lohn Valley, where you have a Church of Christ and a Baptist church and nothing else. I can remember Daddy maybe saying something like, "Get rid of that fiddle, and get him a job, and he might make something of himself." Sleepy was definitely one of my heroes. Watching him play was something else. He would sit back and close his eyes and play from his heart. He could do double stops and harmonies with himself and play all those songs from "Julida Polka" to "The Lone Star Rag" and "Beaumont Rag" and "Orange Blossom Special" and all those great tunes.

Cousin Winford and I worked a lot together in the cotton fields. I would drive the combine, and Winford would haul the stuff in the truck. When Wimp and I—we called Winford "Wimp"—would be harvesting the grain in the summertime, we would eat really fast so we could play music for twenty minutes. We'd grab the instruments and play before we had to go back into the hot field. It was just such hard, hard work, but those few minutes of playing music made it worthwhile.

I started writing songs on the tractor in junior high or high school. I have a song or two I still remember. I had a song that I thought was really good at the time ["Why Did I Ever Go Away?"]. It goes, "Long time ago in my hometown / I didn't want settle down / I wanted to go to a far-off land / And see the world / That was my plan / Why did I ever go away? / I wish that I would go back again / Do the things that I did then / She is the wife of another man / I never can go back again / Why did I ever go away? / If I could live my life again / I wouldn't do like I did then / I love her / I need her so / More than she will ever know / Why did I ever go away?" I still like that.

My father didn't play any instruments, but he was a really good singer. He did church singing. Once a month, we used to have a Lohn Valley sing-in and everybody would come from all over the valley and go to the tabernacle in Lohn. Everybody would pass out the hymnbooks and spend the afternoon singing. Someone would say, "Number Thirty-Seven." We'd turn to Thirty-Seven and it would be "I Come to the Garden Alone." There'd be a pianist playing, but we never had drums or guitar Pentecostal style. The first time I ever sang in public was there at the tabernacle. We had vacation bible school at Fife. There was Billy James Patterson and Francis Cortez and me. We did "Do Lord, O, Do Lord." I really did belt it out.[1]

# 5 | Didn't We Have Us a Time

*"There were mountains to climb, there were songs to be sung. What a time to be living. What a time to be young." ("Didn't We Have Us a Time")*

I got to see some wonderful live music growing up. I went to see Jerry Lee Lewis one time at the brand-new San Angelo Municipal Auditorium. They bought a brand-new grand piano and put it up on the stage. Well, Jerry Lee Lewis was booked there and that S.O.B. got up and started kicking the keys and jumped up on the top of the piano. He was punching the mike stand and doing all the Jerry Lee Lewis stuff, and, of course, he'd kicked the seat all the way across the stage. It's like, "You don't do that." As great as Jerry Lee was in some aspects, boy, I sure didn't take very kindly to him.

I ran into him several times down the line. Much later, we did this show in Proctor, Texas, this outdoor event, and Jerry Lee was the headliner. Emmylou Harris was on that and Freddie King, Frenchie Burke, Kent Finlay and the High Cotton Express, featuring Jesse Ashlock, who played with Bob Wills, his original fiddle player. Well, Jerry Lee got there and came in like you would expect. The manager threw open the door and said, "The man is here." Everybody looked. "Well, okay." They took him another route. He wouldn't associate with anyone out here. They took him to this other room, and he's screaming and cussing and breaking things and throwing things, and it's like, "What all is going on in there?"

The roof of the dressing room is the stage. There are stairs that come up from the inside onto the stage. Well, Jerry Lee wouldn't go up the stairs until everybody's out of the area. So, Emmylou Harris, Freddie King, Frenchie Burke, and Asleep at the Wheel, and we all walked outside for a minute so Jerry Lee Lewis could climb up the stairs. He was a crazy person at the show. Made me think back to the Municipal Auditorium

Poster for Texas Music Reunion, Proctor, Texas, May 29, 1976. Courtesy Finlay family archives

show. They probably still have a beat-up piano there where someone stepped all over the keys.

Johnny Cash said—and I believe it's absolutely true—that there never would've been no rock and roll if it wasn't for the Pentecostal church. Music was hard to come by when Winford, my cousin, and I were living in McCulloch County in Brady. We had to make our own, but you couldn't tell people you're a songwriter. I remember one time I played Mother one of my songs, and she said, "Well, that's all right but play a real song." That wasn't just her. You either had real songs or songs you made up on your own.

Once a year, the Holy Rollers—I would assume that's the Pentecostals or the Church of God, those fundamentalist churches—they would have a tent revival in Brady at this one place. I remember going with Winford. We'd drive up and park and roll the windows down; of course, you always had the windows down because it was hot summertime and no one had air conditioning. We'd listen to that great music. It was rock and roll is what it was, but it was actually gospel. It was Holy Roller gospel music with drums, great guitar players, steel guitar players, great singers, and harmonies amplified. Loud. We didn't go in because we didn't want to get too close. I guess we didn't want the Holy Ghost to get us. I had been around some Holy Roller music before, and, man, it was luring.

Anyway, I have this record at the house [1982's *The Survivors Live*] that proved what Johnny Cash said. Jerry Lee Lewis was in Germany on tour. Johnny Cash and Carl Perkins were also in Germany doing a tour. They had had a night off and went over to where Jerry Lee was playing. Of course, they all got onstage and were singing stuff that they all knew. There's this version of "I'll Fly Away," and it's just rock and roll. It's the traditional gospel, Pentecostal way of playing the song, and it's straight rock and roll, real rock and roll before the Beatles came and tamed it down. I'm talking about the animalistic, wild, crazy, and soulful music that Elvis, Johnny Cash, Jerry Lee, Carl Perkins, and even Sleepy LaBeef, all those guys from the Sun Records days—even Roy Orbison to a certain extent—all the music they were playing came out of that Pentecostal experience. I've tried all my life to write that way, but I grew up in the Church of Christ.

I saw Roy Orbison and the original Ooby Dooby Boys [the Teen Kings]. They had this thing called the Ooby Dooby bug. I don't know if it was part of the show. It's something the audience would do. It looked like someone had a chill run up and down his body, and he would wiggle and shake and give it to someone else, like a wave at a football game. I saw Roy Orbison when he was still living in Wink, Texas, and he had the [Teen Kings], and then they went off to try to make it in Memphis on Sun Records.

If you listen to one of those Elvis records recorded at Sun [Studios] and then you compare it to anything recorded at RCA Victor, it falls flat. That intensity is not there. It's smooth and nice and clean, but that intensity is over at Sun. I've always missed the fact that once it left those kind of recording studios and started getting done in London, England, or wherever, it had great harmonies and great words and all that, but it missed that animal thing. I'm talking about the Beatles and all those bands, even the Rolling Stones. They're pretty raw, but at the same time, it's gotta be a balance between the engineer making it smooth and the musicians making it raw. I prefer the rawness. Chuck Berry's stuff is so raw and nice. The sound of that guitar: it doesn't sound like someone's messing with it and making it pretty. Everything was so simple, three-piece band. Elvis recorded "That's All Right, Mama" and "Blue Moon of Kentucky" with a three-piece: guitar, bass, and another guitar.

When I was in San Angelo, we were listening to Bob Wills—a lot of Hoyle Nix and Bob Wills. My roommate Nick Fletcher was really into Hoyle Nix, who was a Bob Wills disciple. [Nix] played on For the Last Time [1975]. His big song every time he'd play a dance was "Big Balls in Cowtown." Weldon Myrick, who played on my "What Makes Texas Swing" [1975] record in Nashville, came out of the Hoyle Nix band. Bob Wills left a path of disciples. He had never gone away, but he was making a resurgence. Nick would play Hoyle Nix records and Bob Wills records, and we'd listen to them all the time. A friend of ours, Roy Parker, wanted to be a DJ, so we let him be ours in the room. He would talk into a glass. Then he started to learn how to read in a radio voice. He was very serious about it. One day we said, "Why don't you go down to KGKL [960 AM]?" That was the big station. "Why don't you go down there and tell them what your ambitions are and maybe read for them?" He did, and he got the job. It was like, "Wow. That's great." All the rest of his life, he owned radio stations. He owned a station in Comanche, and he owned a radio station in Bronte. We got him started right there in the room talking into the glass. He was great.

Every day when I was in San Angelo, somebody would come by and say, "Hey, Elvis"—they called me Elvis—"we're going to the lake, get your guitar." They would have quarts of beer, and we'd go out there and spend all afternoon out there with me picking and singing. I had a couple original songs that were hits, but I'd play country songs like Hank [Williams] and Johnny Cash especially. Johnny Cash was absolutely one of my big influences. I discovered him with his first record, "Cry, Cry, Cry." When Johnny Cash came out, we liked him better than Elvis. He had that great guitar player [Luther Perkins] who was so simple, but he worked so hard to get that sound.

I saw Johnny Cash in San Angelo. It was great, Johnny Cash and the Tennessee Two—Luther Perkins and Marshall Grant. Neither one were good musicians. Johnny Cash wasn't a good musician. They did funny little things like that one song that has a drum brush in it. He would put a piece of paper in [his guitar's] strings and show everybody how he'd do it. Then he started wearing black. He didn't at first. He had dirty blonde hair at first too.

Jimmie Rodgers carried the music image, and Texas became really, really important, not only in becoming more western. Even the bluegrass guys like Lester Flatt and Earl Scruggs were wearing cowboy hats. When Jimmie Rodgers moved to Kerrville in 1929, he posed for pictures in cowboy hats, and he made a big deal of coming to Texas. Not only did he have these pictures taken, one was in full chaps, full cowboy get-up. This is before the movies. Then he was elected to be an honorary Texas Ranger. It was a big, big deal. Before that, everybody had been wearing clodhopper brogan shoes and overalls and singing "Mountain Dew."

He called it Blue Yodeler's Paradise. I've been in that house. Can you believe that? It was up on a hill. One time we were trying to get together a fund to buy that house and make it a public place. We could send songwriters there to spend a month or a year there to write in the Jimmie Rodgers house. A Schlitz dealer owned the house at the time. He took Art Ables and me through. You go upstairs to Jimmie's room. There's a flat wall with a door, and it opens up to a veranda. It's wide, and it had a wall around it where he could sun himself for his TB. It was a mansion then, but it's a small house now. TB was costing so much money, and he needed to be closer to hospitals, so he sold it and moved closer to San Antonio. I feel blessed that I got to go into that house. Why hasn't the State of Texas bought that house and turned it into a historical monument? You can go where Johnny Horton got killed, and there's no historic marker or anything. Why not? I've stopped where Patsy Cline got killed, went out of my way to get there. That's something that needs to change.[1]

[1] Kent Finlay, interview with Jenni Finlay, January 3, 2014. For more on Jerry Lee Lewis, see Patricia Carr, *The Illustrated History of Country Music* (New York: Random House, 1995); David Cantwell and Bill Friskics-Warren, *Heartaches by the Number: Country Music's 500 Greatest Singles* (Nashville: Vanderbilt University Press, 2003). For more on Emmylou Harris, see Peter Doggett, *Are You Ready for the Country* (New York, Penguin Books, 2000). For more on Fidddlin' Frenchie Burke, see "About Frenchie Burker," CMT, www.cmt.com/artists/frenchie-burke/biography (accessed January 29, 2015). For more on Jesse Ashlock, see Matthew Douglas Moore, "Ashlock, Jess," in *The Handbook of Texas*, Texas State Historical Association, www.tshaonline.org/handbook/online/articles/fashm (accessed January 29, 2015). For more on Asleep at the Wheel, Alan Cackett, *The Harmony Illustrated Encyclopedia of Country Music* (New York: Salamander Books, 1994), 12; Jan Reid, *The Improbable Rise of Redneck Rock* (Austin: University of Texas Press, 2004), 84, 85, 180, 188, 234, 270, 281, 316. For more on Roy Orbison and the Teen Kings, see Tony Byworth, *The Billboard Illustrated Encyclopedia of Country Music* (New York: Watson Guptill, 2006), 149, 158–159, 163, 266. For more on Bob Wills, see Kurt Wolff, *Country Music: The Rough Guide* (Rough Guides: London, 2000), 92–96. For more on Hoyle Nix, see Joe W. Specht, "Nix, Hoyle," in *The Handbook of Texas*, Texas State Historical Association, www.tshaonline.org/handbook/online/articles/fni14. For more on Patsy Cline, see Cantwell and Friskics-Warren, *Heartaches by the Number*.

# 6 | San Angelo to San Marcos

*"With our plans for the future busting out at the seams, we had some incredible dreams" ("Didn't We Have Us a Time")*

My first college band was called the Card Kings. Dennis and Daniel Doucette, two brothers from San Angelo, were in it. They've both become Lutheran priests. A friend of mine named John Barrons was in it. He grew up in Presidio. Not very many people can say that. He spoke very fluent Spanish and English, and he understood the ways of the border very well. He was a drummer. Daniel played lead [guitar]. Dennis played piano and rhythm guitar. That's what happened to my Silvertone. Their father was a violin builder and repair person. He was from a Czech background. Mr. Doucette grew up over in Rowena, where Bonnie Parker [of Bonnie and Clyde fame] was from.

That was a great experience because they had a great respect for music. You could play for real and they understood that. Their parents had been in different polka bands. We wore white sport coats and black pants, as opposed to the rock-and-roll garb that everyone else was wearing. We practiced and got good. We did original songs, mostly Dennis's songs. Dennis was a fine writer. I played [an] upright bass that the Doucettes owned. I played upright bass for two years with that band. There wasn't a moment when I didn't have blisters on both my hands in all that time.

I transferred to Southwest Texas State [now Texas State University] in San Marcos, an easy choice because of the river. Today I say the best thing about San Marcos is the university, [then] the river and the music. Back then, we had the river and the university, but we didn't have music. My friend Mike Mayes and I moved here together from San Angelo. A friend of ours named Jim Boston was already here, and he showed us around. San Marcos was a small town back then and very friendly.

Everybody spoke to everybody else on campus. We all knew each other. There were less than four thousand people. When we came, we lived in the first dorm with air conditioning, Arnold Hall.

When I graduated, Lyndon Johnson was the keynote speaker. I think he was there at both my graduations. I know he was there for my undergraduate. He was also there when I got my master's. I shook his hand then, or maybe he shook mine. I'll say this: I've always been real proud to have the English literature background, and I think it's helped me as a songwriter a lot. I got an English degree and a teaching certificate. I think it helped [Kris] Kristofferson too. I was a Rhodes scholar too, but it was a different kind of road.

I had graduated from college and had the teaching certificate, but, like my friend Philip Bloomer, I was gonna go be a naval pilot and land on those little ships. I sure didn't want to crawl through the jungles, but it was just a fact of life that Vietnam was going on. Anyway, I had applied for that, and they sent me off for my physical. In the meantime, I got drafted and they sent me off for my physical too. Two days before school started, I got a letter of rejection from the navy because I had broken my back in a car wreck.

I didn't get to become a naval officer because of that. I called Mr. Clay Gassid, who used to be the superintendent of schools at Lohn, and he was a principal or an assistant superintendent at Harlandale in San Antonio. I said, "Hey, you have any teaching jobs over there? I just got rejected for what I was planning to do." He said, "Well, yeah, we'll get you a job." I loaded up everything and went to San Antonio. Two days later I was teaching language arts to a bunch of Mexican kids who I didn't understand. I had a lot to learn. Then I got a place to stay not too far away. It was really lonely.

San Antonio's not my town, but I was living in South San Antonio. There was lots of trouble. It's not the worst part of town, but it's not the best. Anyway, I hadn't heard music in four months. There's a place there called The Barn. It had live music all the time. One Saturday night, I thought, I've gotta hear some music. I knew where that place was. It looked okay. I parked, went inside, and ordered a beer. The band started playing in a minute, [a] great, incredible band.

There was this old guy who was singing so well, and he was sitting on a stool not playing a guitar, holding the microphone like it was a baby. He was singing a bunch of Hank Williams tunes. I thought, *If he weren't blind, this guy could be something.* That was one of the great nights of my life, hearing music that I'd been isolated from for a while. I walked out and [the sign] said, "Leon Payne tonight." He had been singing those Hank Williams songs like "They'll Never Take Her Love from Me" and "Lost Highway." Leon Payne's one of the great Texas songwriters who has been far too forgotten.[1]

[1] Kent Finlay, interview with Jenni Finlay, February 8, 2014. For more on Kris Kristofferson, see Tony Byworth, *The Billboard Illustrated Encyclopedia of Country Music* (New York: Watson Guptill, 2006). For more on Leon Payne, see Byworth, *The Billboard Illustrated Encyclopedia of Country Music*, 114; David Cantwell and Bill Friskics-Warren, *Heartaches by the Number: Country Music's 500 Greatest Singles* (Nashville: Vanderbilt University Press, 2003), 2, 104.

# 7 | The High Cotton Express

*"A rusted-out Dodge van with a busted-out light"*
*("Reaching for the Stars and Working for the Door")*

The High Cotton Express was the name of my band and we went on for a number of years. We got to play a lot of cool stuff like Willie [Nelson]'s [Fourth of July] Picnic. If you play Willie's Picnic, then you can quit. The main person in the band was Jesse Ashlock, Bob Wills's original fiddle player. Jesse was one of the great fiddlers of all time, and he was a great songwriter too. My favorite songs were "The Kind of Love I Can't Forget" and "Still Water Runs the Deepest." Jesse was living in Ardmore, Oklahoma. He was in Fort Worth when Asleep at the Wheel played, and afterward he called his wife and said, "Honey, pack yourself, we are moving to Austin." So they did. Lucky me: Jesse came and hit me up for

Kent Finlay's High Cotton Express, 1976. Photographer unknown; courtesy Finlay family archives

a job. Who could not hire him? So for about a year he was in the band.

He found out a month or two after he started playing [that] he had cancer. So I took him to Temple [Texas] for treatments. He told me all these great stories about the Bob Wills days. Little things that would happen and little arguments in the band. One time they were onstage somewhere at a big show, and Bob was up front playing. Jesse stepped up beside him and said, "Bob, your fly's unzipped." He said that Bob spent the rest of the set trying to keep his fly from showing, but it was just a big joke. Another time they were recording in Chicago, and they were all dressed up in their Bob Wills clothes. They were standing on the corner outside the studio and some taxi driver drove by and said, "Hey, Cowboy—where's your horse?" Jesse said, "A jackass will do. Come on." He and Leon McAuliffe had had a falling out. Jesse was always a playful guy. Leon was a couple of years younger and serious. He started in the

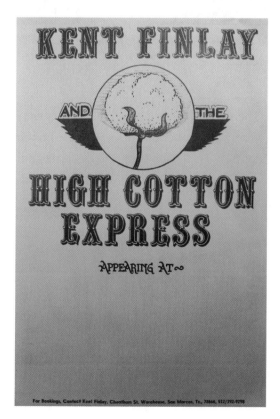

Poster for the High Cotton
Express. Courtesy Finlay
family archives

*Jesse Ashlock (foreground) with the High Cotton Express. Photographer unknown; courtesy Finlay family archives*

band when he was eighteen. There was some bad blood there. They were on the outs for a long, long time. I remember one time, we were on our way to Temple, and Jesse said, "Well, I called up Leon and we settled our differences." It makes me want to cry when I say that because that was so important. Making things right before he passed on.[1]

[1] Kent Finlay, interview with Jenni Finlay, April 22, 2014. For more on Kent Finlay and the High Cotton Express, see "Kent Finlay Plays, and Writes, On and On," *My SA* (*San Antonio Express-News*), www.mysanantonio.com/entertainment/music-stage/article/Kent-Finlay-plays-and-writes-on-and-on-5204468.php (accessed January 29, 2015); Cheatham Street Warehouse, www.cheatham street.com/history.html (accessed January 29, 2015). For more on Leon McAuliffe, see "About Leon McAuliffe," CMT, www.cmt.com/artists/leon-mcauliffe/biography (accessed May 11, 2015).

# 8 | Hondo

*"Dance in the light of the Luckenbach moon" ("Buffalo Gal")*

The first time I ever saw Hondo [Crouch] was at Terlingua, the second chili cook-off they ever had. There was this guy who got up there, and they introduced him. [Hondo] had just bought this town, and it was called Luckenbach. He said that [he and his wife] really wanted to buy Dallas, but they couldn't find anyone who would sell it. They found someone was advertising Luckenbach, so they bought it. They had an egg route and the post office. He said, "But we don't have a graveyard yet. We're looking for volunteers."

Later on, I went with some friends to Luckenbach, and that's when

Hondo Crouch.
Drawing by Charles
Phillip Vaughn;
courtesy Finlay
family archives

I really met Hondo. I was looking through some old pictures I took at Terlingua later, and Hondo was in every picture. I was always amazed that everywhere we went, Hondo was getting his picture taken. "Can I take your picture? Can I be in a picture with you?" It was constant. I looked through those pictures and went, "I did it too." He was just the world's most magnetic person. He could even get along with Jerry Jeff [Walker]. Hondo would invite him out and bring him into the fold.

That first cook-off had so much press because Carroll Shelby had flown all the press corps from the United States out to Terlingua in his airplane and made a big deal out of it. They were only allowed to bring a toothbrush and a sleeping bag, really roughing it. H. Allen Smith wrote an article in the *Saturday Evening Post* about how he made the best chili in the world. He was a Yankee guy, so, of course, his recipe has beans. Wick Fowler and them at the Chili Appreciation Society challenged Smith versus Wick Fowler at the initial chili cook-off in Terlingua. The Chili Appreciation Society was a Friday afternoon Dallas press party. Wick would cook up a batch of chili. All the press people from Dallas would show up there and have some drinks and eat some chili. Wick was always full of fun. I mean, just look at the package of two-alarm chili—that all came out of Wick's head. Anyway, that's how the Terlingua chili cook-off got started. I didn't go to the first one, but I went to the second one and many after that. I ended up being a part of that scene.

I won the Arizona state [chili cooking] championship one year. We played that cook-off, and I happened to cook and win. That was a fair judging. So, on the basis of that, I got to compete at Terlingua. I was up on the stage playing, and I had my chili going there at my feet. I kept taunting the other cooks, telling them how good my chili was. We were right in the middle of some song, and I could smell somebody's chili was burning. I got through with the song and reached down to stir my chili and realized, oh, damn, it was stuck to the bottom. It was my chili that was burning. I scooped off the top to try to keep it from tasting burned, but it wasn't quite successful. I didn't win the world championship, but it was just an accident that I didn't.

I started an annual "rock concert" after the cook-off was over. Everyone brought a log for the fire and sat on a rock and just played songs. Good friends, good songs. Terlingua will always hold a special place in my heart. Hondo was so much a part of it, and his spirit was so much a part of it. I was just totally infatuated with this guy. He was just a magnet, such a magical person. He would talk about his swimming days. He said he learned to swim in a cow track. He was on the [US] Olympic team and the [University of Texas] swim team. He was always full of great fun, always said the right thing. Governor John Connally was in the same class as Hondo at UT. They ran into each other when Hondo had Luckenbach and Connally was governor, and John Connally said, "Hondo, it's just so good to see you. What are you doing these days?" Hondo said, "I'm ranching. What are you doing?"

I always say—and it's almost true—for a while there, every song I wrote, I wrote so I could go play it for Hondo. We all wanted to make him laugh and proud. Praise from Hondo was like manna from heaven. Jim Cunningham told him that I'd written a song that he was going to like better than anything I'd ever written. So they bet Cheatham Street against the Hondo Hilton. The Hondo Hilton was a crumbled abandoned building in the ghost town of Terlingua. Hondo got to be the judge. I sang "Plastic Girl," and we won Hondo Hilton. Hondo went around, "He sang this song and he won my hotel. I was the judge."

I got a lot of songs out of the air around Hondo. "Christmas Time in Luckenbach" has Hondo all over it. "I've Written Some Life" has a whole verse about him: "I once wrote a song with a fun-loving friend / and all things were good but good things all end / We joked and we sang and shared ten thousand beers / And he died laughing and I wrote the tears / See if you read these lines on my face / There are a few verses I'd like to erase / But you can't forget memories even when they go wrong." He wrote under the name Cedar Stacker. One of his sayings was "You can't forget memories." We made a lot of memories at Luckenbach.

I took Jesse [Ashlock] over to Luckenbach one night. It was a great night. Hondo and Jesse were trying to outdo each other. Jesse said,

Luckenbach, Texas, 1976, Kent Finlay at right in front row. Courtesy Finlay family archives

"I want a glass of water." Hondo said, "I'll get it for you. Give me ten cents?" Jesse gave him his dime.

Later we did a big show at the [San Marcos] Civic Center, opening for Willie. I asked Hondo to come out so I could introduce him on the stage. "From Luckenbach, Texas, my good friend, Hondo Crouch." Hondo came up, waving, and then fell flat on his face. Immediately when he fell down—nobody knew that was going to happen—Jesse was standing there and he went, "One, two, three," like he was the referee at a boxing match. Then he took off his hat and was fanning him. I'm standing there, just flabbergasted, but Jesse was such a showman. Hondo got right up, unfazed and said, "Now that I have your attention." He told a story or some little joke. Hondo was my greatest friend ever.

I guess it was Hondo that introduced me and Darrell Staedtler. Darrell is a great songwriter from Llano, Texas. I knew who he was because he had written some really good songs. He had a Lefty Frizzell cut, and Jonathan Edwards had a big pop hit with one of his songs, "Honky-Tonk Stardust Cowboy." I met him in Luckenbach, and we just started hanging out together, of course. When we first met, he got head-over-heels enthralled with chili cooking, and we were having all those big chili cook-offs. The High Cotton Express were playing Terlingua and a whole bunch of other chili cook-offs at that time, [like] the state chili cook-off in San Marcos. We were doing the world championship in Terlingua. Darrell is the kind of person that whatever he gets into, that is what he's into for that period of time. He's totally focused like a laser beam on whatever it is, and it was chili when I met him. We got really close. He was best man when Diana and I got married. We would go to Nashville a lot because he had publishing business.

I wasn't really cowriting then, but now I wish I was. Of course, everyone in Nashville at that time was into cowriting. I know Rory Burke, because I was friends with George Strait, and this is after George got his deal. Rory Burke wanted to cowrite. He had a song idea, and I said, "No, I don't do that." Then a few months later I heard this Rory Burke song on George Strait's album, "You Look So Good in Love" (from Strait's 1983 album Right or Wrong). I said, "My God, that's a great song."

But Darrell and I were disciples of Hondo. We'd just follow him around. Hondo was in a movie not long before he died called *The Pony Express*, about the Pony Express riders, and, you know, those guys usually got killed. The Pony Express was looking for people who were ornery and mean and orphans who didn't have anything to live for when they were looking for Pony Express riders. They didn't want anyone who has anything to live for. Hondo was officiating one of the funerals in the movie. They were laying his body to rest, and he said, "Let us pray." Spit out his tobacco.

He asked if he could keep that coffin, and they said yes. He was very proud of that coffin and kept it in the back of his pick-up. One night Jim [Cunningham] and I stole the coffin out of the back of his pick-up and put it in the van. We were going to present him with one just like it to replace the one that got stolen. He missed the hell out of that coffin, talked about it all the time. We thought we got him good, but you know Hondo. He even got the last laugh there. He went and died before we could give it back. Then Daddy died a month later.[1]

[1] Kent Finlay, interview with Jenni Finlay, March 5, 2014. For more on Hondo Crouch, see Becky Crouch Patterson, *Hondo My Father* (Austin: Shoal Creek Publishers, 1979). For more on Terlingua, Texas, see "Terlingua," Ghost Town Texas, www.ghosttowntexas.com/terlingua.html (accessed January 29, 2015). For more on Jerry Jeff Walker, see Rich Koster, *Texas Music* (New York: St. Martin's Press, 1998), 36–37, 39, 42, 43, 76, 159, 195, 197, 198; Jan Reid, *The Improbable Rise of Redneck Rock* (Austin: University of Texas Press, 2004), 97, 100–103, 108–9. For more on Jerry Jeff Walker and Luckenbach, see Reid, *The Improbable Rise of Redneck Rock*, 92, 93, 104–5. For more on the Terlingua annual chili cook-off, see Original Terlingua International Championship Chili Cookoff, www.abowlofred.com/ (accessed January 29, 2015).

# 9 | Cheatham Street Warehouse

*"I own my own beer joint and sell all the beer I can't drink"*
*("I Own My Own Beer Joint")*

We opened Cheatham Street Warehouse in June 1974. I had been wanting to open a music venue for some time. I was teaching and playing on weekends in Austin, but San Marcos didn't have a music venue. There wasn't such a thing. There was no live music. We'd go to the County Line because they had a jukebox and beer. San Marcos was dry, and it obviously wasn't a good jukebox because I can't remember anything that was on it. They had a pool hall that booked cover bands sometimes, but it wasn't a music venue. There was a restaurant that had solo acts, but it wasn't a music place—just a restaurant. No one ever rose to fame playing a restaurant or a pool hall. San Marcos really needed something. Then my friend Jim Cunningham and I started doing research on places. We'd research Luckenbach and drink beer. I used to drink a lot of Pearl beer. I loved beer. Darrell Staedtler and I drank Pearl. Hondo drank Pearl. Jim drank Pearl. Then when a bunch of us quit drinking beer, Pearl went under.

Luckenbach really nailed it for me because it was pure and all about the music. Luckenbach was absolutely the inspiration for Cheatham Street Warehouse. It could be about music in Luckenbach. You could sit there and not be bothered, play for the chickens and Hondo. It was wonderful. Hondo had a way of saying, "Hey, y'all come listen to this. Come listen to this. This is good."

I also was highly influenced by Mr. [Kenneth] Threadgill's place. Every Wednesday night he'd have a hootenanny out there in his little filling station [on North Lamar Boulevard]. He didn't have restrooms. It was out in the country then so you'd go out behind the cars, and there were all sorts of people there, rednecks and hippies. No one cared about what you were wearing. Everyone loved Threadgill's, and Mr. Threadgill was all about the music. He would do all those old Jimmie Rodgers songs and all that great yodeling. The Split Rail [on South Lamar] was also a big influence. I'd go there and listen to Freda and the Firedogs. I really loved what they were doing. Marcia Ball was lead singer. All those guys in that band became good friends of mine: John X. Reed, Bobby Earl Smith, Steve McDaniels—a lot of great players in that band. They were doing a lot of country covers at the time. I remember they'd do "Okie from Muskogee," and all the hippies would sing along. It was a big anthem for the hippies for different reasons than the strait-laced rednecks had.

I met [Cheatham Street Warehouse co-owner] Jim Cunningham through his first wife, who I worked with at the school. He had just gotten out of the service after serving in Vietnam. He was so afraid of heights. In Vietnam he had been a photographer. They'd hang him out of helicopters from a rope to take pictures.

We didn't know what it was going to be called, but Jim and I had decided to find a place and open it up. We put the word out with some real estate people. They'd show us some god-awful place with a glass front, place without character, something that was "nice." It had to have character, soul, that Luckenbach honesty and reality about it.

That building had been there for years, and I'd seen it a million times. I never would have dreamed it would have wood on the inside. I thought it was just tin, which would not be very conducive to music. Finally, a real estate guy named Hubert Butler got a picture of what we were looking for, and it finally sunk in. He told me one day, "I think I found your building." We walked in and that was it. I remember taking a guitar in and strumming it and thinking *wow*. It sounded just perfect. Nice warm sound, before we even did anything. That old wood is just a perfect conductor for soulful music. Better than the Mormon Tabernacle.

It was built as a cotton warehouse in the early 1900s. I guess mules and wagons would haul the bails of cotton to what we call Cheatham

Street Warehouse so they could be loaded onto the train. There are two different sliding doors that go out to the train tracks. As a matter of fact, when we originally moved in, there was a spur right outside Cheatham Street where they could roll a boxcar up and load it up.

At the time we opened, though, I didn't know it had been a cotton warehouse. I just knew it was perfect for music. In fact, we made up the legend of Homer Cheatham. He was our legendary founder: back in the twenties during Prohibition, he had dreamed of opening up a music hall. He knew Prohibition was not working so he went ahead and built the building and waited. Sure enough, they repealed Prohibition. He was so excited, but what he had failed to foresee was that San Marcos was a Baptist town. So they voted it dry and he didn't get to open his music hall. We carried on for him in 1974 when they voted San Marcos wet. We're [carrying] on his dream. Homer Cheatham was buried on the banks of Purgatory Creek, and he never got to see his dream come true.

Oh, we had a lot of fun. Jim was a journalist and was working at the *San Marcos Daily Record*. He knew all the other journalists and writers everywhere, so when we opened we got a lot of publicity. We did a lot of fun journalism. I remember they ran a feature on April Fool's Day that said we were expanding and turning the building into a four-story high rise. We were always pulling pranks and joking around. Jim had some friends at the *Victoria Advocate*, and they had written Cheatham Street up a few times. They were about to have their Armadillo Confab and Exposition and they were going to select Miss Armadillo of the World and Surrounding Counties. So we talked to our sheriff, who was our friend, and told him we were going to go down there and do this little fun thing. He called the sheriff [in Victoria] and told him we were going to go down and to play along. So we got a cage—an armadillo cage—and got a lock and shot a hole in the lock. Just hung it on there and put a sign on the cage: "Man of Peace racing armadillo."

We showed up with an empty cage with the lock shot off of it. We reported "our armadillo been kidnapped" to the sheriff. I told them that the armadillo had little bitty ears and he had a few little hairs on his stomach. He was grey with a little short tail and had exactly nine bands. The next day it was on the front page of the *Victoria Advocate*. The next day they had the armadillo races. Now, the day before, there were just two sheriff's deputies out there, but all the deputies were out there that day because we had been on the front page of the newspaper. Marti Rowe, who became a TV personality in West Texas, was working at Cheatham Street, and she was just such a great actress. She could cry on demand. We ran up, and she jumped up and down and just started crying, holding that armadillo who had won: "Oh, Man of Peace, we thought you were lost."

It was some radio station in Houston that had really won. They started getting upset, "What do you mean? Like shit that's your armadillo. We caught that armadillo." Finally I had to say, "Hey, have fun. This is an act." Then they started playing along, but then a while later they forgot. So it turned into a little battle because we were claiming the winning armadillo, and the deputies said on the air, "Yeah, that fits the description." Anyway, we got on the front page of the paper again the next day.

That first night we opened was great. . . . We'd been working on it, and we decided, "Well, maybe we shouldn't tell anybody, and whoever comes in, we can practice on them." You know, learn how to do things. So we did that, but everyone had been watching us because we were going to have music."

That first night we didn't have music yet. Three hundred people showed up. It was packed and we didn't have help. We had some volunteers who came back and helped us. I was back there serving beer. It was a madhouse. We all told everyone, "Y'all come back. We're going to have music day after tomorrow." Someone came up and said, "I'll have a Schlitz," and I said, "All right." I found one, and he said, "How much?" I didn't even know. I turned around and had to ask, "How much are we going to charge for this?"

The next night we had Freda and the Firedogs. I remember they got there, and they opened the back door. I remember Marcia [Ball] saying, "All right!"—like, "Wow, what a place." They had a wonderful opening

Freda and the
Firedogs poster,
Cheatham Street
Warehouse opening
night, June 3, 1974

night with a wonderful crowd. It really got us rolling on the right track. All the students were there and lots of other people were too. All the Freda and the Firedog fans were there. They were going to break up real soon after that, so everyone wanted to catch them while they could. Marcia and the whole band continued to play at Cheatham for years . . . in different configurations. Everybody was playing with somebody.

Marcia sings like a bird. She really means it. She was doing country then. I remember that first record she sang, "I Want to Be a Cowboy's Sweetheart," and she yodeled—a great record. She had a record of "Leaving Louisiana in the Broad Daylight," which was the first recording of that. I remember her telling me about meeting this great writer named Rodney Crowell. Boy, she did a great job on that song. But then, you know the music business. It didn't get promoted.

*Willie Nelson and Jerry Jeff Walker at Cheatham Street Warehouse, April 22, 1975.*
*Photo by Hal Odem; courtesy Cheatham Street Warehouse archives (Diana Finlay*
*Hendricks remembers Odem giving photo rights to Cheatham Street in exchange for*
*covering a bar tab)*

One night when Marcia was playing with the Bronco Brothers, I re-member getting the call that Willie [Nelson] and Jerry Jeff [Walker] were on the way. I went up to the bandstand and told the guys, "Hey, guys, let me tell you something. Willie and Jerry Jeff are coming, and they're probably going to want to get up and play." Someone in the band, maybe Jack Rogers, thought I was joking around and said, "What about Waylon? He coming too?" Then he just froze because they had just walked in the door. It was a beautiful night.

At the very beginning, we did mostly country acts: Joe Ely, Asleep at the Wheel, and, of course, George Strait and Joe Bob's Bar and Grill. It was Gram Parsons country, not necessarily Nashville country. Joe Bob was highly influenced by Gram. A lot of people were. That's what we were about. We didn't have anything against the Nashville sound, but we tended to go the other way. There were lots of beginning bands we helped to get started. And they would sometimes switch members. It was a place where people could finally have a chance to open their minds and play whatever they felt like. We didn't have borders. In the seventies I hired Ernest Tubb for a Monday or Tuesday night, and he had a guarantee, of course. I knew we were going to lose money, but it was important to have Ernest Tubb. That night, I met Pete Michaud, who was in the band. They were all such great musicians.

I got to visit with Ernest Tubb a long time on the bus. We talked a little bit about his career. It was such a great night getting to visit with him and talk about the early days of country music. He started out as a Jimmie Rodgers imitator and knew every Jimmie Rodgers song. Then Jimmie's widow helped Ernest Tubb get on one of the radio stations in San Antonio. She got him a fifteen-minute show, and she even loaned him one of Jimmie's Martin guitars. He carried that guitar all through the rest of his life like his security blanket. He was carrying on the next generation.

The seventies and eighties were a magical time for Cheatham Street Warehouse. We had Joe Bob's Bar and Grill, George Strait and Stevie Ray Vaughan once a week, and Asleep at the Wheel once a month. I met Monte [Montgomery] and his mom Maggie in Luckenbach when he was a kid. She left Alabama and moved here. She would play and sing and tell stories. Monte and his brother started singing and joined the circle, and Monte started to play guitar, and before you know it, he was playing real good. Maggie started a band called Family Pride, and they would practice across the creek and at Cheatham Street when Monte was probably eleven or twelve. Monte grew up and really got serious. He moved to San Antonio, and he just holed up and did nothing but learned his guitar. Next time I heard him he was playing incredible acoustic rock and roll. He played a beautiful Alvarez guitar. He is amazing now. It's just awesome to sit and watch him and soak it up. It means a whole lot to me that his first gigs were here. He wrote a song about his mother, "Magnolia."

We had Doug Sahm, Augie Meyers, Billy Joe Shaver, Delbert Mc-Clinton. Delbert played once a month. He would come in and bring that fine seven-or eight-piece band with the horn section and the great

guitar player and the [Hammond] B3 organ. And Delbert on that wonderful harmonica. You know, Delbert taught John Lennon how to play
harmonica. Some people don't know that, but it's pretty impressive.
Delbert is such a great songwriter. He writes those fun backwards lines
that I love like, "She's the same kind of crazy as me."

We had Shake Russell and Dana Cooper. They would play every two
weeks. They always had a huge crowd. They were so good. Then they
decided to break up and have two bands. We booked both of them, but
neither one had a crowd after they broke up. So it just kind of destroyed
that great thing they had going. Everyone was so excited about them. Seems
like when the change came, no one had that same excitement at all.

Oh, and we had the Skunks. We can't leave them out. They were a
punk band, but they were sincere about it. It wasn't exactly what we had
been doing. It wasn't exactly the music that I was into, but they were into
it and that made all the difference. They didn't follow the rules. That's
important across the board, you know. George Strait is the savior of
country music because he didn't do what everyone was doing to country
music at the time. Every label in town passed on George Strait because he
was true to his music and wasn't going to do that pop stuff they wanted
him to do. The Skunks were true to their music too.

*Kent Finlay at
the Cheatham
Street bar, 1976.
Photographer
unknown; courtesy
Finlay family
archives*

Eric Johnson was playing at least once a month. It was always such a treat to have him in the building. He's such a fine person. Such a sincere, artistic soul. He was just a gentleman and a scholar. Such a nice guy. Of course, his guitar playing is beyond reproach. With some bands, people would come in and they'd be loose and wild and loud, but when Eric would play, everyone would come in like they were going to the opera. They'd go sit down, listen and clap nicely at the end of every song. Eric didn't sing as much as they wanted him to, but his guitar playing was captivating. I'm so glad we got to be a part of all that.

At the time, I guess I wasn't really thinking about the impact we were having on the music scene, how many bands and artists we got off the ground who would go on to bigger and better things. I guess I was thinking about how we could be open the next day. At the very beginning, there wasn't another place for music in town, so we happened to be in the right place at the right time.

It was a great music scene. Cheatham Street Warehouse, Split Rail, the Armadillo World Headquarters, [and] Threadgill's were where everybody hung out. We came together to give the music scene a community, a place to happen. We had a way of doing things in a great fun way. We had a really strong presence on [99.3] KOKE FM, which was the music station. Joe Gracey and Candy Kicker were there. We actually went together with Jim Cunningham over at the Split Rail and created the Austin music listings for KOKE. We would cosponsor the announcement of everything that was happening in town. We told who was playing everywhere. We supported each other. There was no competition between the venues. It was one of the things we did that showed our soul because it was all about the music. I remember Jim Cunningham and I went to an *Austin City Limits* one night after we'd been open for about a year. A guy came up and said, "So, y'all are from San Marcos? Tell me. I've been hearing about the Cheatham Street Warehouse." And we thought, "Wow, that was great." On September 12, 1974, Cheatham Street held a Jimmie Rodgers birthday celebration, and Eddie Wilson from Threadgill's came. I met Kenneth Threadgill, and he sang Jimmie Rodgers songs all night long.

Another most memorable night was when Townes Van Zandt and Guy Clark played. It was Townes's gig, and Guy and [his wife] Susanna [Clark] were in town and came out. In a few minutes, Guy was up there, and they were swapping songs and everything. This is back when we had a twelve o'clock closing time. It came closing time that night. Nobody wanted to leave, so we just made a deal with everybody. I told them if everybody chug-a-lugs, they could drink Cokes and coffee or whatever they'd want. They just couldn't have any alcohol. So everybody did, and we just stayed and stayed and stayed and stayed there nearly all night. It was just incredible. It was one of the most magical nights of all time, even though Townes never drew a crowd. Maybe there were forty people. That's okay, you know. The best crowds for a songwriter night are small.

We ended up charging one price for local beer like Lone Star, Pearl, and Shiner, another price for premium, which was Budweiser and Miller and such. Premium beer was a nickel more than local beer. We couldn't give Shiner away at that time. Later on, when Billy Beer was invented, we had that. We ordered ten cases and ended up with most all of it. There's this story Omar [Dykes] tells. Omar and the Howlers played one night at Cheatham Street, and it was god-awful cold. Nobody was there. At the end of the night, I gave them a case of Billy Beer, and they drank it. Omar told me that recently. I said, "Damn. You should have saved it. Think of all the money it would be worth now. Think of what I gave you."

We had the best people come through the doors. Even our audience, a conglomeration of cowboys and hippie cowboys and honky-tonk women and a lot of students, was fun. They really got it. That's really important when you're developing acts. We have students that are at Cheatham Street from Amarillo that start liking George Strait. Well, then they graduate and end up back in Amarillo, and guess what? They're still George Strait fans. So when he'd show up in Houston and other places, he already had a fan base that he had developed here. That happened with everybody.

We would have funny things too. We'd celebrate the invention of the jalapeno lollipop and actually have the inventor there. We'd select Miss

Sweet and Hot of the World and Surrounding Counties. I remember one time we had a contest for Miss Honky-Tonk Angel of the World. It was a very serious beauty contest. The girl that won was a regular at Cheatham, and she called her mother all excited and told her she had won. Her mother said, "Well, that's one hell of a title you have to carry around the rest of your life." It was lots of fun. We were always trying to do something that everyone else wasn't doing. We were pretty successful at it.

We had some great poets come through our bathroom doors. I've stolen some of my favorite song lines from our bathroom graffiti. When Todd Snider and I were writing "Statistician's Blues," he had called me. He said he'd just gotten off an airplane, and he was reading the magazine in the back of the seat. It was about people using just part of their brain. He had written, "They say three percent of the people use five to six percent of their brain / ninety-seven percent use three percent and the rest goes down the drain / I'll never know which one I am but I'll bet you my last dime / ninety-nine percent think we're three percent one hundred percent of the time." I said, "Yeah, and then the next line is: 'Sixty-four percent of all the world's statistics are made up right there on the spot." That was off the ladies' room wall. Todd said, "Yeah. That's perfect.'" We were off and running then.

There was a time I would go every single day to a restaurant called Pick-a-Taco. They had great huevos rancheros. I would sit in a booth way in the back, and it was really magic. I would work for about two hours. Then I would go to Cheatham Street and do that work. I didn't have a guitar. I would just work on paper. I would get to Cheatham before noon every day seven days a week and wouldn't leave until closing time. When I say working, I wasn't just sitting around. I was booking it, making things happen, cleaning out bathrooms, doing all you have to do. I dedicated my whole life to it for several years there.

Eventually I started running out of time. I had children, and I needed to do something to make money. Also, I needed to do something with my own music. Cheatham Street was not necessarily good for me as a musician as much as it was good for everybody else. Instead of being a songwriter, I got thought of as being a club owner, and I never wanted to have that image. So I sold Cheatham in 1988, but for a while it kept coming back like a bad penny.

I sold it one time to some frat boys. They were big guys on campus there for a couple of weeks. They had their grand opening, then nothing else happened. I had gotten my down payment, but I didn't get any more payments. I went back, and it was like they hadn't even cleaned up from that grand opening. It was just a big old mess, so I had to take it back over. There were another couple times. Finally I sold it to someone that did have the money, but then that guy ended up in prison for having money he shouldn't have had. It got passed on to someone else who also ended up in prison for selling cocaine or something.

When I wasn't doing Cheatham Street, I felt like I couldn't help people as much as I had before. I was doing songwriter shows on Sixth Street [in Austin] and different places, and I was running into different people like Slaid Cleaves, for one. I was trying to help him, but I didn't have as much help to give. It just ate at my heart because here I had made Cheatham a place with high integrity. It had always been about the music and had never been about the money, which is why I ended up having to sell it. At the same time, here we had had something special that just sunk down to being just a bar. You know, they had DJ nights every once in a while. It was just so heartbreaking. It wasn't that I missed it. I felt like I had to rescue it to save its reputation.

Fifteen years ago, it became evident that I had to take back Cheatham Street for good. It had taken a turn for the worse for a while. I had put in so much work to give San Marcos our own music scene, and it had all sort of gone away. I was teaching school and dreaming about doing concerts out in the pasture. I was playing a little bit but not as much as I needed to. We had been doing the family band prior to that, but then our fiddle player ran off to Nashville. Somebody told me, "Hey—Cheatham Street is available. Why don't you reopen?" And I said, "Ha. That'll never happen," but by the next day I was already making calls, making it happen. So we reopened. It was a family effort. We put up a sign that said,

Jim Cunningham and Kent Finlay at Cheatham Street Warehouse, 1976. Photographer unknown; courtesy Finlay family archives

"Cheatham Street Warehouse—Under Old Management." We opened New Year's Eve 2000, a grand reopening. I hosted the first songwriters' night in ten or so years at Cheatham Street.

By the time I reopened, the Texas music scene had evolved tremendously. Americana had started to happen. I was liking it because Merle Haggard got played on Americana stations. The format was so much broader. It was more based on songwriting and quality as opposed to how tight your jeans were, which had kind of destroyed country music to a large extent because it was more about what it looks like than what it sounds like. And then the Texas country thing was really kicking into gear. So all of this happened at the same time. Cheatham's main focus at the time was not only to preserve what had happened in the past but to help develop what was happening. We wanted to get on board to help all the new songwriters. We became purely focused on songwriters when we reopened. I'd been gone long enough to be pretty set in my ways. Most everything we have on our stage is something I really and truly believe in.

Since the reopening, we have become more focused on the music. We're no longer thought of as "Austin's Far Out Beer Joint" but more specifically as a music venue. I get thirty or forty e-mails every single day from musicians wanting to get in Cheatham Street. There are only seven nights in the week, so I'm limited in how many people I can help. That also means I can focus on the ones who are really working hard, who deserve the help. We've got so many fine young and unknown bands happening right now. We have the next George Straits coming through. When I look back on an artist that we helped start to make things happen, I'm just so proud.

The physical building has undergone massive renovation and improvement. We've established the Cheatham Street Music Foundation. The Cheatham Street Music Foundation is set up in the long run to hold everything together. We have a whole group of people, a board of directors, who can hopefully hold it all together and keep it as a listening place to develop Texas songwriters and musicians and bands and perpetuate the music. We put on seminars and writing workshops to help up-and-coming musicians and songwriters. We have an annual fund-raiser called BigFest. We have more than a hundred artists that show up and give their time and talents to help raise money for the Cheatham Street Music Foundation. BigFest has turned into such a big deal, a great weekend of music. Big John Mills and Redd Volkaert have their "guitar wars" every year, and it's just amazing, two of the best guitar players in the world. So many really great songwriters show up to do a short set.

It's the coming together of lots of great musicians giving back, all for the music foundation, which will keep Cheatham going as a place to perpetuate and develop our Texas music, especially Texas songwriters.[1]

[1] Kent Finlay, interviews with Jenni Finlay, December 28–29, 2013. For more on Gram Parsons, see Ben Fong-Torres, Hickory Wind: The Life and Times of Gram Parsons (New York: St. Martin's Press, 1998); David N. Meyer, Twenty Thousand Roads: The Ballad of Gram Parsons and His Cosmic American Music (New York: Villard, 2008). For more on Ernest Tubb, see Rich Koster, Texas Music (New York: St. Martin's Press, 1998), 21–22, 27, 29, 69. For more on Maggie Montgomery, see Phil Houseal, "Pickup Truck Texas," Full House January 20, 2010, www.fullhouseproductions. net/ARCHIVE2010/100120Maggie.htm (accessed January 29, 2015). For more on Billy Joe Shaver, see Koster, Texas Music, 33, 35, 40. For more on Shake Russell, see Koster, Texas Music, 200. For more on KOKE FM and Joe Gracey, see "Joe Gracey," KOKE FM, http://kokefm .com/articles/joe-gracey (accessed January 29, 2015). For more on Townes Van Zandt, see Brian T. Atkinson, I'll Be Here in the Morning: The Songwriting Legacy of Townes Van Zandt (College Station: Texas A&M University Press, 2012); Koster, Texas Music, 53, 64, 67, 199, 208. For more on Guy Clark, see Koster, Texas Music, 37, 43, 53, 64, 67, 198, 208; Jan Reid, The Improbable Rise of Redneck Rock (Austin: University of Texas Press, 2004), 99, 100–102, 105, 302, 324, 326, 328–29, 344. For more on Guy Clark and his long friendship with Townes Van Zandt, see Atkinson, I'll Be Here in the Morning, 7–18.

# 10 | Right or Wrong

*"No matter what they do to me now, they can't take that away"*
*("Ride 'Em Cowboy, Life's a Rodeo")*

I took George Strait to Nashville in 1977. George's grandfather had given him one thousand dollars to go do demos, and he wanted us to take him. It was Darrell Staedtler, me, and George. Darrell and I were going quite often at the time, every month or so. We got George and the three of us went and stayed at the Hall of Shame Motor Inn. George even sang downstairs with the band. They always had a band every night back then. Darrell was working for Chappell Music. He had a budget to demo songs, and Darrell got George to demo his songs. George recorded a bunch that day. He did "80-Proof Bottle of Tear Stopper" and a song that was really country, a Merle Haggard kind of a hit that's never come out called "This Morning I'm Hung Over over You." It was straight-ahead country, and George really nailed it. It was a drinking song, and drinking songs were out [of favor] at the moment. Vic McAlpin, a big-time writer who used to write with Hank Williams, said, "That is a hit." Vic was adamant. He said, "Take it from me. I know a hit song when I hear one and that is a hit song." To this day, I totally agree, but it's never come out on a record. Warner-Chappell owns it. They own all the Darrell songs, but they never did work Darrell like they should've. So it's still sitting there.

Buddy Spicher came up to Darrell and me after one of the sessions at [Cowboy Jack Clement's] Clement A Studio, and he said, "You guys aren't going to have any trouble at all getting this guy a deal," but every label passed on George because he wasn't going to do that pop stuff, Ronnie Milsap stuff. [Longtime Strait manager] Erv [Woolsey] had been doing promotions for MCA, and he was in with MCA. He kept talking to George about wanting to sign him to a management deal. When George finally

Promotional poster for Ace in the Hole band performing at Cheatham Street
Warehouse, 1976. Courtesy Finlay family archives

graduated from school, he took a job selling agricultural products out
of Uvalde [Texas]. He couldn't stand it. He had to go back to Nashville
one more time. [George] called Erv and made the deal, made the deal
with the devil, which turned out great for both of them. He signed the
management deal, and then Erv was able to talk MCA into giving George
a deal. Of course, George turned the whole music thing around. All those

pop acts they had signed lost their deal, and they started signing people that sounded country. George [helped] save country music again.

I met George Strait in 1975, but I already knew all the guys in the Ace in the Hole band. When we opened Cheatham Street in '74 we did it so musicians had a place to play. The guys in the Ace in the Hole band were in several different bands. People would be trading out. There was a band called Texas Star that most of the Ace in the Hole guys played in. Then there was a band called Stoney Ridge. Jay Dominguez was the leader of that band, and the guys in Ace in the Hole were playing in that band. They broke up one night, and Jay Dominguez got another group of people for Stoney Ridge, and the other guys were looking for another lead singer, so they were advertising it around.

Ace in the Hole band put out some little cards around campus and places. They were a working band that had gigs, and as soon as they got together they knew they could play at Cheatham Street. So they advertised around. I think George had just gotten out of the army. He and [his wife] Norma had moved to San Marcos to go to school, and George was looking for some country players so he could start a band. Everybody was looking for each other. One day the Ace in the Hole guys said they were going to try out a new guy and see if he'd be a good lead singer. They brought him by right after the tryout and introduced me to George. That started a long, long friendship.

The first night Ace in the Hole played, it was Mike Daily, the grandson of Pappy Daily and the son of Don Daily who owned Big D Distribution, on steel guitar. That family had been in the record business for a long time, and Pappy Daily was a very important person because he's the one who developed George Jones and the Big Bopper and numerous other people. He was the co-owner of Starday Records, which is really important in country music. Then there was Terry Hale, who was from Fredericksburg. He was a bass player, and he was enthusiastic about music, very serious about music. Ron Cabal was a guitar player and also serious about music. Tommy Foote had been the drummer in the Stoney Ridge band, but Tommy had gotten a job in Houston so he was gone when they were putting together the original Ace in the Hole band. Ted Stubblefield, who was my drummer at the time, started the band out for about a month.

Of course, George Strait was the lead singer and rhythm guitar player. He was the new guy in town, a very likeable guy, a real cowboy. He ropes and rides horses, and there's more to being a cowboy than horsing and stuff. Being a cowboy is mental thing, a way of thinking, a lifestyle. It's honor in your heart, honor toward the world. I mean, there are bad cowboys too, but it's a thing about how you live your life, following the code of the West. You have to just understand it. You have to grow up that way. You can't grow up in Houston and ever achieve the cowboy way. George was enthusiastic about music, had a great voice, and looked great, sounded great. He was mighty fine. Ace in the Hole had a good front man, for sure. Their first gig was October 13, 1975. They played practically every week until 1982. We would sit around and talk about music. I had a reel-to-reel back then, so sometimes we would listen to different things. Later on, we'd listen to the [songs] that Erv would send him. I remember listening the first time with George to "Marina Del Rey."

"I told you so" sign outside Cheatham Street Warehouse on October 14, 1985, the night George Strait won the Country Music Association's Male Vocalist of the Year award. Photo by Anita Miller; courtesy Finlay family archives

Single for Ace in the Hole, "(That Don't Change) The Way I Feel about You," written by George Strait, D Records, 1977. Courtesy Finlay family archives

George is more of a songwriter than people seem to realize. At that time, we were just getting it rolling good, and songwriters were really important. George wrote some really nice songs. He wrote several of the songs he recorded on D [Daily] Records. I believe they put out three flip side 45s. George wrote three of them. One of them was "[That] Don't Change the Way I Feel about You, Just the Way You Feel about Me." He wrote a song called "I Don't Want to Talk It Over." He certainly deserves more credit for songwriting than he's received.

I started telling people right away that George was going to be a star. In fact, there's a story that was written in *Action* magazine [in February 1977]. Sam Kindrick wrote it, and it quotes me as saying George is going to be a star. Everyone was like, "Ha. How would he know?" Well, you just know. You can't analyze it. It's like hearing a good song: "Wow. That's a hit. That's a great song." If you . . . overanalyze it, how do you know? That other song has all the same things that *that* one did, but it doesn't have that little pizzazz. George had a certain magic about him. He still does.

We always celebrated the anniversary of [the first] Ace in the Hole [gig], and it was always a big party. We'd have balloons and such. One year we had girls with picket signs marching on campus: "Ace in the Hole Anniversary." On the tenth anniversary we were, of course, going to celebrate it on October 13, 1985, but George couldn't be there because he was nominated for Male Vocalist of the Year. All the guys in the band were there at the party because this was before George was famous enough to use his own band at the awards. I don't think he even got to play. The Ace in the Hole Band except for George was at Cheatham Street, and everybody came out for it. We broke our all-time rule and brought in a TV so we could watch the Country Music Awards because George was nominated. I'll be damned if he didn't win. What a great tenth anniversary. It brings me to tears remembering. I put a sign out on the front porch: "George Strait: Male Vocalist of the Year. I told you so—Kent Finlay."

George had just about outgrown Cheatham Street by that time. By '85, Ace in the Hole were so busy on the road, and they were the hardest working band in the world. At first they had a motor home and just ran the wheels off it, and then finally they got a bus. They were out there all the time, 250 nights of the year out there, playing and selling those records, getting themselves up that ladder. I'd go see them play *Austin City Limits*. I just couldn't have been prouder.

Then, that horrible night [June 25, 1986]. We were having a fundraiser at Cheatham to raise the rent that month, called "Don't Let the Music Die." George and Norma's beautiful daughter, Jenifer, was in high school, and George was doing rather well, very successful. They bought a new house. A couple of her friends came by, and George was at home. Her friends said, "Let's go to Sonic." She said, "Hey, Daddy, can I go to

Sonic?" He said, "Of course, just be careful." Then [she was killed on] that god-awful Hunter Road, where so many wrecks have happened. It was the worst night in the world. I don't know how any of us got through it, but things like that bring out the strength in people.

I believe George's incredible longevity as a performer and all-around good guy is because he's so good and partly because he didn't fall in the trap so many people do and get swallowed up by the business. George kept control. He and Erv kept control of George's career, and he didn't ever move to Nashville. He didn't ever start getting too encumbered with the Nashville music business. The music business sometimes has a way of building someone and then destroying them as quickly as they build them. George has stayed aloof from all of that, and he did it from Texas. That's a big part. Plus, he's just so good. I mean, how are you going to stop George Strait? He's just damned good. George always has been George. He's just lived a straight-ahead honest life. Not only is he a member of the Country Music Hall of Fame, but also he's in the Cowboy Hall of Fame for roping.

I saw him perform at his San Antonio Farewell Show in 2013. There were seventy-something thousand people there. Everyone was eating right out of his hand. George was playing to every one of us like he was standing on the stage at Cheatham Street, talking about our first trip to Nashville and starting at Cheatham Street. He didn't have to give credit like that, but he did. I'm just so proud of George. I knew he was going to be a big, big star from the beginning. I told everyone. I'm really happy he didn't make a liar out of me.[1]

---

[1] Kent Finlay, interview with Jenni Finlay, February 8, 2014. For more on Vic McAlpin, see Nashville Songwriters Hall of Fame, www.nashvillesongwritersfoundation.com/ (accessed January 29, 2015). For more on Ronnie Milsap and his music, see www.ronniemilsap.com/ (accessed January 29, 2015). For more on Buddy Spicher, see "Buddy Spicher," National Fiddler Hall of Fame, www.nationalfiddlerhalloffame.org/HallOfFame/buddyspicherbio.html (accessed January 29, 2015).

# 11 | Texas Flood

*"I got a ring in my ear that you can't see, but it won't go away"*
*("If I Had Known That I Was Gonna Live This Long, I'd Have Taken*
*Better Care of Myself")*

Cheatham wasn't really about blues, but Colleen Edwards, who also booked Marcia Ball at the time, asked if I had a place for Stevie Ray Vaughan. He'd moved to Austin and was playing with the Cobras. I thought about it and gave him a shot. He was so good, but it sounded like he needed a place to start. He played a place every Tuesday called the One Knight on Red River [Street in Austin]. We didn't visit a lot when he played Cheatham. They'd set up, and once he got that guitar in his hand, that's all that mattered. He had that [Fender] Strat, you know, and he played through that Marshall stack. He'd lean right back into it. It'd be so loud that it'd be hurting everybody's ears in here. He'd lean back and shake his head and just soak in the music right in front of the amp, looking up with his eyes closed, playing. It actually really hurt our ears. I know it affected me. I know it took some of the high [pitches] out of my ears for sure. I'm sure we have some loose nails in this building because of Stevie.

The Sexton boys opened with Charlie on guitar and Will on bass. They looked good, sounded good, caught on fast. They called him "Little Charlie." He developed really well. By the time he was fifteen or sixteen, he was on the cover of *Spin* magazine. I've always been really proud of them.

Stevie Ray did a lot of traditional blues. One night we got excited because Tommy Shannon from Johnny Winters's band showed up. A few weeks later, Tommy quit his big-time gig and started playing with Stevie, and they became Double Trouble. It was really good, but we just couldn't

Poster for Stevie Ray Vaughan's five shows in April 1980 at Cheatham Street Warehouse. Courtesy Finlay family archives

get anyone to come. Week after week, there wouldn't be very many people because they'd never heard of him. Stevie who? Then he got a chance to go play the Montreux [Jazz] Festival. There was a built-in huge crowd there. So, naturally, this unknown guy named Stevie Vaughan jumped up there and started playing, and he just won the audience. "Wow. Listen to this guy play." Here we couldn't get but about twenty people to come. They would be into it, but we just couldn't get other people to come. [At Montreux], the people were already there because David Bowie was going to be there. Stevie Ray just won the crowd. He got written up in *Rolling Stone* and David Bowie asked him to open his tour. Then Stevie was gone for a month, and by the time he got back, he'd made such a huge splash. He was already a star.

The last time Stevie played at Cheatham would've been a couple of weeks after he came back from playing with David Bowie. He had a great big crowd and had outgrown us. He started going out on the road and playing huge big shows. It had really happened for him, and it had happened because people finally realized who he was. It wasn't because he was any better. He was always great.

I don't remember exactly where I was when I heard about his horrible death [in a helicopter crash in East Troy, Wisconsin, on August 27, 1990]. It was a sad day when we lost him. It still makes me sad. So many people in the music business seem to have died in plane crashes or helicopter crashes, and this was such a strange thing, flying into the side of a mountain. Trying to get out of the big crowd and everything, and there was a mountain sitting there that somehow the pilot didn't know about—or didn't remember about. Terrible.

I sometimes wonder what the world would be like if we still had him here. I think he would've made a lot more records. He would've kept on playing, and he would've become an elder statesman of the guitar. On the other hand, Will Rogers said that part of being a hero is knowing when to die. So what would we think of Hank Williams if he hadn't died young? What would we think of Buddy Holly, Jim Reeves, Patsy Cline, [and] Will Rogers himself? He got killed in a plane crash, maybe a product of his own prediction. We don't want that to ever happen, but think: Townes is so much bigger than he was when he was alive. When Townes was playing here, we never had a crowd. His tributes pack places now. Maybe the truth is maybe Stevie Ray is bigger than life because he died young. I can tell you this: there's a ring in my ear that never goes away and it's in the key of "Texas Flood."[1]

[1] Kent Finlay, interview by Jenni Finlay, April 22, 2014. For more on Stevie Ray Vaughan, see Joe Nick Patoski and Bill Crawford, *Stevie Ray Vaughan: Caught in the Crossfire* (New York: Little, Brown, 1994), Alan Govenar, *Texas Blues: The Rise of a Contemporary Sound* (College Station: Texas A&M University Press, 2008), 520, 532–40. For more on Johnny Winter, see Govenar, *Texas Blues*, 212, 292–93, 314, 367. For more on Buddy Holly, see Philip Norman, *Rave On: The Biography of Buddy Holly* (New York: Simon & Schuster, 2014). For more on Jim Reeves, see "About Jim Reeves," CMT, www.cmt.com/artists/jim-reeves/biography (accessed January 29, 2015).

# 12 | I've Written Some Life

*"As long as you're listening, I'll keep on singing" ("I'll Sing You a Story, I'll Tell You a Song")*

Back in the seventies, we started songwriters' night. Songwriters just didn't get any recognition at all. There wasn't any place to go and be a songwriter. You just had to write songs and maybe play them in the band like they were cover songs. Then this European friend of mine, name of Alex Abravanel, and I talked about having a night a week for songwriters. Alex was in school at Southwest Texas, and he was a songwriter. We just started off sitting around the woodstove, like it was a campfire. That woodstove was a centerpiece. We would have the warmth of the stove and the magic of the stove, the wood fire, and we would just pass the guitar around and around and do all original songs. Then it got a little bigger. We started meeting to bring in a little PA and setting up a couple speakers and a couple mikes. Eventually, really important writers started coming out of there, and it began to get a good reputation.

The Class of 1987 was really a good group. The regulars in '87 were Terri Hendrix, James McMurtry, Tish Hinojosa, Hal Ketchum, john Arthur martinez, Al Barlow, Aaron Allen, Ike Eikenberg, Todd Snider, me, and a couple others. Bruce Robison would come but wouldn't sing. We didn't know he was a songwriter. He was just bashful and listening. For once they had a place to be serious about what we were doing. Nearly everybody has been a real credit to themselves. They say greatness inspires greatness, and I think that's true.

[Nashville's] Bluebird Cafe opened in 1982. The Bluebird was the first songwriters' venue that I know of in Nashville. It was a big deal when they opened. I remember going there back in the day. I thought it was great. Everybody thought so about a place where you can be a songwriter and go sing your songs, but it got a little snooty. We are not quite as snooty as they are, but everybody knows that we are dead serious about songs and songwriters.[1]

[1] Kent Finlay, interview by Jenni Finlay, February 7, 2014. For more information on Kent Finlay's songwriter circle, see Gregg Andrews, "It's the Music: Kent Finlay's Cheatham Street Warehouse in San Marcos Texas," Journal of Texas Music History 5, no. 1 (Spring 2005): 17–19; "Kent Finlay's Song Writer Circle," Cheatham Street Warehouse, www.cheathamstreet.com/songwriter.html (accessed January 29, 2015).

# 13 | The Sky Above, the Mud Below

*"Saddlesore and weary, riding silent through the night"*
*("Comfort's Just a Rifle Shot Away")*

Tom Russell is a great songwriter. We had some great nights back in the seventies. He had won some national songwriting contest too, so he was starting to be recognized a little bit already. Most of the stuff he did at Cheatham Street was before he started getting things cut, but he's had some really nice songs, like "Tonight We Ride." What a big song.

His songwriting style is absolutely his own. He has great lyrics, great melodies. It was never something he just sat down and scratched out. Obviously he labored intently. He was deliberate. All those great lines like, "Strung out like the tightest wire on a frozen barbed-wire fence." He had a song called "Diamond Red" that I always loved. It was about a wino who always drank Diamond Red because it was twenty-one percent alcohol instead of twenty like Mad Dog. He's such a great songwriter, as the world knows now. Back in the day, I liked him a whole lot. He was a serious guy. He knew where his head was headed, even back then. He's got this western panoramic picture in his head, writing cowboy kind of songs. He's had his stuff covered by so many people, like Johnny Cash ["Veteran's Day"]. He's not like some cookie-cutter writer. It's not like he's getting all these little cuts and a couple of big ones.

Tom Russell was playing once a week back in the seventies. He and his partner—Andrew Hardin and Tom Russell—played every Tuesday. That was great. Not too many people would come out to his show, but it was never about how much money we could make. It was giving everybody a chance. I kind of made myself a promise when we first started that how much money someone was going to bring in wasn't going to have anything to do with it, but I have to admit, sometimes when you get broke you have to make money. I don't think I would have any integrity if I didn't feel that way. I've always felt that way, and everyone knows it. Everybody knows how broke I've always been, but it's a good broke, an honest broke.

He sure has distinguished himself as a visual artist, a painter, and he is a great songwriter. Like Todd Snider, he's become his own universe. Everybody knows who Tom Russell is.[1]

[1] Kent Finlay, interview with Jenni Finlay, March 19, 2015.

# 14 | Twenty-Four Hours a Day

*"His songs are his religion, the lyrics are the word" ("The Songwriter")*

I heard Todd Snider's "Cheatham Street Warehouse" ten years ago when I was in the hospital. Todd was here for a benefit they were having for me at Cheatham Street, and he did it for that. Not too long after, he put it on a record. He says he wrote it when he first heard about me being sick. It's about the music room at the house, [which] is just a big old room. We had all sorts of recording equipment, instruments like guitars and pianos, stacks and stacks of yellow pads with songs written on them, the first two Kristofferson records, all the Bobby Bare stuff, all the Shel Silverstein we could find. There's wonderful stuff out there. Still have most of it. Some of it got away, but I've been able to replace most of it. Todd's song is all about music and a life of music. I just thought, *That's wonderful.* Somewhere close to the top three sentences I always ask people is what they're working on. "How you doing? What's going on? What are you writing now?"

I met Todd Snider in 1986. He was a teenager at the time. He started coming around to the songwriter because he had a new guitar that he'd gotten for Christmas. It was a really gorgeous, mahogany brown Takamine guitar. He had just moved here from Portland, Oregon, to learn to be a songwriter. He was trying to get his feet on the ground. He had a bunch of funny songs. He had a really good presentation, and even then he had a lot of good bullshit. His bullshit was selling his songs. He had some funny songs at first, but they had a smart, witty humor about them. He had this one song called "Fat Chicks on Mopeds." He had another called "Stand Up if You're Eighteen," because the drinking age at that time was eighteen. Then they raised it to nineteen, so it was a protest song. He had a funny song called "Bus Tub Stew." He was working at a restaurant as a bus boy, surviving on what people didn't eat off their plate. I remember

Kent Finlay and Todd Snider, Luckenbach, Texas, 1994.
Photo by Diana Finlay Hendricks

liking Todd from the very beginning. He had his sights set on something really big. Hanging out with Todd is great fun. Once we got to know each other and I had told him that I could help him write songs, he ended up moving in and staying a while. We would write every day.

The first song we ever wrote together—it wasn't really [called] cowriting then, I was just helping him with his song—is called "This Old Guitar." We had several songs that I was just helping him with. I didn't claim any credit for it. That one really has stuck with me: "Popped a Dr. Pepper and drifted away / hopped up on a toolbox, and I began to play." We were doing that stuff together a lot, but it was his song. He was writing really good, really earnest stuff. He had that hunger. We wrote pretty much every day. We listened to Kris Kristofferson and Shel Silverstein and Bobby Bare, which is another way to listen to Shel Silverstein. We listened to other things too, but mostly Kristofferson and Shel Silverstein. We would listen and I would point out what was good. Kristofferson was a great influence on Todd and me. I try not to sound like him, but, wow, all that great alliteration and incredible rhymes that are in there. Some people might not even notice, but they hear it. Rhyme is so important, but it gets thrown out the window by some of the craftsmen. Craftsmen are the people that tend to write in appointments. They're factory writers. Todd's an artist. I consider myself an artist. A craftsman is a factory writer. There's nothing wrong with it. It's a job. You can do black velvet paintings or you can do Picassos.

We started working on a song called "Who Says It's Lonely at the Top" the night I taught Todd how to drink Jack Daniels. He'd always just put Sprite in it. I said, "Todd, you can't do that. God." So we were working on Jack Daniels on the rocks while we were writing that song. Luckily, we got the song done before we got the Jack Daniels done. It turned out to be a pretty good song. I do it all the time. I'm not sure who brought the song idea to the table—probably Jack Daniels. We were definitely channeling Bobby Bare and Shel Silverstein.

Years later, Todd had a deal by then and had already put out [his 1994 MCA Records debut] Songs from the Daily Planet. He was on tour in Arizona. I flew out, and they picked me up at the airport in Phoenix. I got on the bus and headed this way. Wherever we landed the next day, we worked all day on that song in a Wendy's. We sat there all day working pretty hard on that song, and I think we did a great job. I've always been real proud of that song. It started out with a line I'd had written down for a long time: "A skinny young man with born-again eyes and a Jesus tattoo on his arm." That's what we started with. We were trying our hand at writing a "Rosalie's Good Eats Cafe" [written by Silverstein and recorded by Bare], a song full of pieces with no real resolution, leaving the listener with nothing but questions.

One of the songs Todd has written that just blew me away when I first heard it is "Long Year." It still haunts me. Called that [knew it was great] first time I heard the song. What a great song. There are just too many songs that have just knocked me for a loop, and sometimes the really funny ones do the same thing, you know. You write a funny song, and if it's well done enough it's harder to write than something that's real serious. "Waco Moon" is another that knocks me out. Of course, Todd wrote that when [Billy Joe Shaver's son, guitarist] Eddy Shaver died [on December 31, 2000]. Todd called, and that's how I heard about Eddy. That song will make you cry every time you hear it. Eddy had played so many times at Cheatham with Billy Joe. Todd met Eddy at Cheatham Street, and then he played with Todd. I'd seen Eddy about a week and a half before that at Cheatham with a new girlfriend. I still have the note stuck on the bulletin board at the house. It just has his phone number on it. Didn't even have his name.

Writing with Todd began to seem like writing with myself. Since we wrote so much when he was getting started, he knows what I'm thinking and I know what he's thinking. I can foresee where his head is. We're both better writers than we were and write better together than we used to. If you're going to be a sincere writer, you ought to get better as time goes on, up to a certain point. However, there are cases where someone will have a three-year or two-year run, and whatever is eating them is just there. Then maybe they go off and their mind changes. Mine never has. Todd's mind is still working with great ideas and great songs. Todd Snider is absolutely the best there is. He's living in Nashville doing the un-Nashville thing. Everybody on Music Row is looking at Todd as their hero, and he is making fun of Music Row all the way. Of course, I'm proud of Todd. How can anybody not be? He's just knocking it out of the park. I take pride in everything he does. I love Todd, always have. He was like a brother and a son.[1]

[1] Kent Finlay, interview with Jenni Finlay, January 3, 2015.

# 15 | A Voice in the Wilderness

*"If he were doing it for money, he'd be doing something else"*
*("The Songwriter")*

When I listen to songs, I listen for sincerity, even if it's a novelty song. A great song does not have to be true, it just has to contain truth. Even if it's Shel Silverstein's "The Unicorn" or some other made-up thing, there's an underlying truth. It needs to be well-written, well-constructed. I'm blown away by great inner rhymes and all the things that every Kristofferson song has, those great words and the great melodies, the interaction of the words. A perfect example is "Busted flat in Baton Rouge, headed for the train / Feeling near as faded as my jeans" ["Me and Bobby McGee," a posthumous hit for Port Arthur, Texas, native Janis Joplin]. It's full of wonderful inner rhymes, and the words have such great rhythm. With those words, you don't have to have a drummer.

Rhyme always makes it more of a song. That's part of the beauty of the language. Little children love to sing "Ring around the rosy, pockets full of posies." They don't know what it means. It doesn't mean anything, but it rhymes and it sounds pretty. It's got rhythm. That's just a natural thing, even if it's [Billy Ray Cyrus's] "Achy Breaky Heart," which doesn't mean anything. People like it because it all rhymes so well and has that rhythm. It doesn't need to mean anything. I love great alliteration and great rhymes if they're not forced. I hate fake rhymes, forced rhymes. I think rhyme is a very important part of the way a song means, but there's some great unrhymed songs that I love.

There's a moment when a [developing] songwriter writes that song that elevates him. You think, *Wow, he's another one. Wow, its great. Wonder what he's gonna create in the next thirty years.* When Randy Rogers was coming to songwriter night, he had this one song called "Lost and Found."

It was a really good song. I might not have noticed him if not for that song, but it was clear and strong and had a great melody. He's singing with so much feeling, soul, and sincerity. It was a great song no matter who was singing it, but he really sang it too. Another part of a song being good is being able to sell the song. There are some songs that sell themselves, like a Roger Miller song. You couldn't help but listen.

It's harder to write novelty songs than it is to write serious songs. You've got to be sure that you're writing that line without getting silly. I mean some people write silly songs and some silly songs sell. I don't know how to describe it, really. "Plastic Girl" could be considered a dirty song, but it's not. It's about love and loss. I worked as hard on that as I did on "I've Written Some Life."

I'm finding a lot of enjoyment in cowriting lately, something I never was all that good at when I first started out. I started out doing that when I thought I was just helping other people like Todd. Todd and I cowrote some things after he learned to write everything. We cowrote some really good songs. I've cowritten a couple songs with William Clark Green, who is really wonderful. He cowrote "She Likes the Beatles, I Like the Stones," which went number one on the Texas music chart [as did Kent Finlay and William Clark Green's cowritten "Hangin' Around"].

I try to treat songwriters' work with respect. I really do respect whatever creative work they're doing artistically. It's the most important thing there is. I think that everybody that comes to songwriters' night knows that I listen to everybody. I don't care if it's their first song or if they're Slaid Cleaves. I listen to their stuff. I might not be totally impressed by their songs but I'm impressed that they're doing it. A lot of people can't really listen to music. They just pretend to listen.[1]

---

[1] Kent Finlay, interview with Jenni Finlay and Brian T. Atkinson, March 26, 2014; interview with Jenni Finlay, April 3, 2015. For more on Kris Kristofferson's "Me and Bobby McGee," see David Cantwell and Bill Friskics-Warren, *Heartaches by the Number: Country Music's 500 Greatest Singles* (Nashville: Vanderbilt University Press, 2003), 135–36.

# 16 | Good Time Van

*"Building castles in the sand" ("Lovin' You Was Easy")*

Terri Hendrix is the hardest-working songwriter I've ever met. She works so hard at everything she does. She's very deliberate. When she decides that something is going to happen, she makes it happen. She decided—back when she had that little Applause guitar and she was first getting started—that she was going to make it as a songwriter. She did. She said, "Okay, this is what I'm going to do." She made the jump and made it happen. Absolutely. She was not going to be denied. No one could stop her. That's just the way she is.

The first time I met her, she had just moved to San Marcos. She had been going to school, majoring in music, in Abilene at Hardin-Simmons. She had been majoring in music, so she came to songwriters' night. She had an Ovation Applause guitar with probably the original strings on it. She was trying to learn how to write. You know, she'd been majoring in music, so she sounded like she was a music major. That's when I first met her. She sang like you're supposed to, but she was very, very likeable and enthusiastic and so willing and anxious to learn. She started coming out on a regular basis. Somewhere right along about then, maybe just a little after, I took a hiatus from Cheatham Street and doing the songwriter night over at the depot in Katy Station. Katy Station was not the ideal place to be doing a songwriter night. It was always sort of more of a bar than a music place. Betty Elders was a regular there and Eric Moll. Todd and john Arthur martinez. There were a lot of people who were regulars, but it wasn't a good place to do it.

Terri slowly developed the unique style she has now. It was fun to watch that happen. She was always an intentional songwriter and did everything purposefully. I think she was always intent on learning. Honing

# NEW YEAR'S EVE
## CHEATHAM ST. WAREHOUSE
### SAN MARCOS, TEXAS

# TERRI HENDRIX

SUNDAY • DEC. 31, 2000

$15 ADVANCE
$18 AT DOOR

ON SALE NOW
AT SUNDANCE RECORDS
AND CHEATHAM STREET
WAREHOUSE

Photo by Carl H. Deal, III

with special guest

Adam Carroll

WWW.CHEATHAMSTREET.COM
512-353-3777

Poster for Terri Hendrix's New Year's Eve 2000 show with Adam Carroll at Cheatham Street Warehouse. Courtesy Finlay family archives

her skills. I think [Texas State University professor] Grant Mazak taught her a whole lot in the beginning. She was developing her style the whole time. She was always coming up with sweet, fun songs that just made people feel good. It's what she specializes in, making people feel good. Like "Hole in My Pocket." I'm smiling now, thinking about it. Songs like that. It took her a long time for everything to start to click for her, but she was just so persistent. She knew what she wanted to do, and she just kept hammering away at it. My favorite quote: "The harder I work, the luckier I get." That's the way it works in the music business. She's one of the luckiest people I know. Then she and [multi-instrumentalist and producer] Lloyd [Maines] tied up together. That was just a big, big thing for her because Lloyd is a giant musician. It turned into a lucrative and positive thing for both of them.

She recorded a live record at Cheatham Street right after the reopening [2001's *Live in San Marcos*]. She recorded all of her hits, and Lloyd produced it, of course. Incredible live versions. Terri Hendrix live is a beautiful thing. Cheatham Street's got that beautiful sound with all that old wood, just a magic room. I mean, I didn't build it, but I found it, so I take credit. What a great sounding room. It's like finding the Mormon Tabernacle. The acoustics are just great there. It was great to be there for that experience. We did it over two nights and made two versions of it.

Now Terri's creating a really important foundation to give back to our community [the Own Your Own Universe Center]. I'm very proud of her for feeling that need to give back to the San Marcos community. We felt it too. I think her foundation will be quite similar to what we're doing but different. We can support each other. She's such a big part of Cheatham Street's success, and she's spreading our legacy of giving back and bringing up future songwriters. She teaches songwriting seminars, gives back and helps people achieve the things that she achieved on her own. Terri Hendrix is not simply a singer-songwriter, she's also a teacher and an author and someone that makes things happen. I don't know if she got anything from me or not, but I hope I have some of that in me too.[1]

---

[1] Kent Finlay, interview with Jenni Finlay, April 22, 2015. For more on Betty Elders, see www .bettyelders.com/ (accessed May 13, 2015).

# 17 | Purgatory Road

*"Living in the fast lane and writin' night and day"*
*("How Much Abuse Can This Old Body Take")*

I met john Arthur martinez when he was going to school at Southwest Texas State. He came to songwriters' night pretty regularly. He's such a sharp guy, a really smart guy. Real serious about music. He really worked hard on his guitar and his songs. I remember one of his first songs, "Canta Papa," and it's still one of my favorite of his songs. It's about his father, who was a musician. Arthur was not around his father a lot growing up, but he knew that his father was a musician so it had a profound effect on him. He was Arthur Martinez, but then he added the "john."

I got to take him to Nashville the first time he went, and I remember one great night while we were there. There was a little place, more of a restaurant bar, where we saw Ed Bruce, Harlan Howard, and Glenn Ray at a song swap. Ed Bruce was singing "Mamas Don't Let Your Babies Grow Up to Be Cowboys," and Glenn Ray sang his song "I Just Came Home to Count the Memories" [a top-ten hit for John Anderson in 1982]. We just sat there and listened, and john Arthur came back from the restroom. He told me that he had met Harlan Howard in there and they shook hands. I thought that was pretty neat. Only in Nashville can you go to the bathroom and meet Harlan Howard and be on equal ground. The Harlan Howard.

Arthur and I hit it off right away. He's always enthusiastic and positive, and he and I have written many songs together. We had a great trip that time. Went around and heard a lot of music. We played a lot of songwriter open mike kind of things. We were in a contest, and I won the contest, by the way, with "Plastic Girl." I had to be back the next week to defend my title and win a guitar, but I didn't go back.

*john Arthur martinez. Courtesy Finlay family archives*

I'm always so proud of everybody who's gotten their start at Cheatham. It's really nice to feel like you've gotten to be a little part of their development as a songwriter. john Arthur and I are friends forever. We used to meet in Blanco, and we would write. We even, for a while, would meet at a barbecue place in Austin right there on a creek. There were water moccasins everywhere, and one day this water moccasin was up on the deck with us. Really. A damned water moccasin. They come after people. Suffice to say, we don't meet there anymore. We still write together. We have some songs going [that] we need to finish. We've got a beautiful, beautiful song called "Where Do We Go From Here: "Where do we go from here / It is becoming increasingly clear / We can't go on hiding / It's time for deciding / Where do we go from here." It's a cheating song.

I've been so proud to watch john Arthur's evolution as a songwriter. He wasn't as country to start with, but now he's solid country. Of course, he's done that Nashville Star thing and has been highly successful in the music business. You can be highly successful in the music business in so many ways. One way is to sell a lot of records. One way is to have a great career as a dance hall band. There are some dance hall bands who have never had a hit record, but, man, they're great. They pack them in everywhere they go. Sometimes having songs people respect is another kind of success, and they don't have to necessarily be hit songs. Just getting to keep on doing it. john Arthur works all the time, sometimes six nights a week. He's a big success.[1]

---

[1] Kent Finlay, interview with Jenni Finlay, March 19, 2015. For more on Ed Bruce, see www.edbrucemusic.com/ (accessed January 29, 2015). For more on Harlan Howard, see "Harlan Howard," Songwriters Hall of Fame, www.songwritershalloffame.org/exhibits/bio/C136 (accessed January 29, 2015).

# 18 | Home Again

*"I've lived rhymes for reasons and my reasons were strong"*
*("I've Written Some Life")*

I heard Adam Carroll on the radio. I had to turn it up it was so good. Lloyd Maines had produced his first record, and I got a copy of that record as soon as I could. Adam's voice had a quality that just draws you in, and the way it was produced was so wonderful. It kept you interested in everything. He had that great song, "Cain River Blues." I really fell in love with Adam. I met him in New Braunfels before we reopened Cheatham Street, and he was playing that Gibson guitar that I have now. I thoroughly enjoyed it and got to meet him. He was just getting started. Wouldn't you know, it wasn't that long after that that I'd been bit by the bug again, and I reopened Cheatham Street. So there Adam was.

His *Live at Cheatham Street* is one of my favorite records still. It was such a great performance of "Red Bandana Blues." The harmonica is phenomenal. It was like he was just playing off of the top of his head and making it up as he was going. Everyone's heart reaches out to him when he's on stage. He's got that magic thing. I can't describe it, but he's definitely got it. He's so genuine.[1]

---

[1] Kent Finlay, interview with Jenni Finlay and Brian T. Atkinson, March 19, 2015. For more on legendary instrumentalist and producer Lloyd Maines, see Rich Koster, *Texas Music* (New York: St. Martin's Press, 1998), 44; Lydia Hutchinson, "Lloyd Maines," *Performing Songwriter*, June 23, 2013, www.performingsongwriter.com/lloyd-maines (accessed June 2, 2015).

Poster for Adam Carroll at Cheatham Street Warehouse, June 8, 2001. Courtesy Finlay family archives

# 19 | Don't Tell Me

*"So you'll remember me after I'm gone" ("I've Written Some Life")*

Slaid Cleaves was still living in Maine when I met him. He was here checking out Austin, thinking he might want to move here or might want to move to Nashville. I didn't have Cheatham Street, but I was doing a songwriter night at Headliners East on Sixth Street in Austin. Sixth Street was not as bad back then as it is now. Headliners was right in the middle of Sixth Street. Actually, it was the first venue there, something other than a sex shop. Terry Boothe owned the building. Terry is the one that started developing Sixth Street. Terry's vision for Sixth Street was for it to be something representative of Texas, but it all kind of got away from him. Headliners was good, and I was doing a songwriter circle, and someone brought Slaid by there. I got him to do a couple songs. He had a nice old Gibson guitar that had a special pickup on it. Sounded really good.

A few weeks later, here he was. We came back to songwriters' night, and we hit it off real well. He's a likable, talented person. He is very careful and thoughtful about what he writes. He doesn't just jot down the next line that comes through his head. He's very deliberate. He's no craftsman. He likes a little humor, you know. He likes it to have a nice twist. He likes the melody and the lyrics to jive. He and Karen Posten have written some things that are really nice. I love "Drinking Days." My, what a song. It has a nice twist at the end.

Todd had moved on and done real well. I was looking for someone else to work with. I've always been a teacher, schoolteacher, and that kind of carries on into everything else like songwriting. You know, I was trying to help somebody get the next notch up the ladder. I thought Slaid probably needed someone to get in there with him, and I wanted to do it. One of the first songs we wrote together is called "Lost."

*Kent Finlay and Slaid Cleaves, 1990s. Courtesy Finlay family archives*

We started getting together and writing, just once a week. We'd meet over at Camp Ben McCulloch [in Driftwood, Texas], across from the Salt Lick barbecue place about once a week. We'd sit there on one of those tables and work on songs. Sometimes we would get together when [my youngest daughter] HalleyAnna was little, and they had the playscape there in San Marcos by the river. I would take HalleyAnna over to the playscape so she could play, and Slaid and I would sit over there at one of those tables and work on songs. We did that on a religious basis for a while. Slaid's really turned into one of the leading songwriters of the world. Of course, I love "Broke Down," which he wrote with Rod Picott [Cleaves's childhood friend and current Nashville-based songwriter].

We wrote a song that appeared on his [1997] album *No Angel Knows* called "Don't Tell Me It's All Right" ["Don't Tell Me"]. We were actually working on a song called "It's Going to Be All Right" out at Camp Ben

McCulloch. We worked all afternoon on that song. It was coming really good but so slow, and finally we said, "Okay, well, let's call it. We've got to get out of here in about fifteen minutes." So we quit working on that song, and all of a sudden Slaid came up with maybe the idea [of] "Don't tell me it's all right." In fifteen minutes that other song came out like that, real fast. Sometimes you have to grab them when they're coming by.[1]

[1] Kent Finlay, interview with Jenni Finlay, March 19, 2015. For more on Terry Boothe, see "'Empresario' Terry Boothe," Frontier Times Museum, www.frontiertimesmuseum.org/terry-boothe.html (accessed January 29, 2015).

# 20 | Lost and Found

*"The harder I work, the faster it goes"*
*("How Much Abuse Can This Old Body Take")*

Randy Rogers started coming to the songwriter circle in 2000, right after we reopened. He was also coming to the Monday night jam. I met him at that time and started hearing the songs. He sang with so much feeling and soul and sincerity. I told him one day, "Hey, let me buy lunch at Garcia's." So we went to Garcia's the next day. I told him that I was really impressed with that song and his soul, with the sincerity. If he put together a band, I would be happy to help him get it going. I'd give him every Tuesday night like I'd given Stevie Ray [a] night. We called it "the Stevie Ray night" because Stevie Ray started out on Tuesday nights, which means that also Will Sexton and Charlie Sexton started out on Tuesday night too, because they started out opening for him. Tuesdays are just a special night to help new, unknown people get started. It happens over and over. I don't know why it's Tuesday, but it just is. So anyway, I told Randy, "Think about this. I'm talking about, 'You have to work really, really hard.' It's not easy. If you really want to work, I think something could happen. I would be happy to help you and would do what I could do." He said okay, he would think about it.

Later on that same day, he called and said, "I've already got a guitar player." That's how that happened. We started doing every Tuesday night, and we did it for several years. He built up a good, strong fan base. His band got tighter and better. Every time someone would leave the band, he'd find someone better, and the band got really, really good. He was writing lots of other good songs.

One of his first band gigs was a real magical night. There was a thunderstorm and flood in San Marcos the night they were playing. Just as they started their first set, all the power in that part of town went out. Everything

*Randy Rogers at the time of signing his first record contract, Cheatham Street Warehouse, July 30, 2005. Courtesy Finlay family archives*

was blacked out. We found some candles and a couple oil lamps. Someone shined their headlights in the front door to get a little light in there. It was just a little bit of dim light, and there were candles. Randy hopped up on the bar with just his acoustic guitar and started playing. It was wonderful, just wonderful.

There was a guy there that played fiddle. His name was Brady Black. He said, "Hey, I've got my fiddle in the car. Would you like for me to go get it?" Randy said, "Yeah." So Brady ran out and got his fiddle, and he came in. That was the first time Brady and Randy had played together. It was just total by accident by storm. It was probably the best night we ever had, just a magical night. There was rain and thunder and lightning outside, but it was dark inside when they were playing. Brady had been playing with Dub Miller. A few months later, Dub decided he was going to quit and go back to law school, so Randy was able to pick up Brady. He got a big boost in his band based on that accidental night when Brady was playing during the storm.

Brady changed the band entirely. Brady is a big part of the sound of the band, a big part of the look of the band. He totally gave it a whole new excitement. There are lots and lots of people who look to Randy for what their band ought to be. So many bands have a fiddler standing off to the side just like Brady does.

Randy's such a solid, solid person with a great work ethic. He'd always be on the phone all week promoting the next show. He'd be all over town, all over campus putting up posters, personally doing that and getting other people to help. He is really a genuine, personable person and a hard worker. I like him a lot. He always remembers to give me a shout-out at the new show. Randy is always surrounded by other people hanging out with them, all kinds of different people, always good people.

He had recorded "Plastic Girl" and "Hill Country." We wanted to write a song together, and Randy had just gone through a pretty bad experience, and he was angry about it. He wanted to write an angry song. We did. That's how "You Could've Left Me" came about, but I don't think it came across as angry. "You could've left me, before I let you in / You could've let me, before we tried what might've been / You could had left me before you did me wrong / But you can't leave me now, ['cause] I'm already gone." He recorded that. He started featuring "The Hill Country" in his shows, and he taught it to everybody that didn't know. Anywhere I go now, I sing that song, and they sing along with the chorus because of Randy Rogers. I hope that Randy would always give me a shout-out on the song, when everybody sings along, and he turned it into an anthem. Thank you, Randy.

They were really nice to me at MusicFest [in Steamboat Springs, Colorado in January 2014]. They did a special tribute show, and Randy was a big part of it. It was William Clark Green, Wade Bowen and Randy Rogers, Kyle Park, HalleyAnna, and Gary Hartman. Everybody was singing along, a big old standing-room-only crowd. It made me feel wonderful and makes me love my fellow songwriters. Randy did "Lost and Found" at MusicFest. He remembers how much I love it.

As far as what we call Texas music as defined today, Randy Rogers is the top of the heap, for sure. Everybody wants to be Randy Rogers. It's only right that he started at Cheatham Street. Cheatham Street has always been there to try to develop unknown acts, other George Straits and other Stevie Rays. I'm extremely proud of him, extremely proud of the man. He does everything right.[1]

---

[1] Kent Finlay, interview with Jenni Finlay, February 8, 2014.

# 21 | Blanco River Meditation #2

*"A voice in the wilderness" ("The Songwriter")*

Walt Wilkins's secret is his sincerity and his great soul. He's the most soulful singer and writer that I know. Walt is the epitome of soul. He gives off soul when he walks in the room. Such a sincere thinker, writer, singer. He and [Nashville-based songwriter] Davis Raines wrote one of my favorite songs of all time, "Someone Somewhere Tonight." Someone is being born, and someone is dying. "So lay down beside me and tell me you love me and that you always will." I'm crying saying the words. Such a well-written song. Such a sincere, honest, deep-feeling song. Wow. He makes us all connect. He offers us all his powerful soul, and it bounces back. When he's singing to me and I'm feeling it, I'm shooting it back at him.

I knew Walt a little at the time when I was doing that Sixth Street thing at Headliners East. Right around the corner there was a songwriter venue, very much a songwriter venue, called the Chicago House. Walt was playing there some before he moved to Nashville. I didn't see him a lot after he moved, but I did know about him. Then he started coming to Cheatham Street. Ace Ford, Walt, Davis Raines could come do shows at Cheatham Street, and they had come back to this area. So I've come to know him better and better and respect him more and more. Just love him to death.

Writing with Walt is a spiritual experience. The one we wrote that I like the very most is ["Blanco River Meditation #2" from Wilkins's 2008 album *Hopewell*]. "I've got nothing to do / I'm not leaving till I'm done." Walt had that hook, and we sat down and started working on it out on a

*Walt Wilkins at Catfish Concerts, Austin, Texas, October 13, 2013. Photo by Brian T. Atkinson*

river somewhere. "There's a ruckus down the river / I look up to see the sight / Mama duck is gathering up / Her ducklings for the night." You know, everything in its place. This is the last verse: "Twilight is gathering / I've got nothing to do / I'm not leaving till I'm done."

I love swapping songs with Walt because we both know we are paying attention, not making eyes at somebody. Walt is always listening to everything. It's like you are playing to each other. Walt's the guy. He's my hero and a great producer too. As a songwriter, he's just impeccable. As a person he is impeccable. I tell everybody everywhere that he is the most spiritual singer in the world today except for maybe Willie. Actually, I think they are equals.[1]

---

[1] Kent Finlay, interview with Jenni Finlay, March 19, 2014. For more on Davis Raines, see www.davisraines.com/ (accessed January 29, 2015).

# 22 | Legacies

*"My love's completely different than any love I've known before"*
*("New Girl in My Life")*

My youngest daughter, HalleyAnna, has some really great ideas for writing, and sometimes she just really nails it. I'm so proud of her. She nails it with songs like "You Don't Need Me" [from her 2013 self-titled album]. What a wonderful, wonderful song that is. I don't care who wrote it or who would sing it, it's a wonderful song. It's all there and all fits together. What a great song "Peace Is Lonely, Love Is War" is. Sometimes you write twenty songs and nineteen are just real good, but one really does it. That one just jumps out there.

She doesn't like to write with me. She's always been fiercely independent. She wouldn't let me teach her guitar. She'd get in there with a computer and now she plays guitar five times as good as I do. We wrote that one song about setting the bird free ["On My Way to Get You Off My Mind"]. It's a good song. She really sells the songs that she writes. "Peace Is Lonely, Love Is War" [from her 2011 debut *The Country*] is such a powerful song, and it gets you right in the heart. "Back in Your Arms Again" is really a good song, maybe too good. You have to listen to it closely. A lot of people can't listen so they don't hear it. HalleyAnna is going to write some really big hits. She's a much better writer than some of the people she strives to be.

My son, Sterling, is such a natural writer. Music is so easy for him that he doesn't take it as seriously as he should because it's just so easy. He's so talented. You show him the first line of a song, and he knows the whole thing even though he never has heard it before. Most people do charts. Sterling just listens to the song, and he's got it. He'll say, "In the third verse, that second B, we ought to turn it into this." It's like he

*Kent's children, Jenni Sterling, and HalleyAnna at Diana Finlay Hendricks and Mark Hendricks's house, November 29, 2013. Photo by Brian T. Atkinson.*

knows the whole song. He's got a picture of it in his head, and he's right on the money when he's doing a session. He's so quick and makes it look easy.

Sterling was writing songs when he was five and six years old, like "Bubbles for Sale" and "Mr. John." "Mr. John" is just a great song, and so is "The Trail of Tears Still Makes Me Cry." He was six or seven when he wrote it. He could sympathize with the people and created pictures of the people: "Old chief Nighthawk looked so sad / As he buried the best friend he ever had / Then his braids hung down over his ears / As he walked on down the Trail of Tears / Oh, the Trail of Tears still makes me cry / Makes me wonder why, why, why / A hundred years have all passed by / but the Trail of Tears still makes me cry." He was just a little kid. It amazes me to this day how he could achieve that being just a little kid. It was so easy for him.

Jenni was about five years old when Riders in the Sky played Cheatham

Street one night. She sat up there right in the very front row with me and was just spellbound. [The band's fiddler] Woody Paul is who made her want to play the fiddle. When it was over, she said, "Daddy, I want to learn to play the fiddle." Of course, she got a fiddle right away. She started off with a three-eighths size and built up. She got to a three-quarter size pretty quick. It had a better tone. She had some great fiddle teachers, including Fiddlin' Frenchie Burke. Frenchie's still the king of the showmen. He can control a crowd better than anybody I've ever seen. Frenchie taught her all of his show tunes. She played "Orange Blossom Special" exactly like he did, note for note. He's such a showy, exciting fiddle player. His fiddle playing was mostly for show. He could get three thousand people screaming.

I would call her up on stage to do a couple guest appearances where she would play a fiddle tune. Then they started doing a weekend thing in one section of Aquarena Springs. It was still operating as a tourist place at that time. They started doing some short shows, and they hired us to do fifteen or twenty minutes once an hour. Probably by the third show, the people who were there the first time were already gone. That's when we started doing a real show every Saturday and Sunday. We'd be there for several hours doing maybe five or six fifteen-to-twenty-minute shows, cowboy shows with several fiddle tunes. We'd always sign off with "Happy Trails."

Jenni was seven or eight, and Todd Snider had just moved in with us right at that time. She'd already learned the fiddle really well. It was just so rewarding with Jenni being the first child. It was like, *Wow, we're getting to do something featuring her.* We'd dress up like a cowgirl and a cowboy. It was so much fun. We'd come on, and wham, bam, "Happy Trails" and it was over. Sterling would be coming along pretty quickly on bass. What a great thing, to get to be in a band with your kids and grow up with your kids. When you're in a band together, there's a close thing you feel even if you don't like the guy. You feel a closeness. So to feel that closeness, in addition to being family, is pretty wonderful and rewarding, for sure.

Being onstage at such a young age can be pretty intense. Jenni was

Left–right: Clay McNeill, Brian T. Atkinson, Jenni Finlay, Kent Finlay, HalleyAnna
Finlay, Sterling Finlay, and Owen Temple at Catfish Concerts, Austin, February 2014.
Photo by Tiffany Walker

very determined and stubborn. When she sets her head to something, it happens. She was that way even when she was a little girl. She'd practice absolutely every day. That was what she saw as her job. She got really good really early. She was just a little girl, but she played the fiddle like a man. It was her biggest strength. She had a great fiddle and rig too. She had the best sounding fiddle rig. We worked really hard on it and made it big and fat. When she played something on the fiddle, it was big.

We played until she went off to college at Belmont [University of Nashville]. When she graduated from high school, it broke up the family band. Then we would play when she would come home for Christmas, but we didn't go looking for gigs. We did so many festivals and fairs—the strawberry festivals and watermelon festivals, the alligator festival, the freedom festival, the armadillo festival. Every little town has a festival they do. We stayed busy on weekends. We'd go play a couple hours somewhere and then go to Dairy Queen. The kids loved Dairy Queen. Sterling would get the steak fingers. I'd probably get the Hungr-Buster. Jenni liked the dip cone. Every town, no matter how small, has a Dairy Queen.

Santa Claus bought Sterling a Fender Mustang bass one Christmas. Sterling was a natural musician, so he learned it right away. A friend of mine named Stan Ashlock, who used to play in my band, came over and gave Sterling a few lessons. That's all it took. He had it. He'd play and sing harmony. We had a lot of fun. He's not very much younger than Jenni, so he got to be in the band too, not long after we started. Right away, it wasn't any time until he could play. He was right on the money and right on time. We still played the same songs. We had a bass player and that gave more depth to it.

We did two or three weeks at the State Fair, just Jenni and me. We'd go out there every day and do a thirty-minute show. We shared the stage with a magician named Ronnie Cohn. He had this air gauge like you put on a tire, and he'd get up there, and he'd say, "You know, I've been feeling a little pressure." He'd pull it out and stick it in his ear and say, "Oh, my God: 35!" I laughed every time. I guess some people can tell them and some people can't. We met a lot of people at the State Fair—Carl Perkins and William Lee Golden, who the Oak Ridge Boys kicked out of the group. And the carnie act of the century. He's dead now, the World's Fattest Teenage Boy. Three years later he died. We went to see a lot of the sideshows, and one of them was the World's Fattest Teenage Boy. He was in there eating pizza. It was really sad, though, thinking about it all. Here he ended up giving his entire life for show business.

We were invited to play the Democratic National Convention in Atlanta in 1988. We felt very lucky to get to go do it. We played one afternoon, and Travis Tritt, who was unknown at the time, played right after us. It was the first time I heard him and before he had a record deal, but he was really good. After we got through with our set, this guy came up and was talking to Jenni. He said he was a musician too. They talked about being musicians. Then someone said, "And now . . . the governor of Arkansas,

Bill Clinton!" Our musician friend walked up there and talked. Sure enough, I saw him on TV later playing a saxophone. He *was* a musician. That was kind of neat, getting to meet Governor Clinton, who was going to be the president. All of a sudden, he's not just a musician. He was a very friendly, nice guy, outgoing, very humble. He'd just say, "Hello. Nice to meet everybody." He was pretty long-winded. He talked a long time.

I wrote "New Girl in My Life," when Jenni was just a baby. It's a song about falling in love again with another woman [who knows] about my wife. It turns out in the end that the new girl is a baby girl, and that absolutely was Jenni: "There's a new girl in my life/ And she knows about my wife / My wife knows there's another / After all, she's the mother / There's a new girl in my life."

That's the last half-verse in the song where I tell who the new girl is. Up until then, she's just a new girl: "Last night as we were lying / On the bed she started crying / I turned and took her arm / And pulled her closer to my side / She sobbed as I caressed her / And laughed as I undressed her / There's one thing that cannot be denied / I changed her, you see / But not as much as she's changed me / The new girl in my life."

I wrote a song called "Paying My Dues," written from Jenni's perspective as a little girl doing the stuff you do, standing in the port-o-potty line signing autographs. That happened a lot. We had some star clothes. She had real nice shiny shirts, and I always wore a bib front and a big hat. We were dressed up like drugstore cowboys.

At different times in my life, I've had to do some terrible things, like I taught at the prison. I had to get there early in the morning, and I didn't like it. My typical day now begins about ten or ten thirty a.m. I try not to start before then because I typically go to bed by three or four a.m. I stay up when I get home from Cheatham and write or do computer work. I try to always be flexible when I get a song going. I don't always have time for that, depending on what's happening that night. If it's a Cheatham Street night, I get there about eight and stay until closing time. I don't really take a vacation. I'm on vacation permanently.

I sometimes daydream about what Cheatham Street will be like in fifty years. I want it to be sitting there looking just as it does but have a good roof on it. I see it, for one thing, partly as a museum, partly a place to develop songwriters with songwriter concerts. I also see it as a place to develop steel guitar players and guitar players and also to have concerts for all kinds of Texas music, from Texas swing to down-home country to blues and any serious music. Pretty much what we've always been doing. We've had Stevie Ray and George Strait. When you think of the history, you realize you're standing there where Stevie Ray played. Right there. He's in the walls. Those notes are stuck in that wood somewhere.

Same thing with Doug Sahm, Delbert McClinton, Eric Johnson, George Strait, Tom Russell, Todd Snider, and Randy Rogers. Over and over I hear, "Oh it's so nice to be standing right here playing on this spot." I think it maybe makes you play better. I've been a musician all my life, and there are a lot of places you go to play when you're just a worker. I try to always listen. I have great respect for songwriting. It's really important for music to be treated with respect. That doesn't happen everywhere. I see the future songwriters who find a home and inspiration from the old wood boards and the supporters who listen. I'm so proud of the songwriters. Ultimately, that will be Cheatham's legacy.[1]

[1] Kent Finlay, interview with Brian T. Atkinson, April 3, 2014. For more on HalleyAnna Finlay, see Brian T. Atkinson, "HalleyAnna Sneaks Texas Songwriters into *The Country*," CMT *Edge*, November 5, 2012, www.cmtedge.com/2012/11/05/halleyanna-sneaks-texas-songwriters-into-the-country (accessed January 29, 2015); Brian T. Atkinson, "HalleyAnna Captures Her Own Evolution as a Songwriter on New Record," *Austin American-Statesman*, June 5, 2013. For more on Sterling Finlay, see www.sterlingfinlay.com/ (accessed January 29, 2015). For more on Jenni Finlay, see William Harries Graham, "Jenni Finlay Promotions Turns 8: From Sleeping on Pool Tables at Cheatham Street to Radio," *Austin Chronicle*, August 20, 2014; Jenni Finlay Promotions, www.jennifinlaypromotions.com/ (accessed January 29, 2015).

# The Songwriter

V1)
If he was doing it for money,
He'd be doing something else'.
All he wants from life
Is a chance to give himself
To some future generation
Who'll be touched when they have heard —
His rhymes and his rhythms
And the wisdom of his words ...

Chorus)
For yesterday is all we have
That's sure to last forever
Today will end in darkness there's no doubt
But you could never make him stop
Believing in tomorrow
Tomorrow's all today is all about

2)
Sure he'd like a lot more notice
From some more of us today
But he'd never stop doing things
And living his own way
A voice in the wilderness
So many haven't heard
His rhymes are his religion
His lyrics are the word

(Repeat chorus)

Kent Finlay
1985 ??

Kent Finlay's handwritten lyrics for "The Songwriter," 1985.

# PART II

The Players

# 23 | Marcia Ball

Freda and the Firedogs were at the beginning of the Austin scene, and it means a terrific amount to have played the first show at Cheatham Street. I mean, Kent thought enough of us that we could be his club's opening act. There were a few of us who were doing this retro country and classic country, and we had found an audience that was like us: young and long-haired but very reverential about country music and American traditional music. Kent recognized that, and it was exactly what he wanted to do with his club. He was already a musician and songwriter, and he saw something in us that he wanted to encourage. It meant a lot to us. It was validation, something we were craving.

We used to play with that sliding back door open, and the trains would go by and drown out the band. I love the physical aspects of the club. It's a megaphone-shaped building, and it just sounds the best of anywhere to me. There just aren't that many clubs around like that anymore. It's harder for young acts to find a place like that to play. The audiences are less and less available, and the focus is less on live music than it has been in two or three generations. Kent has always struggled and had to close at one point. I'm pretty sure he never made any money long- or short-term, but Cheatham Street is as important as it ever was.

Playing country music was a learned experience, but I truly learned how to sing when I got in the Firedogs. It was my first opportunity to really learn songs and melodies. The gradual moving away from that had to do with the fact that I started my own band in 1975 after the Firedogs, and my natural instinct, my musical memory, is more piano-friendly. I'm a piano player, and it was the music I was going to write and play, and it turned out to be Louisiana Gulf Coast rhythm and blues. It was a gradual move that I did over the five years from 1975 to 1980. I mixed it up with a little bit of western swing and rock and roll and a little bit of New Orleans, Fats Domino–like stuff. In 1980, I just decided to go all in on the R&B.

*Marcia Ball, Austin,
March 24, 2015. Photo by
Jenni Finlay*

Kent watched it happen while I was playing there all through that time. I had really great bands in the late seventies. This was the time when Uncle Walt's band and Alvin Crow would be playing there. We were all friends, and we were all playing together. We played shows with Ace in the Hole and those guys. Willie [Nelson] sat in one time with us. I remember that being a special thing. Walter Hyatt was actually working for me as a roadie for a time because his band wasn't playing, and his wife was expecting, and he needed a job. I particularly remember playing Cheatham Street during that brief interlude, and Walter got up and sang a song. You know, "Here's our roadie who's gonna sing a song," and he swept everyone off their feet with his voice.

Kent supported me through it all. Kent likes music. Period. He understood that I was going to do what was real to me. I've always been fortunate to have a collection of songs that are danceable and seem to be compatible with the same people who like country music. You can almost not find anybody in the world who doesn't like Fats Domino, and I've

Marcia Ball & the Misery Brothers poster, Cheatham Street Warehouse, 1975. Courtesy Finlay family archives

gotten to stay pretty close to that bag. I try to remain in that same place musically. You can call it country or blues or R&B or soul. Kent liked it all because it was real. The more I wrote, the better he liked it. He was very strongly supportive. Also, it's silly but remarkable: Cheatham Street used to have the best graffiti in the ladies' room, more intelligent graffiti than you've ever seen.[1]

[1] Marcia Ball, interview with Brian T. Atkinson, June 2, 2014. For more on Marcia Ball and Freda and the Firedogs, see Kathleen Hudson, *Women in Texas Music: Stories and Songs* (Austin: University of Texas Press, 2007), 82–88; Rich Koster, *Texas Music* (New York: St. Martin's Press, 1998), 180; Jan Reid, *The Improbable Rise of Redneck Rock* (Austin: University of Texas Press, 2004), 81–82, 273–74, 284, 342.

# 24 | Darrell Staedtler

You're in Nashville because you're serious about songwriting. People hanging around Austin bad-mouthing Nashville were just people who couldn't write radio-ready songs. A lot was ill-constructed and you couldn't tell them. You'd say, "You need a really strong first line. Then you need a hook. Then you need to repeat the hook line at the end of the verses so that the last thing people hear is the title of the song so they can request it." People in Austin didn't understand that. They were just knocking around. I went down there looking for writers in 1976, and that's when I met Kent. I didn't meet any writers that I thought were radio-ready. If you want to make it as a writer, you have to go to Nashville. It's like if you're hunting elephants, you have to go to Africa. These people just didn't have it in them to go to Nashville. They'd rather sit on their ass and cuss it.

At that time, country was starting to change. They had not had a fiddle for years, and they started putting fiddle on the records, which made them sound a lot more country. I thought that was a good addition. I think Kent was pretty anti-Nashville and pretty well content with Cheatham Street at that time. Kent and me would meet at Luckenbach a lot and drink beer and play music outside in 1976 and '77 and '78. It was just a really relaxed place. I was best man at Kent's wedding, your standard picture-book wedding. It was like you'd have in a movie wedding. My son was a ring bearer.

I started playing harmonica in Kent's band. He's a good storyteller and uses perfect rhyme, which is really hard. He was always a stickler for perfect rhyme. I don't understand why more people don't cut his songs. We got one cut in Nashville with a major label guy, Mel McDaniel. He cut "Plastic Girl" way back around 1977 or '78. That's the only one we got cut up there. Everybody always liked his songs, but I guess they weren't

Left to right: Kent Finlay, George Strait, and Darrell Staedtler, Wounded Warrior fundraiser, October 2014. Photo by Keenan Christensen Fletcher

radio ready. We never wrote much together because my style of writing is so much different than his. I was taught to [write] radio-ready, formulaic songs. I was trying to make a living doing it.

Lefty Frizzell recording "Honky-Tonk Stardust Cowboy" was a big deal. I got to meet him once. I had written it for him and pitched it to him, and he'd turned it down. Then Bill Rice of Foster and Rice fame recorded it, and it was going up the charts. In fact, it got an award for being on the charts so long. As it was going up, Capitol dropped him, and he met up with Lefty, and he told Lefty he ought to cut the song. We have heard rumors that Merle Haggard taught it to him, but who knows. Lefty started going up the charts, and Columbia dropped him, so the song never was a hit except in Europe. I never got paid anything, so I don't know. One big record was Jonathan Edwards' recording of it. He was the first one who did it in 1972, as the title of his album. He did a real good cut on it.

I met George Strait through Kent in 1976. Kent said, "You ought to listen to this guy." I'd moved out to Texas kind of permanently after living in Nashville off and on for ten years. I had a lot of connections, so we went out to see George, and he was singing "Honky-Tonk Stardust Cowboy," and they were rehearsing it. When Kent told him who I was, he jumped off the stage and shook my hand like I was some icon. We went to Nashville, and I had him do some of my songs on a demo. I wanted to pitch him as an artist, and I had ten major labels turn him down. It wasn't until Erv got there as head of promotions at [MCA] that he got on a label. They were looking for different-sounding voices back then, and George, to his credit, has a nice, vanilla-sounding voice that wouldn't offend anybody. That's one key. Another is that he's a master at picking songs.

Kent has an idea about [Staedtler's unreleased song] "Hung Over Over You," but actually I recorded it [sung by] George . . . at Luckenbach. Gary P. Nunn was there and other artists, except Kent wasn't. At the time, Kent and Kathy Morgan [the manager at Luckenbach] were at war with each other. She didn't invite him up, which was a travesty. We had a bus come in with a recording mechanism, and we put George in the dance hall, and that's where we cut "Hung Over Over You." I've got a CD of the six or seven songs that we recorded that nobody's ever heard. I could make a million off that CD. Of course, the lawsuit would cost another million, so I guess I'd just break even.[1]

---

[1] Darrell Staedtler, interview with Brian T. Atkinson, July 15, 2014. For more on Mel McDaniel, see Peter Cooper, "Mel McDaniel, Singer and Grand Ole Opry Member Dies at 68," *Music* (*Tennessean* blog), April 1, 2011, http://blogs.tennessean.com/tunein/2011/04/01/singer-and-grand-ole-opry-member-mel-mcdaniel-dies-at-68 (accessed January 29, 2015).

# 25 | George Strait

I think it wasn't until the first time we played at Cheatham Street Warehouse that I met Kent. My impression of him at the time was, *This guy's pretty cool to have such a classic little honky-tonk. I want to be friends with him.* I'm sure I was very nervous playing. I don't remember what our set list was or if we even had one. We just knew a lot of songs and were excited to get to go out and start playing them for people. In those days, we would do a forty-five-minute set, take a fifteen-minute break, and then do another set. We would do four sets.

George Strait, Cheatham Street Warehouse, 1970s. Photographer unknown; courtesy Finlay family archives

Kent gave guys like me a place to hone our skills. The live music scene back then was great, and we had some of the best places to play. It doesn't get any better than Cheatham Street, Gruene Hall, and the Broken Spoke, and those old dance halls and honky-tonks were where we learned to play in front of people. I'm not sure I would've been ready to do that if I had been signed to a record label right away. I needed those years to learn how to play and sing on stage.

Kent was friends with a songwriter named Darrell Staedtler, and he introduced us. Darrell was writing for Chappell Music back then and needed to go to Nashville to demo some of his songs and asked me if I would sing on the demos. I had been wanting to go to Nashville forever, so I was excited and ready to go, just to maybe open some doors for us. So Kent and Darrell and me loaded up Kent's delivery van with a few cases of Coors beer since they couldn't get Coors in Nashville at the time. We put a cot in the back, and I think there also was a lawn chair, and off we went. It was a great trip for me and gave me some studio experience, which I needed. I thought the demos turned out great and just knew I would be signed if the right person heard them. I was so wrong. I remember Kent and Darrell were very encouraging, though, and didn't let it get me down. We came back to the great state of Texas and continued to play music and have fun.

Kent was writing, and of course Darrell encouraged me to write as well. I wrote "I Don't Want to Talk It Over" and "[That] Don't Change the Way I Feel about You" back around 1976. I remember how hard it was to introduce them to the band to learn. I mean, you never know how someone else is going to react to your songs, but I still have plans to record those songs again someday. I redid "I Just Can't Go on Dying Like This" on my last record [2013's *Love Is Everything*] and thought it turned out pretty good. I wrote that one about the same time. I'm not sure of the inspiration behind those songs. I guess it was just life in general.

I think about those days all the time. Those memories will be with me forever. It's part of my history as an artist. I think about the great old music we were playing back then and how we would order some beers to the stage during the set if we were thirsty. Beer was free for the band, and we were always thirsty, it seemed. I think about all of the great crowds we had and people filling up the dance floor. That's how you knew you were doing well. If they weren't dancing, you were doing something wrong. We didn't make a lot of money, but we were doing something we loved and getting paid for it.

The reason I thanked Kent from the stage on the [2014 farewell] tour was because I wanted people to know some of those stories and know who played a part in my career. Kent was a very important part of that. He is a friend and was an inspiration to me and a whole slew of others he let on that stage at Cheatham Street Warehouse. He knows good songs and knows good music. I went there a lot as a spectator, and I never once saw a band there that sucked. He wasn't going to let you play there if you sucked. I mean, just look at the amazing list of people who have played there. I saw Ernest Tubb at Cheatham Street. How cool is that? I think that was a dream of Kent's all along: to give a platform to artists to develop their skills and just have a damn fun way to make a living. Kent and his band would play there as well, and it gave him a chance to introduce some of the songs that he was writing at the time. That's how I think Kent will be remembered, a guy who was a friend to the songwriters and artists in our great state of Texas, who believed in our music and was willing to do his part to help you get to wherever it was you wanted to be.[1]

[1] George Strait, email interview with Brian T. Atkinson and Jenni Finlay, July 10, 2014. For more on George Strait, see Austin Teutch, *King George: The Triumphs and Tragedies in the Life of George Strait* (JRAB Press, 2010); Rich Koster, *Texas Music* (New York: St. Martin's Press, 1998), 52–53, 56; Patricia Carr, *The Illustrated History of Country Music* (New York: Random House, 1995); Tony Byworth, *The Billboard Illustrated Encyclopedia of Country Music* (New York: Watson Guptill, 2006), 125, 239, 252–53, 259, 266, 294.

# 26 | Ray Wylie Hubbard

We used to play Cheatham Street in the seventies. That whole progressive country thing was happening with Michael [Martin] Murphey and Jerry Jeff [Walker] and all those cats. We probably played that first year when my record [1975's *Ray Wylie Hubbard and the Cowboy Twinkies*] came out. I'd show up and play my gig, and all of a sudden Willie Nelson and Jerry Jeff and Murphey would show up. Everybody would just kind of sit in. Kent's got a picture of Jerry Jeff and Willie on his wall, and that was at my gig, and I always kid him that he cut me out of the picture. In fact, that's my guitar that Willie's playing. I always kid Kent, "Man, I can't believe you cut me out of a picture of my own gig." It was an exciting time. You'd show up and play and the audience was like another member of the band. It was just an incredible down-home, cool feeling.

Progressive country really was progressive. You had all these folk singers like Michael Murphey and Jerry Jeff, who were adding steel guitars and electric guitars, and Willie Nelson, who had Mickey Raphael as a blues harp player. Nobody had been doing that before. You had full-tilt pot-smoking hippies with long hair in the audience, but they were wearing cowboy boots and cowboy hats. The crowd was very aware of the music. They were very knowledgeable about who was writing the songs. Everybody was great songwriters: Willie, Jerry Jeff, Murphey and B. W. [Stevenson] and Rusty [Weir]. Cheatham Street had this reputation. It wasn't cover bands. These guys were songwriters. It's a reputation that's held up to this day. It's about the songwriters. Kent, being a songwriter himself, he has the heart, the soul of a songwriter. He knows what it's like, but he was very selective in who he let play there. You couldn't be a hack. You had to have your songwriting teeth. You had to have your chops together. That was because of Kent. He was very aware of it.

As a songwriter starting off, playing Cheatham Street's a feather in

Ray Wylie
Hubbard, Long
Center, Austin,
September 19,
2010. Photo by
Brian T. Atkinson

your cap. It puts you in a good roster of real songwriters. Kent called
me up seven, eight years ago and said, "Would you come over and do a
songwriters' circle with some of these kids?" I said, "Sure." I think Randy
Rogers was in the circle, and it was his second or third gig or something.
For Kent, it's not about what he can get from this but about what he can
give, what he can contribute to the music. What he's doing for the young
songwriters is saying, "Hey, you need to write songs." He's a guru, a
Yoda, one of the cats the young guys look up to. He has an incredible
sense of the craft of songwriting, and he has the right inspiration for
why he does it. He has a very noble purpose. He shares what he knows
with these young cats to put them on the right track. It's not about, *Hey,*

*I'm gonna get a guitar and write some songs and get some beer and girls.* It's, hey, write some songs that hopefully have some significance.[1]

In Buddhism, the term "Bodhisattva" [means] an enlightened being who helps others without selfish attachment. I think that's Kent. He helped a lot of young writers without doing it selfishly. He was just trying to get these young writers to be the best they could. It keeps me on my toes to write with younger writers too. I write with a guy like Jonathan Tyler or those cats from the Dirty River Boys or Hayes [Carll]. I can't get lazy, and I have so much respect for them as writers that I have to bring my A game to the table. You say, "Hey, man, instead of making that E like that, try making it like this." You see their eyes light up when you show them an old blues lick or a weird chord.[2]

There's been this bar that's been set by Lightnin' Hopkins, Mance Lipscomb, Townes Van Zandt, of course. Townes was a great storyteller. Cheatham Street is very important because it combines the songwriter and the personality. The audience gets to know them. Kent is a master at that. He's got these great songs he's written, and when he talks about them you begin to know him and learn about him. Kent has that ability to marry the inspiration and the craft together. He knows how to write a song, and his inspiration comes from a very heartfelt look at the world, very knowledgeable about what's going on around him. His songs are well written and significant and have some depth and weight.[3]

---

[1] Ray Wylie Hubbard, interview with Brian T. Atkinson, March 7, 2014.

[2] Ray Wylie Hubbard, interview with Brian T. Atkinson, March 12, 2015.

[3] Ray Wylie Hubbard, interview with Brian T. Atkinson, March 7, 2014. For more on Ray Wylie Hubbard and his role in the Texas progressive country movement in the 1970s, see Brian T. Atkinson, *I'll Be Here in the Morning: The Songwriting Legacy of Townes Van Zandt* (College Station: Texas A&M University Press, 2012), 19–24; Brian T. Atkinson, "Interview: Ray Wylie Hubbard," *Austin Music + Entertainment*, July/August 2006, 26. For more on Ray Wylie Hubbard achieving sobriety and his creative rebirth, see Grant Alden and Peter Blackstock, *The Best of No Depression: Writing about American Music* (Austin: University of Texas Press, 2005), 60–63.

# 27 | Omar Dykes
## (Omar and the Howlers)

I was in a band called the Howlers in 1976 when we moved from Hattiesburg, Mississippi, to Austin, Texas, and we met up with Kent Finlay. Kent brought us down to Cheatham Street in San Marcos, and we just loved it. He was really good to us, and that was one of the first places we played in Texas. Kent booked us every week. I think George Strait played every [Tuesday] and we played every Thursday in 1976. Sometimes the crowd wasn't that great, but he had us back the next week. If the crowd was a little short, he'd throw in two cases of Billy Beer. He said he couldn't sell the stuff, which is funny because it's worth two hundred

Omar Dykes, Cheatham Street Warehouse, 1980s. Photographer unknown; courtesy Finlay family archives

to three hundred dollars a can now. He'd give us two cases, and the band would drink it before we got back to Austin. They didn't know they were drinking up a fortune.

Cheatham Street was a funny place. It had two crowds: the college crowd and the Texas shufflers and twirl dance people. Omar and the Howlers play blues, but the Howlers played blues and rock, and we had two guys who played fiddle. We'd lean into the country music and western swing a little more. Kent always made it fun and let us do anything. It didn't make any difference to him, and Cheatham Street gave us a chance to work on our material. Kent was always right there with a hand out to help you. I've never seen anybody love music more than him. I don't think he cared what you played as long as you played it good.

We usually didn't draw a full house, but we'd draw enough to make it worthwhile. One night, we had the whole placed packed with college kids. You couldn't walk through. I'm not sure why, the day after exams or school got out, and you couldn't move in there. We usually drew the twist dancers and the Texas shuffle people and played country and country blues, but that night we took off our cowboy hats and were a rock band. The place was electric. We played a song we had called "Shout Bama Lama" and we used to play that song "Money": "The best things in life are free."

I think Kent liked our original stuff. A lot of what we wrote in the original Howlers was western swing–oriented. You knew if he liked you because he'd have you back just about whenever you wanted to play. You didn't have to beg for a job with Kent. If he liked you, you called him about a job, and he would see to it in the next two weeks or so you'd be playing there. At the time, that was good because Omar and the Howlers went out on the road extensively. We were gone, so when we came back sometimes we didn't have a lot of time to book it because we didn't know when we'd be home, but he'd have us down there. Cheatham Street really is the original Texas honky-tonk, a place with a bare lightbulb onstage.[1]

---

[1] Omar Dykes, interview with Brian T. Atkinson, June 16, 2014. For more on Omar and the Howlers, see Rich Koster, *Texas Music* (New York: St. Martin's Press, 1998), 182; www.omarandthehowlers .com/.

# 28 | Cleve Hattersley (Greezy Wheels)

In the blur of history, it seemed like we always played Cheatham Street Warehouse and Kent was always there. In those days, you played Friday nights until midnight and Saturday nights until one in the morning. We always considered those really good gigs because Austin was changing, and you had to play until two o'clock. Every time we would end the night with "Orange Blossom Special" [the Ervin T. Rouse song popularized by Johnny Cash], and the train went by whether it was midnight or one. I mean, that train went by the club every time we played that fucking song. We went back and did a Greezy Wheels gig there eight years ago, and we got to "Orange Blossom Special," and, sure enough, the train went by as soon as we started playing.

You always smell old beer and new expectations when you walk into

Cleve Hattersley (second from left) with Greezy Wheels. Photo by Erin Houser

Cheatham Street. The joint has not changed in all this time. In a way, Kent hasn't either. I mean, the PA's a little better, and stuff improves, but it's the same feel. You load in the same place. The train goes by. It makes you feel like home. You always load in from the back because that's where the band parks. Nobody bothers to drive around from the front where there's an actual parking lot. You load right into the stage, so there's no secret that you're there when you show up. Anybody that's there for happy hour is watching you load in. You have to be very careful on stage . . . because there's a low-hanging beam that I swear I have run into every night in all the years I've played there. They put signs up there: "Watch out." "Duck." I still hit it every time.

Kent is one of the sweetest people on the planet. When you're talking about a guy who's taken such time to promote and allow artist nights for people to just play, for forty years, you're talking about a pretty good guy. He's never put making huge success out of the club in front of making it a good place for you to play. It's always been about the artist, and Kent's never gonna separate himself from Cheatham Street Warehouse because of that. That's his thing. I don't know if Kent will ever get the recognition as a songwriter himself that he sought—that we all sought—originally, but I think he should be very proud of the fact that he's promulgated a whole lot of fucking great music.

When we used to play, we had a couple fans who came out to see us every time we played: George Strait and Steve Earle. They started out there just like everybody else, but I never knew they were fans until afterward. I went up to New York City to run the Lone Star Café for several years, and they both came through. George was making his first big trip up to New York to do a live recording for WHN [1050 AM] radio, and he came up to me and said, "Do you remember me?" I kind of recognized him and said, "Yeah, yeah." He said, "I'm George Strait, and I used to come see you every time you played Cheatham Street Warehouse." Steve Earle told me the same thing years later.

I had broken up the band by then. Chris Layton had moved on to work with Stevie Ray [Vaughan], and Chip Dill decided he wanted to retire, and

I didn't want to have a revolving band. I had seen what Mort [Cooperman], the owner of the Lone Star, had been up to. He was really trying to put Texas right in the middle of Manhattan. It wasn't country music; it was Texas music. That's what he was looking for. That's the thing that Kent had going from day one. It didn't matter what kind of band you were, it just mattered that you were real and part of the Texas landscape in a way. So Mort put me in charge. I immediately started booking bands like Fabulous Thunderbirds and Stevie Ray Vaughan and Marcia Ball and Doug Sahm.

Mort wanted something that Kent understood: Texas was a giant state with a huge mix of great music. If you limit it to one kind or another, you limit your club. We were hot dogs for years, man. The Yankees hung out there. Every Sunday night, Kinky Friedman had people like Robin Williams onstage with him. The Blues Brothers did all their rehearsing there at the Lone Star. John Belushi and Dan Aykroyd had a little club on the West Side, but it wasn't functional, a bar without beer and booze. So, every night after *Saturday Night Live* finished taping, we would take cases of beer over there and jam all night with whoever played that night on the show. They were part of this crazy New York thing that was the roots of Americana in a way. We really were riding the wave for a good while.

When you get real good Texas music, whether it's Joe "King" Carrasco or Delbert McClinton, you're getting real, honest-to-god stuff played by guys who learned it from the time they could pick up a guitar or harmonica. There's no mistaking it. As soon as we identified ourselves as a Texas club up there, everybody wanted to be a part of it. Texas music was everything from Steve Miller and Boz Scaggs in the Dallas area to the Conjunto of the [Rio Grande] valley. You can't get away from how influential that's been on the music business, and Mort understood that at the Lone Star. Kent was all about that.[1]

---

[1] Cleve Hattersley, interview with Brian T. Atkinson, April 21, 2014. For more on Cleve Hattersley and Greezy Wheels, see Donna Marie Miller, "Cleve Hattersley: Sex, Drugs and Greezy Wheels," December 18, 2013, http://austinfusionmagazine.com/2013/12/18/cleve-hattersley-sex-drugs-and-greezy-wheels (accessed January 29, 2015).

# 29 | Jon Dee Graham (The Skunks)

It was 1978 or '79 and I was in a punk band called the Skunks. At that time in Texas, there were a limited number of places a punk rock band could play. You had Raul's in Austin, DJ's in Dallas, Paradise Island in Houston, and Cheatham Street Warehouse in San Marcos. The punk rock thing was so new, and people were so unclear on what it was about. People were casting it this way and that way. Kent never seemed to differentiate between us and any other rock bands that would come through Cheatham Street. He would never talk down to us. He would hang out with us and talk. It was weird because Texas was so polarized between the cosmic country culture and the punk rock. Joe Ely had not yet played

Jon Dee Graham and Jenni Finlay, Catfish Concerts, Austin, September 6, 2013. Photo by Brian T. Atkinson

with the Clash, so there was no melding of the cultures. We never felt anything from Kent except this open-armed "Yeah, come play."

Honestly, I think it was that [Skunks bassist] Jesse [Sublett] grew up in Johnson City, the drummer [Billy Blackmon] grew up in Beeville, and I grew up on the border. We were all guys who grew up in these little Texas towns, and in some weird way I think it was an avuncular thing, like he was this uncle taking us under his wing and giving us a place to play. I wouldn't say he's known for promoting punk rock, but look at all the stuff Todd Snider has done. He pushed the boundaries of the singer-songwriter thing as far as he can go. Several of his records are pretty avant garde as far as singer-songwriter things, and Kent loved him. I just think Kent is a really open-minded, open-hearted fellow who took an interest in us. He could sense that we were testing boundaries and seeing how far we could go. There's nothing more outlaw than that. Kent Finlay likes people who fuck with the rules.[1]

[1] Jon Dee Graham, interview with Brian T. Atkinson and Jenni Finlay, March 30, 2014. For more on Jon Dee Graham, see www.jondeegraham.com/.

# 30 | Jesse Sublett (The Skunks)

I met my girlfriend in fall 1972 when I went to Southwest Texas State. She was my first love, and she was murdered in San Marcos. That's what a lot of my book *Never the Same Again* [Boaz Publishing, 2004] is about. In fact, she was an artist and a poet, and she painted a couple things in Cheatham Street. One was an ad for the Hungry Sticks, which was a pool hall on the square. I don't suppose the painting's still there, but it was there for a long time. Kent let people paint advertisements for places on the wall there, and she got hired to do it.

We went to the Nickel Keg a lot, a place right on LBJ on the other side of the square. This band Krackerjack played there a lot. Stevie Ray Vaughan was in that band a while. They influenced me to want to play. Blackbird was another band that included Stevie Ray. I never saw him at Cheatham Street, but I remember his early days really well. He kind of reminded me of a young Steve McQueen, a raw, boyish look about him. Stevie played in bands in San Marcos quite a bit.

The Skunks played there for the first time in 1980. I suppose Kent might've contacted us. We had a buzz going for some reason, maybe a story had just come out. We got good press in the *University Star*. We played there and it was packed. I remember, vividly, taking home like nine hundred dollars after Kent's take, and I doubt we charged more than two bucks. I remember really well because there weren't a lot of places paying that kind of money on the door. It was great, and we made decent money later but never that much again. We probably played a dozen, two dozen shows at Cheatham Street.

We played there with Jon Dee, and then he was out of the band, and we played with other configurations. You have probably read in various

Jesse Sublett and Jon Dee Graham, Continental Club, Austin, September 18, 2014. Photo by Brian T. Atkinson

places that he left the Skunks because he was "frustrated" over his lack of input in the band, but actually he was a big influence. He's a big talent, and he had to move on anyway. The big song we wrote together is "What Do You Want," and we wrote that during a horrible three-week stint living in our leaky, cold RV parked in a trailer park in New Jersey, just over the Manhattan line. We had some good gigs booked in New York City and a few elsewhere, but several of them fell through, so we had lots of down time and no money. We were living on one meal a day and the cheapest whiskey we could buy. Not long after we wrote it we played Cheatham Street the first time.

We played all our hits at Cheatham Street: "Gimme Some," "Cheap Girl," "Something about You Scares Me." I remember Kent liking "Something about You Scares Me," which was one of the earliest songs I wrote for the Skunks. It's basically about a dim-witted friend of Bela Lugosi as Dracula, the dimwit taking four verses of the song to put it all together that he's a vampire: "Your skin is a little too white / Is it 'cause you only go out at night? / You're richer than a Rockefeller / Then how come you're sleeping in a cellar?"

When the band started with Eddie Munoz in '78, we were playing a lot of covers, and I wanted to do the Stones' "Stupid Girl," but I couldn't figure it out. I had no ear, no training, except a half-dozen lessons from a lady named Boots Maldin, who had played on the *Louisiana Hayride*. I really got nowhere, so I made up my own song, "Cheap Girl," the same basic, snotty, irreverent sentiment. We caught a lot of flack for the lyrics because it's really unkind and politically incorrect, but there was no hatred behind it. You could say sexism, yeah, but at the time I didn't think of it. The lyrics came from hanging out with these women at clubs. Eddie and I would just talk trash with these girls: "I wouldn't fuck you with his dick" and stuff like that ended up going into the song.

The song started out being largely improvised. I had that hook: "You're not choosy where you sleep / [Trash] like you [is] cheap, cheap, cheap." That's what sold the song. The first time we played it was at a club in San Antonio, and [former *Austin Chronicle* music writer] Margaret Moser and her friends were there, and they were dancing and hollering, and it was barely put together. It wasn't even called "Cheap Girl." It was called "Pretentious Girl." After playing it that night, I thought about it and made it "Cheap Girl."

A lot of people who weren't part of that scene wouldn't like us because we weren't trying to be in the scene, [but] we knew that we hadn't just bought guitars because we'd just heard the Sex Pistols and we were mad or political. We just wanted to play music. Kent was an anomaly to me. He was really sweet and easy-going, and I just love the guy. You'd think it wouldn't be his cup of tea at all, but Kent just liked the band, and he wouldn't just pay me and I'd leave. We talked after the gigs for a while. That's another reason I like him: he's really genuine.[1]

---

[1] Jesse Sublett, interview with Brian T. Atkinson, April 17, 2014. For more on Jesse Sublett, see his *Never the Same Again: A Rock and Roll Gothic* (Albany, CA: Boaz, 2004); www.jessesublett.com/ (accessed January 30, 2015).

# 31 | Will Sexton

My brother [Charlie] and I were playing every Tuesday at Cheatham Street when Stevie Vaughan was playing there. We'd come and sit in with [Vaughan's band] Double Trouble. Hundreds and hundreds of people have told me that they used to go see those shows when Charlie and I would play with Stevie. Impossible. There would be one biker chick and one drunken frat guy and another random person. No one was ever there. I was nine and ten years old, and we only did those gigs for a couple months, but I played there for so many years, and it's incredible because [it still has] the exact same integrity that it ever had. I've heard so many people comment when it's a slow night, "Do you know Kent?" "Yeah, I've known Kent forever." "God, he's just treated us amazingly. He said, 'It's one of my best shows I've had and you're welcome back any time.' There were only like four people there and I was feeling like it

Left to right: Will Sexton, Tim Easton, and J. T. Van Zandt at Catfish Concerts, Austin, March 18, 2014. Photo by Brian T. Atkinson

was a total failure, and the night ended in total kindness and generosity."

Kent was really supportive of my brother and me when we were little and playing with Stevie. The Fabulous Thunderbirds were huge, and they were the darling band in Austin. Stevie just played in little funky places, literally for no one. It's an interesting perspective because when you look at his life, at least eighty percent if not more was playing at little bars in front of no one. It happened very fast. The Stevie I remember at Cheatham was a weekday, and it was just trying something out. It's the perfect example of Kent's spirit and his heart. It doesn't faze him. He ferrets out the talent and the music and supports the hell out of it whether it's lucrative or not for him.

There were a lot of sleazeballs who owned the Austin bars. Kent was very paternal. It was a whole different thing. It's been great having that relationship with Kent, and it's spanned such a long period of time. Cheatham's still so much the same, but I don't get to go play that often, so when I do play there it's such a great feel. There's this insane nostalgia every time I play there. I think the last time I played there was with John Evans, and I just wanted to go be in his band that night. I said, "John, I want to go to San Marcos and play at Cheatham." We had a ball.

I was doing a lot of gigs with Joe Ely when I did my first record with him [2001's *Scenes from Nothing*]. Some of my favorite Ely shows ever were at Cheatham Street. Amazing. It's such a perfect place right on the railroad tracks. It starts hopping, and it can make you feel like you're in more of a juke joint than anywhere you've ever been. On the nights when it's really hopping and rocking, you feel the energy like you're in rural Mississippi all of a sudden. It can have that feel. The aesthetic of the building and the train tracks and the wood floors and the ancient smells are pretty exciting. It feels so good, so good. A structure like that with the roadhouse feel is one of those things people wish they could bottle and emulate. You can tell the difference with a place like Cheatham that's the real deal.

After he died and I'd started playing around Texas, people would get drunk and want to hear a Stevie Ray Vaughan song, and it would annoy me. Then one day I realized, you know, remember back when we used to do that thing in Kent's place? Now that I think about it, the irony and the beauty of that request is that whenever Stevie would be playing at Cheatham, there'd be one person in there wanting him to play a ZZ Top or Johnny Winter song. It made me appreciate it to where I actually laugh about it and enjoy the request.[1]

[1] Will Sexton, interview with Brian T. Atkinson, April 11, 2014. For more on Will Sexton, see Jan Reid, *The Improbable Rise of Redneck Rock* (Austin: University of Texas Press, 2004), 360; www .willsexton.com/ (accessed January 30, 2015).

# 32 | Joe Ely

Cheatham Street had become the talk of the Austin songwriter bunch by around 1985. I used to go down and see Will and Charlie Sexton play. It was totally unique and had this vibe and being on the main road between San Antonio and Austin, the perfect stopover. We would all go to Cheatham Street because here was something that we knew we couldn't hear anywhere else. It was a big inspiration and an eye-opener to all of the guys who appreciated a good song and were learning the craft of how to make one. Cheatham Street has always been an amazing place where stories are passed onstage and off. I think there's some magic in that old wood that holds these stories.

I was onstage one night, and I started playing Butch [Hancock]'s

Left to right: Kent Finlay, Joe Ely, and Butch Hancock, Cheatham Street Warehouse, San Marcos, April 6, 2014. Photo by Brian T. Atkinson

"Boxcars" with this rumbling bottom beat. Right as we hit that chorus, a train was rumbling down the track and blew its whistle. We all looked at each other. "Wow, that was great timing." We kept playing the song and got through another verse and heard it coming closer. The whistle was just going like crazy. All of a sudden, there's this big *ka-bamb!*—sounded like the train ran into the building. *Boom.* I stopped the song and opened that big sliding door on the back of the stage. Some drunk had parked his car on the tracks, and the train had hit the car and knocked the car over into my rent-a-car. So there was this double train wreck, and my rent-a-car was totaled. It almost seemed like the song attracted the train.[1]

---

[1] Joe Ely, interview with Brian T. Atkinson, October 30, 2014. For more on Joe Ely and his role in the progressive country music movement, see Jan Reid, *The Improbable Rise of Redneck Rock* (Austin: University of Texas Press, 2004), 48, 302–7, 328, 340, 346; Rich Koster, *Texas Music* (New York: St. Martin's Press, 1998), 66, 102–3, 109, 111, 112, 196–97; Peter Doggett, *Are You Ready for the Country* (New York, Penguin Books, 2000); 280, 438, 439, 454, 466–69; www.ely.com/ (accessed January 30, 2015).

# 33 | Monte Montgomery

Kent would swap songs at Luckenbach and Cheatham Street. He was one of those guys who would break out his guitar every time you'd see him back in those days. So my earliest memories of Kent are just as him as a musician. I remember the stuff he'd play would have a sense of humor, amusing and cool and clever. I appreciated being exposed to that more folky songwriter back then that my mom [singer-songwriter Maggie "Magnolia Thunder Blossom" Montgomery] exposed me to at an early age because it helped my appreciation for crafting a song.

I grew up playing those kind of places, like Luckenbach Dance Hall, that had more of the Texas country vibe that I was into in my earlier years as a performer. I didn't play guitar until I was thirteen or fourteen, but my mom used to drag me around to all of her gigs when I was younger. You know, I came from Alabama. When I got to Texas and was thrust into my mom's world with all these musicians and cowboys and people she used to hang out with, it was quite a cultural shock. She always hung out with talented people.

In those days, Luckenbach was more of a secret. I learned how to play guitar out there hanging out with my mom and her friends underneath the trees and watching them play. It was real loose and had no shortage of talented people back then. I learned so much from a guitar-playing and songwriting standpoint. It was such a genuine, easy, special place to hang out. It wasn't all commercialized and touristy like it is now. I met some genuine people, and Kent certainly was a part of that scene. I was just the young kid who knew a few chords, more of an observer back then. Luckenbach had some hippies and that cosmic cowboy vibe. Everybody was wearing cowboy hats and smoking weed and drinking beer. It was Jerry Jeff Walker and Rusty Weir and Gary P. Nunn and Kent Finlay and Guy Clark and all those songwriters. They were poets, troubadours.

*Monte Montgomery tour poster from the 1990s. Courtesy Finlay family archives*

I definitely do my own thing, and I've made my whole career on do-ing things that nobody else does, so I guess it's true that I fall into the category of Kent looking for people who break the rules. I play electric stuff on an acoustic and do my own brand of music. It makes sense that he'd dig that. Initially, I used to just be a big fan of "Romeo and Juliet" when I was younger. Then I came across a live version on the Dire Straits' [1980 concert video] *Alchemy: Live*. Of course, I was drawn to the fact that Mark Knopfler was playing it on an old National guitar. It was one of those songs I was doing when I played cover gigs in restaurants in San Antonio when I lived there.

I did it for so long that it became what it is. Obviously, I do a lot more stretching out on guitar than Mark Knopfler does. Over time, it just turned into that, a song that I played every night because everyone wanted to hear it. I became synonymous with that song for many years. I did more and more involved guitar, which will happen when you play the same song over and over every night. You get a little bored with it and look for ways to freshen it up for yourself. It ended up being this ten-, twelve-[minute] saga, but it's all melodic and beautiful, and it obviously took me years to land on all that stuff where it all works together.

I still go to Cheatham Street every once in a while to play. It's a very unassuming, very Texas juke joint, and that's because of Kent. I think of him as a mentor first. That's probably the most important thing that he does, the way he takes people under his wing and gives them a place to play and helps them along. He's helped a lot of people, and a lot of those people have gone on to do really big things. Kent said, "Man, you're on a level where you're gonna be out of here soon. You're taking off. You're so good and do your own thing that's very energetic. You're destined for big things and bigger stages."[1]

---

[1] Monte Montgomery, interview with Brian T. Atkinson, July 14, 2014. For more on Monte Montgomery, see Brian T. Atkinson, "Monte Montgomery at Antone's," *Austin American-Statesman*, March 19, 2010; www.montemontgomery.com/.

Cheatham Street's a real laid-back Texas honky-tonk with this sliding door in the back, a barn door where you opened and slid all the gear in. It's right next to the train tracks, literally twenty, thirty feet away. There'd be certain times in the set when we'd have to stop playing because the train would go by, and it'd be so loud. Also, I remember the ceiling was really low, and there'd be these light bulbs hanging down, and a couple times I knocked the lights out with the headstock of my guitar, just accidentally, turning around. One time we played two nights in a row, and we went home after the first gig and left our whole gear set up all night. The next day we discovered that we hadn't locked the sliding barn door. Everything was still there.

We mostly played rock, but we experimented. We got into playing there a whole bunch, and I could go down there and try out new stuff and new combinations. I would've been playing "Cliffs of Dover," "Zap," "Bristol Shore," "Trail of Tears." We did some Weather Report songs and Eddie Harris's "Freedom Jazz Dance," some Jimi Hendrix songs. I started writing "Cliffs of Dover" in the early eighties, and then I just played it onstage for years but never recorded it until my second solo record. During the time I was playing Cheatham Street, I wrote a lot of those songs that came out on my first and second records. I knew Kent was a songwriter and guitar player, and we used to talk about songwriting, and he was really into that.

I think being so fervent about music goes a long way with any artist. You can feel the support and encouragement from somebody, and when you emit that kind of energy it inspires people to keep going. I remember many times playing in the club, and Kent would come over with a smile on his face. You know, you feel like you're going forward, and if somebody comes over smiling it's like a pat on the back. "Keep going."

*Eric Johnson*

Photo Credit: Mary Beth Greenwood

Eric Johnson promotional photograph from the 1980s. Photo by Mary Beth Greenwood; courtesy Finlay family archives

It's like getting a drink of water in a marathon race. He was one of the artistic people who supplied a venue, an outlet, a chance, an opportunity for a lot of musicians to continue and flourish.

Kent's just a music lover, such a sweet guy, very affable and easygoing. He was always, like, "Let's just do this and have fun." I think he's one of those rare gems. He comes from that Texas singer-songwriter gang, and a lot of those guys are great players: Rusty Weir and Willie Nelson and Michael Murphey. I think the rare thing about Kent is he lit up about all kinds of music. The Texas songwriter folk and country crowd might've been his thing, but you could just tell in his eyes and his appreciation that he just likes music. That's a good commentary on how it should be: you just support and enjoy all music, any music that's good and can be enjoyed.

I love bluegrass and country, and I'm a big fan of jazz and classical and blues. There's always something in every style that I can enjoy, and it moves me. It's the spirit behind it. That's why it's not really an issue of what you're playing. You'll go hear a band that only knows one chord or two, and they come out, and they're not together, and they're all over the map, but they're great, and people love them because they've got the spirit behind it. It's nice to be a great musician or have really interesting orchestration and color, but it's all smoke and mirrors if you don't have spirit. If you have that, you've got it all.[1]

---

[1] Eric Johnson, interview with Brian T. Atkinson, June 17, 2014. For more on Eric Johnson's pioneering guitar work, see Rich Koster, *Texas Music* (New York: St. Martin's Press, 1998), 98, 101, 107, 109, 110; "Eric Johnson," *Guitar World*, www.guitarworld.com/eric-johnson (accessed January 30, 2015); www.ericjohnson.com/ (accessed January 30, 2015).

# 35 | Joe "King" Carrasco

The first time I went to Cheatham Street was to see Gatemouth Brown in 1975. How cool is that? Gatemouth was older, and he was playing country and blues on fiddle and less guitar, which was pretty amazing. He was primarily a blues guy, so I was surprised. You'd always see stuff like [that] there. I saw Doug Sahm there too. It's an institution, man. You can't make up something that cool, the way the stage door slides out, the ambiance. It's real comfortable. I know the stage, the room, the layout. You know where the railings are when you move around the crowd. Plus, they serve good Mexican Coke.

I started playing there in the early eighties. The Crowns got real big in '83, and Southwest [Texas State University] was the party capital of the world. I was throwing myself in the audience, diving off the stage into that audience. You know that's not a really high ceiling, right? It was insane at that time. I can't imagine we'll ever see that craziness again. Then Southwest changed their policy and became less of a party school, but I still like the audience we get there. It was always interesting when the train came by and rumbled the building. I always liked that the warehouse doors slid back. When you think about San Marcos, you think about Cheatham Street. That's the only music place I've gone to in San Marcos. There may have been other places, but that was the only one where I wanted to go.

There was the Soap Creek Saloon in Austin and Cheatham Street in San Marcos when the [1983] album *Party Weekend* came out. Soap Creek didn't survive, but Cheatham Street's still going. Kent gave original Texas music a laboratory where you could experiment with stuff. I'm sure that's what George Strait did. He could try out songs and see if they worked or not. George Strait basically started out playing at the same time. It's interesting: there's George Strait playing one night, and then there's Joe "King" Carrasco playing to the crazy college kids.

Joe "King" Carrasco, Cheatham Street Warehouse, 1985. Promotional photograph; courtesy Finlay family archives

Doug Sahm and those guys defined that Texas sound that came out of Austin. Soap Creek did that, and so did Cheatham. It was so important because that's where the music developed live. Cheatham Street was one of the places where it was a real authentic thing. It wasn't in a mall or some brand-new building. It had a lot of soul. That's what it's all about, right? Doug's my favorite Texas musician. Those guys always brought their own cooler full of drinks to Cheatham. I remember that. It was always so hot, man, and they'd have the sliding doors on the stage open. You could watch Doug from inside, but if you really wanted to see how the musicians were you'd go back and watch them from behind the stage through the sliding doors. I loved the down-home vibe.[1]

[1] Joe "King" Carrasco, interview with Brian T. Atkinson, July 2, 2015. For more on Joe "King" Carrasco, see Rich Koster, *Texas Music* (New York: St. Martin's Press, 1998), 124; Courtney Harrell, *Westword*, August 26, 2014, http://blogs.westword.com/backbeat/2014/08/joe_king_carrasco_interview_profile.php (accessed January 30, 2015); www.joeking.com/ (accessed January 30, 2015).

# 36 | Ernie Durawa
## (Texas Tornadoes)

We played at Cheatham Street Warehouse in the late 1970s when I first came to Austin. Doug Sahm might've played there more with the Sir Douglas Quintet, but I remember being there with the Tornadoes. Texas Tornadoes actually started in San Marcos at Fire Station Studios. That's where we recorded our first record [1990's *Texas Tornadoes*], the one that won a [Best Mexican/Mexican-American Album] Grammy for us. Lucky Tomblin was the owner of the studio, and he was a friend and fan of the band. Doug called and said, "Come down and record a record." That was the launching pad.

We'd always play the hits like "Mendocino" and "She's About a Mover," but what I liked best was when we did the blues with the horns. He did a lot of Bobby "Blue" Bland–like songs, basically Texas blues, Texas double-shuffle. I really enjoyed playing that. He also did his country where he played fiddle. That band we took to Europe in 1984, '85, was really amazing. We had Larry Campbell, the guy who ended up producing Levon Helm and was with Bob Dylan forever, on guitar. He was with us before he did all that. That was a heck of a band. We took Europe by storm.

I grew up playing with Doug Sahm in San Antonio. I was fifteen and he was sixteen. Doug was electrifying, charismatic onstage, played great guitar. I remember people like Stevie Ray Vaughan in the very early days coming to watch him play. He influenced a lot of musicians. He was a genius musician, an entertainer. He was demanding. He wanted to hear certain things certain ways, and there were times when we would have disagreements onstage, but then we're having dinner together later, and it's like nothing happened. We were like a married couple almost.

Ernie Durawa, Strange Brew, Austin, March 17, 2015. Photo by Brian T. Atkinson

Doug was versatile. When we'd be in New York, we'd go to the jazz clubs. He was a big jazz fan. He wanted to have a country band, a blues band, a Tex-Mex band. We all grew up that way. Growing up in Texas, you have a melting pot of cultures and styles and food. Barbecue and Italian and Mexican food is all here. That's the way the music was. We could play anything we wanted, and we had the talent to do it because we started so young. Doug was well respected by guys like Bob Dylan and Bruce Springsteen. Everybody had a tremendous respect for his musical abilities.

He died when he was fifty-eight, and we lost a lot of music with him. When he left here, he left two messages. One said, "Ernie, I'm going far away, so far away you're gonna have to send a bird out to find me." I just went, "Oh, shit, I don't know what he means by that, but I'm not gonna worry about it." Later on, there was anther message that said, "Get ready. We're going to Europe in February." Those were the last two messages I got. [Sahm passed away on November 18, 1999.]

I was giving drum lessons the day that he died. I got this really bad stomachache at the end. I went up and told the lady, "Cancel my last two lessons. I'm going home. I'm sick." I came to my house, and I told my wife, "I need to lay down. I don't feel good." I lay down and about thirty minutes later the phone rang, and it was Clifford Antone calling me. I was surprised because he never called me for anything. He said, "Hey, did you hear about Doug?" I said, "What do you mean? Yeah, he said he was going to California or something." "No, no, they found him in a motel. They found him dead." I went, "What?" Just about the time they found him in the hotel was when I was having the severe stomachaches. How do you explain that?[1]

---

[1] Ernie Durawa, interview with Brian T. Atkinson, October 21, 2014. For more on Ernie Durawa, see www.erniedurawadrums.com/ (accessed May 15, 2015). For more on Doug Sahm, see David Goodman, *Modern Twang: An Alternative Country Guide & Directory* (Nashville: Dowling Press, 1999), 275. For more on both Sahm and the Sir Douglas Quintet, see Jan Reid, *The Improbable Rise of Redneck Rock* (Austin: University of Texas Press, 2004); Austin Powell and Doug Freeman, *The Austin Chronicle Music Anthology* (Austin: University of Texas, 2011).

# Diana Finlay Hendricks

I ran into Kent again at Hondo's wake [in September 1976]. He said, "Hey, do you want to be in the movies?" I said, "Yeah. I want to be in the movies." He said, "Well, this week, I'm filming [the 1977 Warner Brothers film] *Outlaw Blues*. I'm in the band in this movie with Peter Fonda and Susan St. James that's being filmed in Austin, and I have a speaking role, and I can get you to be an extra." "Okay." So my roommate Cissy and I show up to go be in the movie, and they say, "Okay, today you're at Soap Creek Saloon and the band's playing. Do you have prom dresses? If you could come tomorrow dressed very fancy like for a prom, you're gonna be in a wedding scene at the Driskill Hotel." Kent got me in the movies, and I got two scenes.

*Diana Finlay Hendricks at her home in San Marcos, 2014. Courtesy Diana Finlay Hendricks*

We'd drive up to Luckenbach two or three times a week because Hondo had this magical world there. People would just come play songs for him, and if you made him laugh, it was so great. Kent was an incredibly good songwriter and probably the first songwriter I knew well. I'd first seen songwriters at Willie's first picnic: Billy Joe Shaver and Kris Kristofferson and all those guys. So, there's Kent, who's writing really great songs and was highly influenced by Kris and Billy Joe. Kent had what I loved about Kristofferson and his internal rhyming. He had a master's in English and was working on a PhD when he quit college. He was sitting in a Shakespeare class listening to a long, dry lecture about why it took so long for Hamlet to get his revenge, and Kent said, "All I wanted to say was, 'because everybody had to get their penny and a half of entertainment.' Instead of raising my hand and being a smart aleck, I wrote 'Bumblebee.'"

The song that was the most popular with everyone in Luckenbach was "Plastic Girl" because he had just written that. As a journalist, I was saying, "How do you write those things? How do you write like that?" He would explain what gave him the ideas. He was really good at novelty songs and making people laugh. Look at when that was: Jan Reid was writing *Redneck Rock*. *Texas Monthly* started in 1973. All this was building on a magazine level, and the literary world was moving over to a journalistic style in Texas. Kent was in a good place, and he had so much talent and so much energy.

Cheatham was 100 percent influenced by Luckenbach. Cheatham was like Luckenbach and Armadillo World Headquarters and Soap Creek Saloon. All those places had the same kind of push back from the culture of old Texas. You know, they're all playing songs they made up, and the beginnings are not tight, and the endings are a train wreck, and it's this new sound that they were calling the progressive country movement coming out. It was more of a moment than a movement, though. It evolved pretty quickly, a snapshot in time when songwriters reared their heads and said, "You know what? We're gonna play our songs, and we're gonna get these good guys together, and we're not gonna do a whole lot of practicing." It was raw and great, and Kent was pulling bands together.

I think every one of those people from George Strait to Randy Rogers would say the words are the most important thing, because we are story-tellers. The thing we have is the story, and the words are the most important thing. I don't think George Strait ever sang a song that didn't have words that meant something to him. I don't think Todd Snider ever sang a song that didn't have words that meant something to him. The story is what Texas music is and what Cheatham Street has always been about.

I was there the night Townes and Guy played late. We closed and took all the beer off the table and just let them keep playing. They sat down on the edge of the stage and kept playing and kept playing. The most memorable Townes story about Cheatham was about our arcade games in there. They were always coming in with these new used video games, and they came with this one called Cowboy or Fast Draw or High Noon. It was like the original Pong except it was two cowboys. They'd shoot at you, and you'd shoot at them, and whoever killed the guy first got a point. One night I was there when Townes was playing. He's standing there alone feeding quarters, but it's a two-person game. He was just playing the one side and he kept dying because the other one kept shoot-ing him. He was just trying to run away. He wasn't trying to shoot back. I said, "You want me to play that with you?" He said, "No, I'm good." I said, "You're losing." He said, "Yeah, I know." That was Townes.

I always worked Joe "King" Carrasco nights. They asked to play, and Kent said, "Yeah, sure. We'll let anybody play once." Little did we know, they had an incredible cult following. You know, we have Stevie Ray every Tuesday, but he's not drawing a crowd. Wednesday is George Strait, and it's ladies free. Joe "King" came and people were literally hanging from the rafters right by the bar. The whole place is a dance floor. It was ab-solutely crazy. I'm counting stacks of twenties, going, "We're gonna pay the rent this month." At that time in the 1980s, Texas beer was probably seventy-five cents, and it's hard to pay the $400 rent at seventy-five cents a beer, so somewhere along there we had to learn that the Joe "King" Carrascos made us able to afford the Townes Van Zandts.

The Skunks would come in and were just the coolest of the cool. What they brought to the table was great music, good songwriting, and they were Texas boys. They knew. They could go as far as they wanted, but they'd all been in a beer joint before. When they came in, they understood it. We didn't have air conditioning. They said, "This is gonna be fun." Some other bands came in and said, "You don't have air conditioning, and I'm playing on September 3?" The Skunks said, "We're packing the house." Jesse Sublett's girlfriend Diane painted the Happy Trails mural advertisement. She was a great artist, a little, skinny hippie girl. In every effort to raise money, we'd decided to sell space on the wall for advertisements. Diane was the one who said, "Can I have the air space?" She was quiet and very talented.

Eric Johnson would want to come in early. We opened at noon, and he'd come in at one o'clock to set up his amps, which were measurably where he wanted them to be to get the sound he wanted. It was true artistry. Stevie Ray would play and crank to eleven and it was good, but Eric would come in and practically use a tape measure to find out where his amps were gonna be. It was art. I can only compare it to the fact that you can be Jackson Pollock and use splashes of paint, and you can be successful, or you can draw those lines to the miracle triangle and you have art. That's what Eric did. He was this skinny little guy introducing those songs like "Cliffs of Dover." Listeners who would come in for Eric were like pilgrims. They would sit and soak it in.

I was following George Strait before I knew Kent. It was Ace in the Hole band all the way until George got his record deal. Then he said, "It will be George Strait and Ace in the Hole." That band is still playing together. That says a lot about George. They were the nicest guys. Norma was the sweetest, nicest band wife you ever saw. Jenifer, their daughter, was their little girl, and Norma was working at an insurance company, and George was finishing school and being a musician and coming in early to set up. He was the caretaker for Jenifer, and she was the sweetest thing. In fact, January 18, 1979, Kent and Mother and I were talking about names for my first daughter. If it was a boy, it would be James Finlay III. If it was a girl, all these names came up, and I said, I want her to have a name like Jenifer Strait. That's how we came up with the name.

The first time George went to Nashville with Darrell and Kent, Kent had some great songs that would've been perfect for George. George said, "I'd really like to do 'What Makes Texas Swing' and 'I Don't Want to Talk It Over,'" two of Kent's songs. Kent said, "No, I'm gonna save those for myself." On that same trip, Kent did some sessions, and George did some sessions, and Kent didn't recognize the fact that that could've been a big thing. Eight, ten years later, he still couldn't say, "Why don't you do 'Texas Swing'?" He wanted to do it his way. He wasn't gonna go to Nashville, but he was waiting for them to knock on his door and say, "What do you got?" The world doesn't do that.

Kent had a lot of heartache when Gruene Hall wanted them. Gruene Hall had hit the map as a big regional venue. We were local. For whatever reason, they figured out how to get good marketing early and they were an old-time dance hall. In reality, the Gruene Hall we know today opened after Cheatham Street. It had always been there—I slept on the floors at Gruene Hall when I was a kid—it was just closed for a while. All of a sudden, George and Ace in the Hole get a call and are invited to play there, and that was the first time I can see that Kent was hurt by somebody leaving the nest. He didn't want them to go there. It's like, "That's competition for me. That's not fair. I've done all this for them." It was a betrayal. "Why would you go there? Aren't you getting enough here? I'm not done with you. I don't think you're ready yet."

Todd Snider had started coming to songwriter night, and he was working at Peppers at the Falls. He was a cute, lanky, clumsy kid, friends with all the frat rats. He had a couple songs: "Fat Chicks on Mopeds" and "Bus Tub Stew." He got it. He got it like how I got it when I met Kent. Kent recognized people who understood good music. Todd's very first songs were rough, but they were great. He had this gypsy charm, and he could talk anybody out of anything, yet he had this vulnerability. He was eighteen and became one of ours and was there all the time. Kent not only could teach, but he could write. He could do both, and he worked to make other people better than he was, which is a great element of a teacher, but when Todd got good enough and thought he could take the next step, it was a horrible betrayal. Todd was the biggest one he told, "You're not ready yet." He said, "Todd's gone crazy. I don't know what he's doing. He's talking to these other people and I don't know what's happened to him."

They did do some fun things. Todd didn't wear his seatbelt right after they passed the seatbelt law in Texas and got a ticket, and Kent said, "Go to jail." I called [longtime *Austin American-Statesman* columnist] John Kelso, and Kelso came down and did a story on Todd being in jail for not wearing a seatbelt. I turned him in at the highway patrol office in San Marcos. They handcuffed him, and we took pictures, which are still in the music room at the house. They put him in the jail outfit, and Kelso came down. Our neighbor was a plumber who worked at the jail, and he snuck him in a pencil, and Todd wrote songs on the wall in jail, [like] "Hays County Jailhouse Blues."

So Kent is the spokesperson and he's talking to people everywhere: "Yeah, we have this great, young songwriter, and he just got arrested for not wearing his seatbelt. Here's the song he wrote." We snuck out a version of the song. There was a "Todd was released" party at Cheatham Street. Somewhere down the line, you look back at that and think, *Huh, what are the lessons there?* Todd made Kent feel young. I made Kent feel young. He has his annual twenty-ninth birthday party to this day. Age was something he fought for a very long time, and he has a hard time letting go. He had trouble letting go of Jenni [when she was] going to Nashville. She got a lot of good scholarships, and she's the queen of the class at Belmont, and she wins all the awards, and Kent's going, "Don't listen to anything they say because that's Nashville and they're gonna mess you up."

Kent had Cheatham Street. Period. He had songwriters at the house. He was working. He was writing a song. He's helped so many people, and he's done so much for so many, but unless our children were between the bar and stage at Cheatham Street Warehouse, he didn't see them. Whatever family issues are there kind of fall in the wasteland beyond Cheatham and his musicians. For instance, we got Jenni on Super Bowl Sunday. I was in labor that Saturday, and I had gone to Cheatham and opened, but I didn't feel very well, so I went home. Kent was resting because Alex Harvey was playing at Cheatham Street that night. I said, "I'm not feeling very well." He said, "You're not going to see Alex Harvey tonight?" I said, "No." "But Alex wrote 'Delta Dawn.'"

Kent went to Cheatham Street. Well, I got to feel[ling] worse and worse, and my high school best friend came to the house and said, "Shit. Are you in labor?" I said, "I don't know." She got all drunk and couldn't drive, and it was eleven o'clock that night. Kent said, "Can you wait so I can close? We have Alex Harvey." I said, "Pretty much not." He said, "I'll get there as soon as I can." So I drove myself to the hospital. Kent and Alex and several other people showed up after closing. My mother brought the motor home over. They all were celebrating and doing whatever, and I was having a baby, but there's something odd about having to drive yourself to the hospital.

Kent opened a lot of doors for a lot of people. Should I say it was all rainbows and yellow brick roads? No. I will say a hundred times over, I hope my kids find a Kent Finlay in their lives to inspire them and make them be more than they ever thought they could be. What I learned from Kent was the realization that his answer wasn't always the final answer. I think Todd and George and a litany of people can say that. Cheatham Street was a stop along their journey. Kent's a good person, but our marriage was a business. Today we're friends. We've had a lot of differences as anybody who's ever raised kids together will have. I'm so grateful for my husband, Mark Hendricks, who taught me what love was like and has done a lot of the heavy lifting in the lives of my kids and their friends to create that world of expectations. I'm so proud that Mark is proud of all of my kids, but Kent will always be dear to me because he's given me three incredible kids. What a ride it was.[1]

---

[1] Diana Finlay Hendricks, interview with Brian T. Atkinson and Jenni Finlay, July 16, 2014. See also www.dianahendricks.com/ (accessed January 30, 2015); Diana Finlay, "Daydreams" column, *San Marcos Daily Record*, 1991–99.

# 38 | Travis Warren (Blind Melon)

My mom and dad got divorced when I was really young. My mom would come meet me at Cheatham Street. I remember my dad being there a lot. My mom was going to pick me up and take me back to where she lived in Dallas, but she stood me up twice. I had my bags packed, and every time a car would pull in I thought it was her. Naturally, her not showing up caused friction between my dad and mom. So I have this dark memory, a sad feeling about Cheatham Street. I ended up writing a song called "Cheetum Street" about it, the last song on the Blind Melon For My Friends record [in 2008]. It was a melancholy song. Rogers [Stevens] had written the music to it, and the lyrics just came naturally. It's something that stuck with me through the years.

I didn't have any memories of my mom up until that point. I was one when they got divorced, and my mom got custody, but within a few months she came back to Dad and said, "I can't take care of him." She was really young when she had me too, about seventeen or eighteen. My dad was a little older. So my dad was, like, "Yeah, I'll take him. No problem." My dad was a nomad, a gypsy. We were up in Amarillo, and we just packed up and moved to San Marcos.

Kent let my dad and I stay in the trailer in the back of his house in Martindale, Texas. Kent was a pretty big fan of my dad's music, and I'm sure my dad didn't have a whole lot of cash at the time. My dad would give me some change, and I'd walk to the corner market, and the owners there would just load me up full of food. In retrospect, I'm sure they felt sorry for me and gave me more food than I could afford. I never knew those folks who ran that store, but I'm still grateful. We never could have afforded that food. I remember we used to go out to the river and light

Left to right: Terry Warren, Mark Luke Daniels, Travis Warren, John Arthur martinez, Erik Moll (obscured), Olin Murrell (obscured), Kent Finlay, Todd Snider, Jenni Finlay, Raven's, Austin, 1989. Photo by Diana Finlay Hendricks; courtesy Finlay family archives

firecrackers and cherry bombs and throw them in the river and watch them swell up and change colors. I remember tubing down the San Marcos River.

I saw the Killer Bees and Chris Duarte at Cheatham Street during that time. My dad introducing me to Gatemouth Brown sticks out like a sore thumb. He was this really old dude. I think he was smoking pot. Of course, they were all into that. My dad had a buddy who was growing a massive amount of herb. I think the feds found out about it, and he basically took off on a motorcycle and went to Mexico. There was crazy shit. When all that erupted, he sent my ass back to Amarillo.

When my dad passed, I was going through a lot of his things, like lyrics from the sixties. I found some Cheatham Street posters that I have framed, and my favorite one has my dad playing on a Saturday and then Townes Van Zandt playing on Thursday the fourteenth. I'm a huge Townes Van Zandt fan. I wish I [had been] a little older during that time because I think there were a lot of magic things going on. Of course, I would have loved to see Townes play at Cheatham Street.

Townes was awesome, a musician's musician. My dad was a huge Townes fan. Toward the end, I had burned a lot of vinyl to CDs and made my dad this book with some Dylan and all the Townes Van Zandt records. He was sitting there in his room going through all of them, and it was really cool watching him sing the songs. I was watching the Townes documentary *Be Here to Love Me* with my dad, and I was watching my dad more than the show. He was so into it. My dad was so bummed when Townes passed away. He used to tell me that he'd played shows with Townes, and I never knew because sometimes he was telling the truth, and sometimes he was exaggerating. I never really knew, but then I was talking to my dad's publishers at his funeral. They said, "Yeah, we're who introduced your dad to Townes." I was like, "Holy shit, he wasn't bullshitting about that."[1]

[1] Travis Warren, interview with Brian T. Atkinson, April 9, 2014. For more on Travis Warren's role in the popular rock group Blind Melon, see "Blind Melon Recording Album with New Singer," *Billboard*, October 20, 2006, www.billboard.com/articles/news/56893/blind-melon-recording-album-with-new-singer (accessed January 30, 2015). For more on Chris Duarte, see www.thechrisduartegroup.com/ (accessed January 30, 2015). For more on Gatemouth Brown, see Alan Govenar, *Texas Blues: The Rise of a Contemporary Sound* (College Station: Texas A&M University Press, 2008), 256, 374–377, 379, 456, 497; Ben Ratliff, "Guitarist Clarence Gatemouth Brown Dies at 81," www.nytimes.com/2005/09/12/arts/music/12brown.html?_r=0 (accessed January 30, 2015).

# 39 | Radney Foster

Kent Finlay's not had the fame of Guy Clark or Townes Van Zandt, but I'd put him in that same generation. He's written some brilliant songs. When we recorded "Hill Country" with the Randy Rogers Band, I was like, "That's a cool song." I moved to Nashville when I was twenty, so I wasn't around when George Strait and the Ace in the Hole band were playing there. I was already either going to college or trying to figure out how to make it work in Nashville. It wasn't until after I'd started an independent career that I played at Cheatham Street Warehouse. The thing I love about [Kent] is how many young writers and musicians he's mentored over the years. It's a staggering list.

*Radney Foster and Bill Lloyd, Waterloo Records, Austin, June 25, 2011. Photo by Brian T. Atkinson*

I think the first time I played there I was working with Randy Rogers Band. Randy and [fiddler] Brady [Black] still had their Tuesday-night gig. They were playing every Tuesday when we were making [Rogers's 2004 album] *Rollercoaster*. Randy said, "Hey, man, do you know about Cheatham Street Warehouse?" I said, "Yes, I do, but I've never played there." He said, "Will you come be my surprise guest?" I was coming down on a Tuesday to write on that Tuesday and Wednesday and was going to play Thursday, Friday, Saturday. I said, "Yeah, sure." So the first time I played there was ten years ago. I met Kent that night. I said, "I'll come back here and play anytime, Kent. This is awesome."

Cheatham Street's the Bluebird Cafe of Texas. It's a place where you can call Kent and say, "Hey, I have a bunch of new stuff I want to try out. Can I come on a Wednesday night?" He'll say, "Well, you can sell out a Friday night." "Yeah, but I want to come in with my guitar on Wednesday night and try stuff out, new songs." He's like, "Absolutely. You can do it." It is the one place that I go that feels like and looks like and walks like and talks like a honky-tonk bar, but when you're playing a song, even with a full band, you don't hear the din of cocktail parties like there are at a lot of other bars in Texas.

There are places down here where you can play with you and your guitar, and it's fine, but there [is] always gonna be a level of conversation. It's the thing to do. Also, they really want to hear the hits. The other places where you can hear a pin drop usually are much smaller than Cheatham Street. They're folkie listening rooms by their very nature, like the Mucky Duck in Houston. Cheatham Street's a honky-tonk bar where everybody listens. People get pissed because they can't hear the lyrics. It's like, "Nope, you can't do that in here. Hey, take it outside."[1]

---

[1] Radney Foster, interview with Brian T. Atkinson, April 4, 2014. For more on Radney Foster, see Rich Koster, *Texas Music* (New York: St. Martin's Press, 1998), 54, 225; Brian T. Atkinson, "Radney Foster Faces the Muse, Finds a New Album," *CMT Edge*, May 15, 2014, www.cmtedge. com/2014/05/15/radney-foster-faces-the-muse-finds-a-new-album (accessed January 30, 2015); Brian T. Atkinson, "Radney Foster Revisits Del Rio, *Texas* 1959," *CMT Edge*, September 18, 2012, www.cmtedge.com/2012/09/18/radney-foster-revisits-del-rio-tx-1959 (accessed January 30, 2015); Brian T. Atkinson, "Radney Foster and the Circle of Life," *Austin American-Statesman*, July 15, 2009.

I met Kent when I started making my first organized trips from Nashville back to Texas around Fire, Honey and Angels [2000]. I played a gig at Cheatham Street, and there were probably six people there, but Kent treated me with such respect. He said, "Call when you're headed this way." At one point, we talked about writing. On one of my trips down, I came in and had a hook line [for "Blanco River Meditation 2"]: "I've got nothing to do and I'm not leaving until I'm done." It was a spring morning, and I was driving down following the Blanco River. I said, "I've got this hook." Then Kent just wrote the song. He'd say something, and I'd go, "That's really good." I'd have an idea that wasn't that good, and he'd go, "How about this?" The last verse goes, "There's a ruckus downriver and I look down to see the sight of mama duck." He just said it all at once like Walter Hyatt would do sometimes. I was like, "Well, shit, that's good."

It's so corny to say this, but Kent has a twinkle in his eye. You can meet people, and they know when you're real. Kent immediately treated me like I was good enough to be in the club. I was serious about it and came prepared to work. I played a good set even though there weren't people there. There was no shadow over it from Kent. After a show like that, someone might say, "Hey, sorry it didn't work out, but give us a call." You know they're never having you back, but Kent said, "Can't wait to have you back," and he meant it.

I was out with Pat Green after his first national release. He recorded three or four of my songs, and I'd sung a bunch of harmonies, and he wanted me in the band. We went all over the country. [My son] Luke was ten weeks old when I got on the bus, and I missed a bunch of firsts, including the first steps. No doubt that was on my mind, but Pat was so cool. He gave me the back room. I didn't sleep in a bunk the first couple

*Walt Wilkins, Cheatham Street Warehouse, San Marcos, February 10, 2015.*
*Photo by Brian T. Atkinson*

months. So I slept in the back, and I always carried my idea book, and I had the idea for "Someone Somewhere Tonight." It was five or five thirty in the morning. I was looking out at the lights as we were passing through this town and thinking about all these stories. You know, every house has maybe four stories going on. At any given moment, every house has some joy, even if it's just the stillness of another day. Each house has unimaginable pain. I wrote the first and second verses in their entirety. I was missing my son.

Most people will say Kent provided this cradle for people, including me, to get better. Secondary for a lot of people is just that he's a great songwriter. Also, his singing knocks me out. He's full on and hits the note dead center with that beautiful vibrato, all those ancient beautiful things you don't hear on the radio anymore, like Marty Robbins and those guys. Why wasn't Kent on the radio? It's all luck, and, well, life's not fair, and he's not ambitious in that way. It always seemed to me that he likes his life pretty well, but when you hear him play, you're, like, "Wait a minute. You're great." There's no one in the room who can play a song as good as that. He's upper-tier. When you hear him sing one of his songs, you're like, "This guy is of the ages." Kent is like Jimmie Rodgers and Lefty Frizzell. He's connecting from generation to generation.[1]

The last song I wrote with Kent, "Mother Nature, Father Time and Me," was a little unfocused, so we meandered a bit. I didn't realize he [had] live[d] in that house so long. That's where the kids were raised. We were talking about the river there, and we started writing about nature. Kent had a great line already that'll probably end up being the first line of the song, "Ten thousand years before Jesus." We were talking about the wisdom of the land and describing that particular land in another time, a thousand, two thousand, five thousand years ago, and the people who were there. We'd been working on it for a couple hours, and Kent said, "You know what, I've had this title for a couple years. I saw it the other day: 'Mother Nature, Father Time and Me.'" I said, "That's heavy, man." I will be working on it. I will finish it.

He was awesome that day. He was pretty cheerful. I hadn't seen him in a while, and when I came in the house I was pretty shocked, pretty stunned at how he looked. He had a nurse there checking on his vital signs. He said, "I'm just gonna tell you man to man what's going on." He was talking about his heart. He said, "Well, the doctor told me if there were songs laying around that I needed to finish, now's the time to do it." He knew his time was short. He was, like, "I'm working on these songs." Who knows what it feels like when you're down to days? There's this compulsion to finish what you have around. You have things that are in their idea form. You have a title and a verse started on another thing.

I love "Bright Lights of Brady" because it's told with such a wink. On one hand, it's a really sincere song about a kid, but when an older man sings it it's funny and still really sweet. I heard him sing that for the first time at Cheatham Street when we sang together. We were talking years later, and I said, "I'd love a copy of that." It was hard to not imitate him. I don't have that voice, that pure, clear voice like Kent. I recorded it and just tried to get his melody. He was particular about things like melody. I pretty much just did it in one take. I realized that I did a couple things different than him that I don't think he would've minded. We were keeping it simple and uncluttered to tell that great story. There's an arc. It starts one way and has this great twist. I enjoy playing it. Kent's a great songwriter. I've been playing it, and I'll play it forever. I played it last night in Fort Worth, and that was the first night I played it when it really worked. It's getting better.[2]

[1] Walt Wilkins, interview with Brian T. Atkinson, May 7, 2014. For more on Walt Wilkins, see Richard Skanse, "Walt Wilkins Q&A," Lone Star Music, March 2006, www.lonestarmusic.com/index.php?file=interview_det&p=a&iInterviewId=38&page=4, (accessed February 26, 2015); Brian McElhiney, "Walt Wilkins Enjoys Simpler Life after Moving Back to Texas," Daily Gazette (Schenectady, NY), October 3, 2013, www.dailygazette.com/news/2013/oct/03/1003_WaltWilkins (accessed February 26, 2015).
[2] Walt Wilkins, interview with Brian T. Atkinson, March 9, 2015.

# 41 | Bruce Robison

I went to college for a semester or two at Southwest Texas State, and I guess I was thinking about writing songs, and I would go over to Cheatham Street and watch open mikes. I didn't have the guts to get up and play. I'm not sure—I had hardly any songs then, and I couldn't imagine how it'd . . . go to play your own songs. It wasn't until I moved to Austin and joined a band that I thought about putting in my own song. I was singing harmony and playing rhythm guitar because I don't think I had any idea of what else to do with my life.

Bruce Robison and Kent Finlay, Texas Music Theater, San Marcos, April 27, 2014. Photo by Brian T. Atkinson

When I started playing in Austin, the big thing Kent did was to give me encouragement and let me know that he liked my songs. He booked me when I didn't have any shows. He really is a friend of the songwriter. You feel like you're doing good when he gives you some positive feedback because he's heard so much and been involved in this area for such a long time. He reminds me of the people you'd hear about in Greenwich Village back in the day who would get people a gig and encourage folks when they thought they were worthwhile.

Cheatham Street feels like a labor of love in this community. I know what it's like to want to be a part of that. When I was a kid, Guy Clark and Jerry Jeff and Willie and Waylon [Jennings] and Emmylou [Harris] and Townes Van Zandt were mythical to me. When you find yourself sticking your toe into it, Kent's always been doing it for the right reasons and not to make a million dollars and not trying to go off to Nashville or anything. He's the grassroots mobilizer.

Cheatham Street really is the nuts and bolts of the music scene at any given moment in the past decades, whether it was George Strait or Hal Ketchum on the stage or Todd Snider or [James] McMurtry. I don't want to call it a proving ground because it never felt competitive. It's a place that nurtured you, and that's what you get from him. The open mike was the same as any open mike I've been to: there's good and bad. I wasn't ready, but I didn't walk away thinking, *Oh, I can never do that.* That's where I [was] starting to think, *Gosh, some other people are doing this. Maybe I could. Maybe they won't laugh.*

The Class of '87 reunion [at Cheatham Street in 2007] was a huge thing for me. There are these moments when it really is great to think that you have made a little mark. Kent really did that for me. The people onstage were so accomplished, such good songwriters, and, God, I can't imagine a more varied group. They're people who really took a different approach to things. I was really honored to be a part of that. I think it was a nice representation of Texas music, and one thing I love about Texas music and this area in particular is that it's so varied—and worthwhile too.

Funny songs seem to be a real big part of the vibe down here. It's really difficult to do. I have one that I'm proud of. There are a lot of angles to it. You know, it's difficult to write a love song, and a concept for a funny song that's gonna hold up is probably even harder, but it's a big part of Texas music. Jerry Jeff doesn't like me to say it, but "Pissing in the Wind" is one of my favorite songs of his. I love "Gotta Get Drunk" that Willie did. Todd's halfway to being a stand-up comic. I think that comes out of trying to put on a good show. You don't want to go up there and bring everybody down for ninety minutes like I do.

I didn't know Todd cowrote Kent's "Who Says It's Lonely at the Top." There are a couple lines that are really creative. There's that one about sitting there and playing your songs for people, and that guy says, "Well, what else you got?" It's one of those moments you know if you've been in that horrible situation with somebody sitting there at a desk, and you're playing songs for them and trying to impress them. It's Kent playing that part, which he never would [actually] play to anyone.[1]

[1] Bruce Robison, interview with Brian T. Atkinson, March 22, 2014. For more on the Cheatham Street Class of 1987, see Brian T. Atkinson, "Todd Snider's Return to Cheatham Street," Austin American-Statesman, November 29, 2007. For more on Bruce Robison, see Chris Willman, Rednecks & Bluenecks: The Politics of Country Music (New York: New Press, 2005), 16, 23, 120–23, 238.

# 42 | Terri Hendrix

I found out about Cheatham Street because of Todd Snider. I had a job at Peppers at the Falls [in San Marcos], and Todd was a busboy and a waiter there. Todd was Todd. He was only there because he had to be there to earn money. His head was really into the songs, and he was already starting to get a following, and he was getting ready to launch into his career. He was very hippie. So I had heard about this open mike night, and I had always played guitar and written songs. I was nineteen years old when I started.

People knew that I had majored in music at Hardin-Simmons University, and they knew that I wrote songs. Somewhere along the line, someone said, "You should go to the songwriter night at Cheatham Street Warehouse." I did. People would sit around this [wood]stove and play songs. I was really nervous [my first time]. I had a hard time getting through my songs and was definitely not performing out at that time. I hadn't written a lot of songs. I had written a lot of poems, but nothing I was really comfortable playing on guitar and singing at the same time.

I would write political and religious songs. It wasn't like I turned people on their heads. It was really like they were polite to me, but it was obvious I didn't know what I was doing. I just thought, *Why not just jump into it?* I remember I played "Sister's Song" [and] a gospel song, "Medicine Man." Kent knew I was nervous and just getting started. I said one day, "You know, I really want to do this." Kent said, "Well, you have to be really hungry for it, and you have to be able to not do anything else." It took me a long time to realize what he really meant, but it's true. In order to want this career, you do have to be hungry and really work. That was really great advice for me. Kent was an important figure in songwriting, and I liked the way he crafted his songs. He set the bar as far as musicianship coupled with lyrics.

*Terri Hendrix, Cheatham Street Warehouse, San Marcos, February 7, 2015. Photo by Brian T. Atkinson*

I played a house concert a long time ago that was more like a house party. Scott Biram was booked on it as well. He did these traditional folk songs, but they were so funky, like [Leadbelly's] "Pick a Bale of Cotton." I like that style a ton, and that had a lasting impact on me. I've always bought Scott's music, and there were a few other shows we did together, but I don't think he realized I had turned into such a fan. He introduced me to Elder Roma Wilson, the acoustic blues player. He was an inspiration to learn harmonica because I liked his style so much. I love "Ain't It a Shame."

I met Adam Carroll at the Larry Joe Taylor festival and was just floored by his songs. I think he's one of my favorite songwriters in Texas and one of my favorite people. What's really great is he doesn't think he's all that. He doesn't think he has a handle on songwriting. He never has. He's always in search of something to write about, and he's not high on himself, which is something that gets on my nerves with our Texas songwriters. I feel like they don't listen to other people. They listen to themselves. Adam Carroll turned me on to [jazz trumpeter] Kermit Ruffins, and [Carroll] recently . . . had a sellout at Cheatham Street. People were just clamoring to hear those lyrics. It's been a great place for him to sink his roots into the ground and further his career.

By the time '93 rolled around, I quit waiting tables and was playing full time. It was just my pickup truck and PA. I met Lloyd Maines around '97, and we started to work together. We did that *Live in San Marcos* record in 2001. I had been playing for a long time and had a fan base built up to warrant two sold-out nights to record it. I wanted to give people who had been following my career a chance to be in on a recording. I picked Cheatham Street because it was in my hometown, and Kent has been really important about supporting songwriters. It felt like the perfect home to sing my songs and record them.

Kent's never booked artists based on their beer sales, and that's always been really appealing to me. He really cares about the people who come into his building as long as they respect the songwriter. It was the perfect place to do the fan appreciation party [for the release of *The Ring* in 2001]. I wanted to make a free event where nobody paid. We just sat around and played songs, and it was a record release. I ordered pizzas and food for everyone, and people brought their kids. I'm looking at a photo right now of me singing with these two little girls. That's what playing music's all about to me: down-home, in town, hometown party.

The Class of '87 reunion was really relaxed. I really enjoyed watching everyone joke with one another. There's no real backstage at Cheatham Street, so the place where people were joking "backstage" was right onstage. People really enjoyed it, and I was honored to be a part of it.

It was interesting to think back to when I first played there. We set up around a circle. It was kind of like when I was nineteen years old. I kept thinking to myself, *Wow, if you [had] told me that I was going to be doing this, that I would have traveled as much and had the opportunities that I have had and played music for a living, I would have never believed you.* I was pretty in awe the whole night.

I think that when something's done for the right reasons, good things happen. Kent loves songs. He loves lyrics and thinks about every word he writes. When you have a venue that's all about the songs and you just love songs, you create this magical atmosphere that continues. I think it's really important that Cheatham Street is seen as a historical site and not something that you can mow down and put a condo on. It's important to American music. When people talk about San Marcos, people talk about the outlet mall and the river and the university and Cheatham Street. Sometimes Cheatham Street comes in first before the outlet mall. I could see a statue of Kent Finlay in bronze by it. Kent started it.[1]

[1] Terri Hendrix, interview by Brian T. Atkinson, May 22, 2015. For more on Terri Hendrix, see Kathleen Hudson, *Women in Texas Music: Stories and Songs* (Austin: University of Texas Press, 2007), 20–28; Brian T. Atkinson, *I'll Be Here in the Morning: The Songwriting Legacy of Townes Van Zandt* (College Station: Texas A&M University Press, 2012), 187–92; Gary Hartman, *The History of Texas Music* (College Station: Texas A&M University Press, 2008), 191–92; Brian T. Atkinson, "Hendrix Puts Lively Mix in New Album," *Austin American-Statesman*, May 20, 2010; Brian T. Atkinson, "Terri Hendrix Gives *Wallpaper* a Modern Makeover," *CMT Edge*, March 27, 2013, www.cmtedge. com/2013/03/27/terri-hendrix-gives-wallpaper-a-modern-makeover (accessed January 30, 2015). For more on Elder Roma Wilson, see "Elder Roma Wilson," NEA National Heritage Fellowships, http://arts.gov/honors/heritage/fellows/elder-roma-wilson (accessed January 30, 2015).

# 43 | Todd Snider

I don't come from what I would call the most honest family. A big part of their dishonesty is showing more than you have, keeping your best jacket on all the time. I fell out of that, or was sort of chased out of that world. I was busing tables and making up songs about it, and I was sitting in with this band called the Martin Brothers at Peppers at the Falls. They were finally like, "Hey, man, this isn't how you do it. You don't just jam out on someone else's gig. You have to go to open mike and Cheatham Street's the best one." I went there and sang three songs that night, and Kent told me I was really good that very first time. He asked me where I lived.

At the time, I was living with Trog [Snider's friend made popular in the live version of his song "The Devil's Backbone Tavern"], but my answer was that I didn't really live anywhere. He took me to his house that night, and him and Diana played me the Shel [Silverstein] and Kris [Kristofferson] and [John] Prine. I'd never heard any of them, but from my three songs he said I reminded him of them. So he showed that to me, and I stayed there that night. Then I just slowly eased into staying there all the time. He gave me a PA system, and I started working.

We wrote or talked about writing all day, every day, for two or three years. He would have me do weird shit, too, like "wax on, wax off" sensei shit that I still to this day wonder whether it was for his amusement. He had me walk to a tree that was about six hundred yards from his house and wanted me to spend the whole day doing it. I felt that he was trying to teach me to be observant. Don't just zip down there and back. Check it out. Be able to talk about the whole trip. That's what I took from it. Then years later I thought, *Was that guy fucking with me? Was that some Hondo joke?* Maybe both. That's a lesson there too: the sense in the senseless, the linear and abstract. He's a deep cat and he thinks that shit through.

Todd Snider and Kent Finlay at Finlay's house, Martindale, Texas, November 6, 2014.
Photo by Brian T. Atkinson

The main thing got instilled into me almost family-like. You can see it in Sterling's face: "You can't buy me, man." I would take that over poems. That lesson that he just rode into me, [and} I would take that over the songwriting. I would reapply it to mowing yards. He had a real balance between what Willie Nelson used to say: do it for the love, but then don't be above the money. Do it for the right reasons, but then don't sabotage it for the wrong reason. Don't be a wuss, either. Don't horde it. The songwriting part, maybe somebody else could show somebody else how to do it the way he did.

Kent reminds me of a Hondo from Luckenbach, a very funny guy, pulling his hair out and pacing around. I remember in the eighties, people would talk about him because you could just see a little glimpse into the window of his office. There'd be some band playing, but if you looked in there Kent would very sincerely be marching to his own beat in there.

He'd be yelling and working on some song. I watched him many times get into that place where we're all trying to write songs or play music. If a hurricane whistle went off, he wouldn't hear it. Someone would have to go get him.

He saw me at my gig one time drinking whiskey with 7-Up in it. I was out on the patio, and I thought Kent was going to yell at me about drinking, but he was yelling about me drinking wrong. He said I had to meet him back at the house [the next day] and I should probably have an idea for a good song. I got out there, and he said, "Okay, I'm gonna show you how to drink whiskey and mix it with 7-Up and ice. He came out with a tray with ice and 7-Up and two glasses and a big thing of Jack Daniels. He goes, "Now, I'm gonna show you how to mix 7-Up and ice and Jack Daniels. Are you ready?" He takes out the Jack Daniels and pours two big glasses and hands me the other one. He says, "That's how you drink Jack Daniels with 7-Up and ice." I was, like, "What about the ice and the 7-Up?" He goes, "Yeah, what about them?" Then after two glasses of that, we made up "Who Says It's Lonely at the Top."

He's one of the great lyric guys. I love Bobby Bare, and I think they'd be a great team, but that's just one guy's opinion. I think Kent's lyrics are really strong, and people are really taken by them. More importantly, people who want to have them in their lives seem to instinctively see something in his eyes—that he's pulling the joy out of it and he's also getting attention and money for it and has been for a long time. You look at him, and you see the same look that Willie Nelson has on his face: "You can throw me in the middle of a hurricane and I'd still have this grin that says, 'Yeah, I kind of make up songs when I'm bored, and it makes me happy.'" I think he's very Kristofferson-like in that he's an even truer testament to the saying that if you do what you love to do, you'll never have to work. He's also an even truer testament to how much work you can get done if you do.

I was reading a magazine on an airplane one day, and there was an article that said that we only use a percentage of our brain. I wrote that down and thought I could make it a song. I must've been on my way to

Kent or away from Kent because I called him during a layover and told him what I had written down. Then he said, "Sixty percent of all statistics are made up on the spot." We were off running on our second verse. Graffiti isn't a song, you know, so that makes it legal. So we had a verse and a half by the time my plane took back off. When I landed, I got back on the phone and kept going.

"24 Hours a Day" was [written] during the first time I got to tour in a bus. I called Kent and said, "I got a bus," which meant he could come. He flew out and met me somewhere in Arizona, and we got something to eat and sat outdoors at Wendy's. It was across the street from a gas station, and there was some kid leaning up against a pay phone, and we were trying to be Shel Silverstein and just started imagining what was going on. He had this line that he'd kept for years about the born-again eyes, and that might apply. Once we thought it would apply, that started being the foundation for the whole thing. We put that onto the person we were seeing. He didn't have that tattoo, or if he could've we were too far to see it, but we connected those two people. I don't feel like I delivered as much of my personal heart to that as I could've. I feel like I was still trying to learn things. I still am trying to learn things.

I remember that my wife was really mad at me on the telephone the night [of the Class of '87 reunion]. We'd just gotten past a health scare as well. I remember it was good to see Hal [Ketchum]. I hadn't seen him in so long, and then James [McMurtry] and all of them. Stuff like that's intimidating to me. I came into music to get away from anything that seemed jockey. Guitar pulls are the hardest. They're not jockey, it's just that I always feel like someone plays a song, and I like it better than mine and then think that it's relevant, and it's not. I sat there the whole night going, *Man, fuck. I need to work on my guitar playing. I need to rework these songs. I need some new songs.* That's how I used to feel at songwriter night, really.

There was a period there when Kent and I got as sideways as we ever got. Songs like [Snider's unreleased] "Feeling at Home" are harder for me to listen to because I could hear him wanting me to really not like this new crowd. He wanted me to really see the value of my older friends. One of the places where Kent and me didn't have similar experience in life was when I got hooked into Nashville. I got hooked in with a guy from England named Bob Mercer, and he was as Kent Finlay as anybody as anyone I'd ever met, and yet he was the president of a record company. After I met Mercer, if I made up a new poem, I'd send it to him and I'd send it to Kent.

Neither of us knew much about the music game then, and Kent was even more suspicious than I was. I think from that point forward I stayed in it, and even as that was happening, there were more and more people coming out of Cheatham. There have been some kids who have come out after me who have gone on to do—let's say a metaphor like they have two buses and a truck. I like to think that that's one of the places where we grew back together in the nineties. So those songs are a little bittersweet for me because they're tinged in guilt and a little anger, but we got through that.

My friendship with everybody was bad when I was making *Viva Satellite* [1998] except for my band. That's where Kent was calling the most bullshit and trying to get me to sing myself out of it, really. Then I told everyone to get fucked at this show that was supposed to be the big show, and everyone was there, and I'd made this big plan to piss on the whole thing. I still think it was semi-logical as a plan, maybe not executed well. Maybe I could've used a partner to plan it, but that knocked me into a place where I [thought] . . . *I'm gonna turn them in to John Prine. That's gonna settle these arguments between Kent and me,* and it did. In his mind, it was, like, "Okay. Now you're on the right track. Now you're not asking Jimmy Buffett's wasted right-hand man 'What the fuck?' At least you're asking John Prine now." It was like, "All right. We're back."

As soon as I found out he was sick the first time, "Cheatham Street Warehouse" started to come out. I was playing on a piano, and I always think for the worst. All of it's true. There's no artistic part. You can hear the phones [at Finlay's house] if it gets hot. I'd wake up in my room to that phone and his boots and the sound of those pedals because they'd squeak, and he'd be working on a song. I thought, I'm not gonna play this for him. Then he called while I was working on it, and that part worked its way in. Then he got better, and I thought, *Well, maybe I can play it for him.* I don't know if it was a good idea. I don't know if it's good to show somebody the song you wrote for [his] funeral.[1]

[1] Todd Snider, interview with Brian T. Atkinson and Jenni Finlay, June 13, 2014. For more on Todd Snider, see Chris Willman, *Rednecks & Bluenecks: The Politics of Country Music* (New York: New Press, 2005), 233–36; Brian T. Atkinson, *I'll Be Here in the Morning: The Songwriting Legacy of Townes Van Zandt* (College Station: Texas A&M University Press, 2012), 89–92; Brian T. Atkinson, "Todd Snider's Return to Cheatham Street," *Austin American-Statesman*, November 29, 2007; Brian T. Atkinson, "Snider and the Politics of Brevity," *Austin American-Statesman*, October 8, 2008; Brian T. Atkinson, "Tirelessly Seeking, Helplessly Hoping," *American Songwriter*, September/October 2006, 24. For more on Bobby Bare, Shel Silverstein, and John Prine, see Patricia Carr, *The Illustrated History of Country Music* (New York: Random House, 1995).

# 44 | James McMurtry

Kent is what makes the venue unique. When you're starting out, it's not so much about money. It's more about getting your chops, getting out in front of people, and figuring out that you're not just playing the guitar. You're playing the room. The room's the instrument. I think that might be where I learned that: it's the room and the people in it and whatever energy you can feed off. It took me a long time to really implement that.

I was living in San Antonio in 1987 and looking for anybody who would let me play my stuff. Cheatham Street was very important to me. I might've come up with Tish Hinojosa because that was when she was living in San Antonio and before she moved to Taos. I was playing guitar with her. I probably would've played "Crazy Wind" and something that would become "Talkin' at the Texaco" at the first open mike because those were the first two songs I wrote. Maybe "Terry." I start with two lines and a melody. If the combination is cool enough to keep me up at night, I might finish the song.

Kent just let everybody do their thing and was pretty much universally supportive. Todd Snider was around then, but I never ran into him. We were there on different nights. I had seen Hal Ketchum around, but I never ran into him at Cheatham Street. I didn't know about Todd until he had that big record, *Songs for the Daily Planet* [1994]. At those early shows, Kent would just say, "How are you doing? Thanks for coming out." He was pretty much running the bar. I didn't get the hook, so I figured it was okay. It's much easier to play Cheatham now because I'm not near as nervous as I used to be. Songwriter night all happened somewhere in space light years away. Time is not just time; it's movement. The earth is not where it was then. Most of the places I go now that I played back then just don't register as the same place. The Class of 1987 reunion show was a good night because we had survived the music business. Hal pretty well stole the show. Great night.

*James McMurtry and Steve Earle, Sirius XM broadcast booth, Moody Theater, Austin, February 11, 2015. Photo by Brian T. Atkinson*

I had to mess with "Comfort's Just a Rifle Shot Away" for the [2014 tribute to Kent Finlay at Threadgill's in Austin.] I took some liberty with the lyric: "A diamond in the night" instead of "like a lady of the night." Sorry, I was not going to call Mexico a whore. Not a good time in history to be doing that. When I first saw "comfort" [in] the title, and you're in Central Texas, you think Comfort, Texas, down there west of Boerne, west of San Antonio. I thought maybe Kent was out there shooting at the city limit sign in Comfort, Texas. Didn't turn out that way. I could just picture him there, though, pulled off the road, sandbags on the hood, aiming for one of the o's in Comfort.

I heard him do "You Bring the Condoms and I'll Bring the Wine" [a Finlay cowrite with Todd Snider] quite a bit. That's when the AIDS thing really hit. Kent said he believed in responsible cheating. Kent's mellowed some. He once told my bass player, "You'll never play in San

Marcos again," and Ronnie [Johnson] didn't play in San Marcos for another twenty years. I don't remember what led up to that, but they got into some kind of a tiff. I've never seen that side of Kent, and I'm glad I haven't.

I first saw Adam Carroll at the Cibolo Creek Country Club, which was owned by Tim Holt, who's now my road manager and sound man. That's the one place that's on par with Cheatham as far as vibe. It's gone now. Gruene Hall doesn't have that. It's too touristy down there. There's one out in Swiss Alp that's sort of the same, but it's so far out and a different culture. You go out there and they try to two-step to "Too Long in the Wasteland." It's real country people out there, and there's no air conditioning. It's just a big exhaust fan. I don't know another place like Cheatham Street. The train track beside it helps.[1]

[1] James McMurtry, interview with Brian T. Atkinson and Jenni Finlay, April 30, 2014. For more on James McMurtry, see Gary Hartman, *The History of Texas Music* (College Station: Texas A&M University Press, 2008), 189–91; Jan Reid, *The Improbable Rise of Redneck Rock* (Austin: University of Texas Press, 2004), 337–41; David Goodman, *Modern Twang: An Alternative Country Guide & Directory* (Nashville: Dowling Press, 1999), 214; Chris Willman, *Rednecks & Bluenecks: The Politics of Country Music* (New York: New Press, 2005), 229–32; Brian T. Atkinson, *I'll Be Here in the Morning: The Songwriting Legacy of Townes Van Zandt* (College Station: Texas A&M University Press, 2012), 102–5; Brian T. Atkinson, "South by Southwest Brings Out the Best in Musicians," *CMT Edge*, March 18, 2013, www.cmtedge.com/2013/03/18/south-by-southwest-performances-bring-out-the-best-in-musicians (accessed January 30, 2015); Brian T. Atkinson, "James McMurtry Is a Craftsman of Complicated Stories," *CMT Edge*, March 4, 2015, www.cmtedge.com/2015/03/04/james-mcmurtry-is-a-craftsman-of-complicated-stories (accessed March 5, 2015). For more on Tish Hinojosa, see www.mundotish.com/.

# 45 | john Arthur martinez

I was a student at Southwest Texas State University, and I heard about the songwriters' night at Cheatham Street Warehouse, and I showed up to find a quiet room around a pot-bellied, wood-burning stove in the back. I was impressed that the focus was on the original song and not turning out as many beer sales as possible. I thought, *Wow, what a unique concept.* Kent did not want any talking during the songs. I remember him saying, "It's okay if you want to visit, but do that outside. This is a listening night." I became a passionate follower of the Kent Finlay philosophy from that moment on.

There were a lot of great songwriters hanging out around the Class of '87. If you know Todd Snider, you know he stands out no matter where he is, even among those other giants. I think Todd was the one I was closest to, the one other than myself who showed up the most often, although I think Terri Hendrix started showing up more after I left. Todd hasn't changed much. He may kill me for saying this, but he had some ridiculous songs he'd probably never sing now. Nonetheless, they were filled with things you wouldn't hear from any other writer, like "Fat Chicks on Mopeds." That always brought the house down.

As with any songwriter, when you first show up at an event you want to play what you feel is your best song. I played one I wrote for my father, called "Canta Papa." I remember Kent commenting about the song. Of course, if someone tells you your child is an excellent athlete or great student, you take notice. For a songwriter, that child was my song. The fact that Kent liked my child provided a window into which we connected immediately.

My dad is a musician who played through the late fifties and sixties and seventies and even into the eighties with various regional bands in the Austin area. Some had national significance later, but that influence

John Arthur Martinez, Threadgill's World Headquarters, Austin, March 17, 2014.
Photo by Brian T. Atkinson

was minimal upon me early on. "Canta Papa" is about my dad's influence upon my music. My mother left my dad and married a more "reasonable" man. Music wasn't a part of my stepfather's life in the way it was my real father's. It wasn't until I was an adult that I allowed that influence to come back into my life. That song is a tribute to my dad, who may never grow up, but he has such a passion for song and music.

I remember when I showed up at Cheatham Street to have a writing session with Kent. He's always interested in hearing your latest song, and I played him "Closer to My Dream." It really moved him. It's about a songwriter coming from West Texas and making a long journey to get to the place where he felt his dreams could be realized, and that was Austin, Texas. Rather than make a scene in his home in West Texas, he leaves a note for his mother underneath her favorite coffee cup, knowing that would be the first thing she sees when she gets up. The song progresses and says, "By the time you have your second cup of coffee I'll be close to Austin and closer to my dream." Kent always liked that.

For Kent, it undoubtedly would be that those songs are real, and they're of the writer, as opposed to taking an arbitrary hook we hear somebody saying and writing a song around it just because you can. Those are wonderful exercises in writing, but for Kent if a song has an emotional or spiritual tie to the writer then that's more significant.

Kent never does what perhaps some mentors or cowriters would do in a writing session. He would never chastise you or beat down an idea or line. He would rather celebrate the good lines or the good ideas. One of the things he told me early on is that while Nashville has some good writers, there was a lot of writing you could hear on country radio that was inferior or sub-par. He always told me that we had to do better than that. That was his way of encouraging me without beating me down.

"I Watched You Break My Heart" [is a story]—a friend of mine in the Marble Falls area told me that had happened to him. He had gone to a bar in the . . . community of Round Mountain, Texas, which is in the country. Everything else was dry, but Round Mountain had decided that they would allow honky-tonks to flourish. My buddy Roland Ray Schroeder went to one of those bars called the Lazy A and he happened to sit underneath a broken Old Milwaukee sign. He was basically nursing his beer in the dark when he saw his wife walk in with another man, and the whole story unfolded. Kent loved the story when I shared it, and we turned it into that song. That's another one that's born out of something real and painful, but sometimes those make the best songs.

"Purgatory Road" came when I was driving through the Hill Country. I live in Marble Falls, and I was taking Highway 32 from Blanco, and there's an area called the Devil's Backbone because the road winds like a snake there. I remember driving through there and passing Devil's Backbone Tavern and passing the intersection where Purgatory Road leads you to Gruene. All the while, I was thinking about an episode where my daughter had her vehicle repossessed by one of those payday loans. All that was swirling in my head, and I got close to Cheatham Street, and a train stopped me at the tracks. I thought, *Maybe this song is already writing itself.* So when Kent and I got together, it just poured out. It's one of those songs that you hear other writers talk about that almost instantaneously happened.

The ones we've cowritten that I have chosen to perform are the ones where I came in to Kent with the idea that was close to me. It only makes sense that the singer in the equation of singer-songwriter is most likely to sing one of those songs I brought to the table, but Kent and I have worked on many, many songs, not just ones I brought to the table. He brought in "Where Do We Go from Here?," in the tradition of the great country and western cheating songs. It's a song about two people trying to figure out how they can move forward without hurting the other people they love in their lives. "Our love never sees the light / It hides behind the veil of the night / And goes no further than the dawn / How long can this keep going on?"

Kent took me to Nashville for the first time. It was a magical journey. That kind of thing seems to follow the Finlays. I remember Kent driving around to some of his old favorite spots, and nothing was happening. I noticed a place near Belmont University, and I said, "If I were a songwriter or artist, that's the kind of funky place I'd hang out." Because the other places didn't seem to have anything going on, he said, "Well, let's stop in there and grab a beer." I needed to go to the gentleman's room, and as I was at the urinal, a fairly tall fellow said, "Are you new in town?" I said, "Yes, sir." "Are you a songwriter?" "Yes, sir." As we were leaving the restroom, he said what I thought was, "My name is Arland Howard." Kent corrected me after. He said, "No, that's Harlan Howard." Kent started listing all the songs he'd written. Kent said, "That's Ed Bruce over there." All the guys gathered around for an impromptu song pull. Kent told me, "This is going to be a great night." Then he whispered, "This is not the night where you try to join in. Let's just listen. You're about to hear some great songs."

I have a mentor in tennis, and my pastor was talking about how his legacy would continue on years and years beyond his life. Kent's gonna be the same way. He affected folks like Bruce Robison and Tish Hinojosa and Todd Snider and James McMurtry. Ace Ford was another coming around during that time. Those people have affected another generation that's followed them. Who knows what great one will come from the second generation that touches the next generation? Legacy is a great way to describe it. When you have a mentor like Kent, it's not a casual influence that he imparts to people like the Class of '87. It's a real, heartfelt, spiritual thing that Kent's passing on.[1]

# 46 | Hal Ketchum

I had the great pleasure of meeting Kent at a pivotal point in my life. I was a struggling carpenter and thought, *Why not be a struggling songwriter as well?* Upon our first meeting, Kent welcomed me with open arms, and [that welcoming] continues to this day. If you line up every songwriter and musician he's helped over the years, they would stretch from here to Lubbock and back with room to spare. Our first meeting was when I went up to a gathering at Cheatham Street for the *Texas Summer Nights* [compilation] album. My friends Mickey Merkins and Brian Wood had played on the album and asked if I would come up and sing with them. Kent welcomed everybody at the door, and he and I hit it off immediately. He's an easy man to love, and he was cooler than he could possibly be. He was like the godfather of the Texas singer-songwriter scene at that time.

The first time I played at my own gig [at] Cheatham Street was 1986, when I did an in-the-round with people like Todd Snider, Lloyd Maines and James McMurtry, and it was just the absolute best. We used to sit in the middle of the room, not up on the stage, and I was immediately taken with Todd Snider, and his intellect and his power of retention really amazed me. My stuff's really simple by comparison. I write pretty much three chords and the truth in my mind. It was really inspiring to see these articulate young men up there, especially since I was just getting going. Lyle Lovett told me I could probably write a few songs, and I'd just written nine songs in the course of two weeks. I played all of them in the course of that sit-down.

Todd had a depth of humor that reminded me very much of John Prine. I've had the good fortune of getting to know John Prine well, and there's a certain intellectual tongue-in-cheek that Todd carries that I really admire. I've tried writing funny songs a few times, but I write from an alter ego because I'm not known for funny songs. I wrote one called

Hal Ketchum (r), Gibson Showroom, Austin, August 23, 2014. Photo by Brian T. Atkinson

"The Continental Farewell." The crowd seems to enjoy that very much, but it's hard to be genuinely frivolous on that level.

My friend Owen Temple writes pretty serious songs but has an alter ego called Gary Floater, and that stuff's just hilarious. My alter ego's name is Dick Tater. The quote on the first part of the Dick Tater show is, "I had a record deal once, but I realized there's more money in poetry." He does all his stuff as spoken word like, "Mama's Out Swinging Pasties." It's about his mother finding gainful employment.

I learned a lot from the environment at Cheatham Street and Kent's acceptance of songwriters. He's one of the first people who told me I could do this. He's seen a lot of writers come and go, so I admired the fact that he would encourage me on that level. He saw something that I didn't see at that point in time. I think his impact's based on the fact that he's created this atmosphere that has allowed so many great songwriters to pass through his doors. He makes us believers in ourselves.

I've known a lot of guys who have owned clubs, and it's very rare to find someone as genuine and generous as he is. There are a lot of other places that support songwriting, but I think Cheatham Street is a unique venue. It's very rare to find a place that nurtures songwriters to that degree. You don't have to be at the top of your game to walk in there, but you want to be. He encourages you to be. You can feel the notes just floating around in there from so many great artists who've played there, like Joe Ely and the Flatlanders and Todd and McMurtry.[1]

[1] Hal Ketchum, interview with Brian T. Atkinson, March 25, 2014. For more on Hal Ketchum, see Rich Koster, *Texas Music* (New York: St. Martin's Press, 1998); Alan Cackett, *The Harmony Illustrated Encyclopedia of Country Music* (New York: Salamander Books, 1994), 89–90; Brian T. Atkinson, "Hal Ketchum Trades the Factory for the Back Porch," CMT Edge, October 7, 2014, www.cmtedge.com/2014/10/07/hal-ketchum-trades-the-factory-for-the-back-porch (accessed January 30, 2015).

# 47 | Slaid Cleaves

I played at Kent's open mike in the early part of 1992 down on Sixth Street in Austin at a place called Headliners East. He had a weekly thing. I was an observer a couple times, and then somebody recommended me to Kent. As soon as he heard me, there was an instant bond. He was very effusive in his enthusiasm for what I was doing. Of course, that meant a lot to me when I was just starting out and I was getting a lot of rejection. He said, "I've seen a lot of musicians and you have something a lot of them don't have." He was very encouraging and offered his help right away.

He didn't own it at the time, so I didn't know about the legend of Cheatham Street until I got to know Kent. I remember him telling me that he was buying his old club back and starting it up again. That's when I started hearing about it. I'm sure I would have played there soon after

*Owen Temple and Slaid Cleaves, Strange Brew, Austin, October 19, 2014. Photo by Brian T. Atkinson*

he opened it again because in the late nineties we were getting together to write songs. I remember being around him quite a bit when he was getting ready to open up the place, because he was so excited about it.

A lot of what I learned was the business side of songwriting. He helped me set up my performing rights at BMI. He would provide advice on how to get my publishing set up so that if somebody cut one of my songs I'd get paid for it. He explained that system to me. He was that kind of a business mentor on that side. In other ways, we would trade song ideas back and forth and pick at each other's project songs. He was one of the first people I cowrote with. I wrote with Rod Picott first and Karen Poston early on and Kent. Those were the only three I wrote with when I was starting out. So he was one of the people who introduced me to the style, sitting at a picnic table and banging song ideas out.

I brought a fragment of the song "Don't Tell Me" to him around 1995. We were down at Camp Ben McCulloch on a nice day, and HalleyAnna was playing around in the creek. She was a baby, basically. I presented my song idea, and he guided me. I remember I had about half of the song written—the melody and the words, the first verse—and I didn't know where it could go. He coached me. It wasn't like he was throwing out specific words to fill up the next verse. It was more he was trying to shape a description of what the next verse should be, where I should take it, what direction the song should go and what it should accomplish, the direction I needed to shoot for.

There are other songs we've written together, that weren't released, where he was more "here's this word" and "let's try that line" and back-and-forth, nuts-and-bolts songwriting. I've done that with him too, but in my relationship with him, his strength is as a mentor, someone who had been doing it a long time and knew the business and had written with a lot of people. When I met him, he was talking about this kid Todd Snider who he had helped out, and he thought big things were gonna come for Todd. Eventually, of course, they did. It was exciting to see that happen. I said, "I've gotta listen to this guy. He knows what he's talking about."

"Lost" was the one where we worked on it face-to-face and then later shot ideas back and forth. That was more hammering it out line by line. Sometimes when you're cowriting you have to make a case for a change you want to make or even a word you want to use. Sometimes your cowriter doesn't agree, and you have to lobby for it. You don't want to insult anyone or dismiss people. It's a delicate place to be when you're being creative. In hindsight, that was a lesson in how to do that, how to cowrite.

Cheatham Street is an embodiment of all he's done, his history of mentoring and promoting young songwriters. The fact that that building is so funky and has the railroad track next to it fits Kent's personality. He's not a fancy guy. He's a humble guy, and it's a humble building, but I love the fact that the building's been there so long and so many songwriters have come up through the place. So many people have memories of going there back so many years. There's a gal who does massage therapy in Wimberley, and I mentioned Cheatham Street to her. Her son is named Sterling. She didn't know Kent, but she said, "Oh, yeah, I grew up at Cheatham Street. My parents took me there as a kid." It's a cross-generational place now, and that adds to the legend of the place, but I think mentoring is his greatest contribution. It's a long list of people who have benefited from his mentoring and championing.[1]

[1] Slaid Cleaves, interview with Brian T. Atkinson and Jenni Finlay, May 11, 2014. For more on Slaid Cleaves, see Rich Koster, *Texas Music* (New York: St. Martin's Press, 1998), 210; Brian T. Atkinson, "Slaid Cleaves Seasons His Songs with Love and War," CMT Edge, June 19, 2013, www.cmtedge.com/2013/06/19/slaid-cleaves-seasons-his-songs-with-love-and-war (accessed January 30, 2015). For more on Rod Picott, see Brian T. Atkinson, "Rod Picott Follows a Crooked Road," *CMT Edge*, February 12, 2015, www.cmtedge.com/2014/02/12/rod-picott-follows-a-crooked-road (accessed January 30, 2015).

I met Terri Hendrix and Slaid Cleaves, and people like that started help-ing me out. Slaid was actually the first person who said, "Hey, man, you gotta meet Kent Finlay." Aaron Allen, a radio DJ on KCTI [AM 1450] in Gonzalez and a character cut from the same cloth as Willie Nelson, asked me to do the gig at this place Landis Station that used to be in New Braunfels. It had a stripper pole and a stage. Kent and Sterling and Aaron Allen and a couple other people that I can't remember were there, but I remember that stripper pole. No one was dancing on it, but we were doing the gig and the pole was right in the way. I think somebody had given Kent my first CD, so he knew some of my songs.

I started hanging around Cheatham Street right off the bat. I used to live right by it, and I used to go over all the time. It was a home away from home. As he's done with so many people, Kent made me feel a part of his family. Kent has so many stories, and being around him—driving to gigs and hearing about the Hill Country and people he knows—never gets old. He's so interesting and in a real natural way. I consider him a really good friend. Right from the get-go he's been fatherly, for lack of a better term. I've seen him be that way with other people too. He's a real natural at bringing out the best in songwriters, a real inspiration. Some people do this for a little while and get older and move on, but it's Kent's lifeblood. That's how I want to be, and I admire a guy who does what he does forever. He's like one big song that never quits writing itself.

Of course, he encouraged me by being a fan of my songs. As a person, his passion for songwriting is infectious. It makes me want to stick with it. It helps to have a venue where you can have the rituals like at the Wood-shed, where his studio is. We'd go over there and write songs. It doesn't always work, but I've always dreamed of having a place like that. "This is a music place, where the music happens. Here's some coffee and here's a cigarette and here's a guitar." He has the capability to provide that for

Adam Carroll, Cheatham
Street Warehouse, San
Marcos, February 8, 2015.
Photo by Brian T. Atkinson

us. You see all the old coffee cans laying around and the old pictures of
Cheatham Street. Here's the environment. It's like, "This guy's serious
about this. Let's write a song."

I really think, for me and for Kent, it's a lifestyle. That's what I want
it to be. I mean, it's a business and it's a spiritual thing, but it can be the
way you live your life, kind of like ranchers do. They do it because they
like that lifestyle. They either go broke, or they figure out a way to do
it. That's what I'm trying to do and Kent does by providing that venue
and that space that says, "Hey, man, this is all about the songwriter, all
about the song." We all have our limits, our strengths and weaknesses.
There are things that I'm pretty good at and there are things I can't do,
but when I have the right venue I can be pretty successful. Kent helps by
making that venue all about songwriters. We need a guy like that, who
makes us understand how important that is. It's a lifestyle choice. He
makes it that, and it's really a gift.

As a cowriter, Kent's a really good listener. He's a good audience.
Usually I'll have about half a song or a chorus or a verse or two. "Here's
what I got. What do you think?" He has a real oddball sense of humor,
which I gravitate toward. For some reason, it locks into what I'm doing.

He can connect with the oddball ideas I can't figure out how to use in a song. Also, he's patient. Even if it doesn't seem like it's going anywhere, he will sit and work on it and give it the time. He's persistent to see the song through, and he'll contribute his own ideas. Sometimes we haven't been successful, but we keep trying and trying at the same idea. Sometimes we do get a song. There's one we wrote called "Dear John (You Can Keep the John Deere)." I've never played it, but he has, and it's funny. It's right up his alley. I'd like to learn it, but I just can't see how I could do it any funnier than him.

"Poor Boy Blues" is another we wrote that I haven't ever worked up on my own, but it's got a lot of good Kent Finlay lines. That was just a good idea about a guy that can't afford anything and how he's supposed to get by. Sometimes it sounds more Kent Finlay than me, so maybe it's a Kent Finlay song. He's just his own original guy, and he's really good at helping craft a song when he figures out how he can contribute. He's good at helping me take a song from an idea through the verses and chorus. He's good at hammering it down and walking away with an actual song, rather than just, "Oh, I see what you're saying." He'll just sit there and go over it in his head, and he's so quiet. It's eerie sometimes. He's always thinking about what to do. He has the space and the willingness to make it happen.

Randy Rogers was recording "Plastic Girl," and he was pretty local still before he hit it really big. He asked me to sing a verse, the part where the character comes home from making pizza and he finds the plastic girl with his best friend. I just put my own spin on it. I sang that one line where he comes in and finds his doll cheating with his best friend. I just think it's funny where he says, "When I'd come home late at night all tired from making pizza / Wendy, she'd be waiting there for me." That's a line that only Kent Finlay would come up with. It makes it real.[1]

---

[1] Adam Carroll, interview with Brian T. Atkinson, February 11, 2014. For more on Adam Carroll, see "Adam Carroll," Lone Star Music, www.lonestarmusic.com/adamcarroll (accessed January 30, 2015); William Harries Graham, "Adam Carroll: Let It Choose You," Austin Chronicle, August 26, 2014, www.austinchronicle.com/daily/music/2014–08–26/adam-carroll-let-it-choose-you (accessed January 30, 2015)

# 49 | Randy Rogers

I heard an ad for his songwriters' night at Cheatham Street on the radio. I was writing songs and thought, *I'll go down there and try that out.* I went in and sang my songs, and he came up to me afterward, and I didn't even know who Kent Finlay was at the time. He said, "Hey, man, you're good. I'd love for you to come back next week." That began our friendship and eventually led to me starting a band. I gravitated toward Kent because I felt like he was a source of knowledge in the music business, and I did my research about Cheatham Street and the other folks who'd been through there. I just wanted to know what Kent knew about the music business, and he provided that for me.

"Lost and Found" was the first song I played that first night. I had written that maybe four or five months before I walked into Cheatham Street for the first time. A girl in San Marcos I was going steady with inspired it. I eventually broke up with her, and it was a pretty rough time. It was my first relationship in college and really the first time my heart had really been broken.

I didn't realize how important getting Kent's approval was that first songwriters' night. I knew "Lost and Found" was a good song, but I just thought Kent was just being nice and encouraging. Obviously, I didn't know that things were gonna turn out like they have. I just thought, *Wow, this is a great place to try out new songs.* Another thing is he encouraged me each week to write another song, and that really was more important than anything. He kept saying, "Write this week and bring a new one when you come back next week." It was almost a challenge. I started doing that and really stacking the catalog.

Our first gig at Cheatham Street as the Randy Rogers Band was October 3, 2000. I'd been going pretty regularly to those on Wednesday nights, and friends of mine would get word that I was playing, and all

Kent Finlay and Randy Rogers, Cheatham Street Warehouse, San Marcos, June 9, 2014. Photo by Brian T. Atkinson

of a sudden open mike night was packed with drunk college kids, and that's probably not the atmosphere that place needs. So I think my loud, rowdy friends played a pretty big role in making up Kent's mind to give me the Tuesday residency. We had lunch across the street at Garcia's, and he basically told me that he believed in me enough to offer me the night if I could put a band together.

We had a lot of memorable evenings. We had a storm and the power go off one time, so we played acoustic on top of the bar with candles all around us. Brady and I were friends and had had jam sessions at the house, but we'd never played a show before that night. Brady just happened to be in the crowd that night, and he had his fiddle, and we knew we needed more acoustic instruments. He just ran out and got his fiddle, and that was it. We started playing regularly together soon after that. The five of us who stuck it out in the band today are equal members. Brady's a partner, as equal as I am. I mean, he's essential, vital.

Early on, Kent's trick was: "Tell all your friends to drive so the parking lot looks full." We did that for a long time. You have ten friends coming, you say, "Hey, man, bring your car so it looks like it's a good time." So fifty people turned into a hundred, and a hundred turned into two hundred pretty quick. We weren't great by any means, but there wasn't anywhere else in town doing live music like that. You know, Nephew's and a few other bars there would have live music, but it was predominantly cover songs, and it wasn't necessary based on original music. People who had the taste for that kind of thing gravitated toward Cheatham Street.

Kent vouched for me too. The first few other places I played were Wichita Falls and Fort Worth and Houston. At the time, I was a booking agent, and I would use my middle name, Wade, for a fake name: Randall Wade. I'd book several acts like Adam Carroll. I worked for a publicity company called Propaganda Music Group and a lady named Vickie Lucero. I worked my way into booking, and I'd call clubs and say, "Hey, this is Randall Wade and I represent the Randy Rogers Band. We'd like to open for Pat Green May 3, and if you need a reference, the guys have been playing Cheatham Street Warehouse. You can call Kent Finlay, and here's his number."

Kent would stick his neck out there for me and say we were professional and up-and-coming. He played an instrumental part in that. At the time, we didn't have a CD, so there's no other way to know other than word of mouth. It was a resume builder. "Hey, man, we played Cheatham Street." Cheatham's very well known throughout the state, and it helped to have that on my resume. Also, Kent's ex-wife Diana was the first person to put together a press kit so I could send out mailers. After we recorded *Live at Cheatham Street* [2000], we would send that out with the little bio and band photo and try to get gigs. She helped me out with that.

Todd Snider's version of "Plastic Girl" drew me to the song and also hearing Kent do it constantly. He made me laugh out loud every time. [Writing funny songs is] not something I do very well. I think I have a pretty good sense of humor, but I've never written anything funny. So that let me take from someone else's work and be funny. I like that. We cut "Plastic Girl" in the studio with Adam Carroll. I don't think Kent was there. We just ran one microphone and cut it live and let it roll. It was a lot of fun. Adam sang a whole verse and ad-libbed a little and made it even better.

I remember "Hill Country" from songwriter night. I told Kent, "If I ever get my shit together, I'm gonna play that song every night." He said, "Go do it, man." I just think that that song is timeless, a song that will be around through the ages. People in this area will always have an affiliation with that. Living down here as long as I have and seeing the leveling of fifteen acres of land to build a WalMart and things like that make me want to hold on to the beautiful landscape we have as long as we can. It's definitely important. I'm raising my family here. I wouldn't have recorded it if it wasn't a great song. I don't know if I did anything for him other than take what was already a fantastic piece of work and do my best to promote it and get it out there. I also love "To See Sara Smile" and the one that goes "I'd rather take an enema than lose Diane / If I lost Diane I'd just shit," from the "worst song ever" competition ["If I Ever Lose Diane"]. It's pretty hard to beat.

We wrote "You Could've Left Me" across the street [from the Cheatham Street Warehouse] at the Woodshed [recording studio]. I think we wrote it back and forth over the phone, if my memory serves me correctly. I just wanted to sit down and get something together since I love Kent so much and wanted him to have a cut on a record of mine. That's a barnburner song too. It's fun to think that Kent and I wrote that one together. That's not really my forte, and I don't know that that's his forte either, but that's what we came up with.

I think he understands the songwriting formula, which is to write and rewrite and finish. I don't know how many songs in my life I've started and not finished. Kent's always been good about getting an idea down and completing it. Not every song's gonna be your best, and you have to understand that and go with it. Get it down and get it out even if it's not gonna be your best song. That's something I really suck at. It may be because my attention span is short. If I'm in it for a couple hours, I'll get bored and quit or think my idea sucks.

We made *Rollercoaster* in 2004, and that put me on the map. Radney Foster was writing with us and producing, and we were selling that album because of a song called "Tonight's Not the Night." It was on the radio and in the forties on the *Billboard* airplay chart. It was unheard of: an unsigned independent artist cracking *Billboard*. It was pretty damn exciting. We had all these suits fly down from these labels, and eventually we had our pick. There were a couple labels willing to give us a deal, and we picked the one we believed in and liked the most, which was MCA or Mercury Universal Music Group.

When they decided to ink the deal, I felt like as a way to respect our roots and our home and all that Kent had done for us through the years, we decided to sign at Cheatham Street. We made the label guy and the attorney come down and the lady doing A&R on my project. We had some cheap champagne and plastic champagne glasses, and we inked our deal on the stage. Our band and girlfriends at the time were there and the folks from Nashville and my manager and just the people who were really important to us, like Kent and his family. I remember thinking I could conquer the world, and my life was about to completely change. I signed a record deal, which was my goal since I was a little boy. It was a huge day, and I wanted to do that with Kent. Without him there wouldn't have been a band or a venue or literally a stage to sign a record deal on. My life has changed since then. Absolutely. It's craziness.

I didn't understand a lot of things at first, like publishing and statutory rates and having your songs on records. There's so much true bullshit in the music business, so, between Kent Finlay and Radney Foster, I really got schooled, and I'm very thankful for that. There were some hard decisions I had to make during the first years, with different managers and booking agents, and Kent had been around long enough to know who was who and what was what and what a bullshit deal looked like and a good deal looked like. He absolutely taught me all that stuff.

If I play a new song these days at Cheatham, I definitely still look back to see if it sparked his attention. Playing Cheatham Street is still sacred to me. It's the real deal. I cherish those times I get to be there. I've been doing those secret songwriter nights when I bring somebody different in, and we're gonna try to pick those up again soon. It's a special night any time you get to play there. I've had great things happen and ideas come to me about the show and the songs there. It's a creative little spot. I feel like I'm creative there, like I'm at home there. It's easy to say, because it says "Welcome home" out front, but for me it truly does feel like it. I'm very comfortable there.

Plus, think about his impact on music. I mean, I played that show with George Strait at the Houston Astrodome last year, and George stopped the whole show and said, "Hey, if it wasn't for Kent and Cheatham Street Warehouse, there wouldn't be a George Strait. Thank you for taking me to Nashville for the first time ever." You know, in some way, shape, or form, George Strait has impacted your life. How could he have not impacted every person who likes country music with those songs and their relationships revolving around those songs? In a way, Kent Finlay has been a part of everyone's life. Just take that one situation with George Strait. The impact's immeasurable. I mean, if there hadn't . . . been a George Strait, I wouldn't have had a hero.[1]

[1] Randy Rogers, interview with Brian T. Atkinson and Jenni Finlay, April 2, 2014. For more on Randy Rogers, see Randy Rogers, "Kent Finlay: A Songwriter's Songwriter," *Mavrik Magazine* (Lone Star Music), May/June 2007, 17–19; Kent Finlay, "Son of a Preacher Man: The Randy Rogers Band, a Band of Brothers," *Mavrik Magazine* (Lone Star Music), May/June 2007, 20–25; Brandy McDonnell, "Interview: Randy Rogers Band Gets into *Trouble* with New Album, Plays Stillwater Calf Fry Tonight," *NewsOK*, http://newsok.com/interview-randy-rogers-band-gets-into-trouble-with-new-album-plays-stillwater-calf-fry-tonight/article/3833072, May 22, 2013 (accessed January 30, 2015); John Goodspeed, "Randy Rogers Band Showing a Taste for Tamales," March 21, 2014, *My SA* (*San Antonio Express-News*), www.mysanantonio.com/entertainment/entertainment_columnists/john_goodspeed/article/Randy-Rogers-Band-showing-a-taste-for-tamales-5331859.php (accessed January 30, 2015); www.randyrogersband.com/ (accessed January 30, 2015).

# 50 | Cody Canada (Cross Canadian Ragweed, The Departed)

I moved to New Braunfels, and Randy Rogers took me to Cheatham Street for the first time about 2002. The rest has been history. Any time Mr. Finlay calls, I'm all over it. We know a lot of the same people, and he's just a good soul. When somebody really cares about music as he does, I gravitate toward those people, people that really care about a song's structure and lyrics. A lot of people in the music business just want to make money or get drunk. He just wants you to do good. He cares for the artist, for the songs. You'll never hear a bad word about Kent. He's a massive figure, as important as Ray Benson is to the Texas scene.

My first gig at Cheatham was acoustic with Randy. I probably would have played "17" because that was right around the time that Cross Canadian Ragweed's [2002's eponymous] purple album came out. I had gotten married and had moved back to my hometown, Yukon, Oklahoma, not a very supportive town for music. Jason Boland was driving through, coming back from a gig in Fort Worth, and we were over at our bass player Jeremy [Plato]'s house, and when Jason got there we decided we had to go get some more beer. I saw a cop, and I froze because I knew he was gonna recognize my truck and was gonna pull me over. Jason said, "What's wrong with you, man?" I said, "I feel like I'm seventeen all over again." He said, "You're always seventeen in your hometown." We had that look: "Shit, that could be a tune, man."

We did a lot of full-band shows with Randy at Cheatham Street, and then Randy signed on with my wife's management company, and he lived in New Braunfels, and we hung out all the time together. We've

Poster for Cody Canada and Stoney LaRue song swap at Cheatham Street
Warehouse. Courtesy Finlay family archives

only written two songs together, both on the same night on the front
porch of the office. After that night, we started booking more acoustic
shows together. There's something to be said about a place where the
owner gets up on the mike, and before he introduces the band playing
he tells everybody to shut their phone off. That's high respect in my

book. Ninety percent of the shows, people are in the front row on their phones.

I saw Todd Snider on *Late Night with David Letterman* in '94. I thought, *Holy shit*. It sounds really hippie, but I think it was the free spirit, not-give-a-shit attitude. That's how music should be approached: This is my music. If you don't like it, fine. If you do, come on, let's go. That's what I loved. Todd was really writing these songs for himself. If other people dug them, it's a bonus. After that, I probably saw him ten, twelve times a year for three or four years. I'd see where he was playing and drive over or fly in. I very fortunately got to be friends with the guy over the years. I really had some of that anyway, but watching Todd and [Nervous Wrecks guitarist] Will Kimbrough together really helped shape what we've done over the last twenty years.

We went to all those shows together, and Jeremy and I still could play the first two records—[Todd's] *Songs from the Daily Planet* and [1996's] *Step Right Up*—front to back. We were doing a sound check one day, and we brought out [Snider's] "I Believe You." There were a few fans, and they asked what song that was and who it was and if it was gonna be recorded. We just said, "Yeah. Yeah, we're gonna record it." We'd been playing that song for years. "Late Last Night" really felt like the perfect song for where Ragweed was. I'm all over anything with a Chuck Berry riff. I learned "Alright Guy" a long time ago, up in Stillwater, [Oklahoma], at the Wormy Dog [Saloon]. I played that every Tuesday night for like six years. Everybody loved that song, so I learned it and never forgot it.[1]

---

[1] Cody Canada, interview with Brian T. Atkinson, June 28, 2014. For more on Cody Canada and his bands Cross Canadian Ragweed and the Departed, see Andrew Leahey, "Cody Canada Steers New Band toward Familiar Sound with HippieLovePunk," *Rolling Stone*, October 14, 2014, www.rollingstone.com/music/features/cody-canada-the-departed-hippielovepunk-in-betweener-20141014 (accessed January 30, 2015).

# 51 | Willy Braun (Reckless Kelly)

We moved to Austin in the first place to play six or seven nights a week, and we were able to do that. A lot of the smaller joints like Cheatham allowed us to go out and fill holes and play for four hours a night and really get the sound of the band together and tighten up the ship and try out new songs we'd been writing. Kent's always been a guy to give a new kid a chance. He gave us a place to play like countless others, like Randy Rogers and George Strait. It was cool to be the new band in town and have places like that to go to where the crowd's pretty young, drink-

*Willy Braun, Strange Brew, Austin, March 6, 2015. Photo by Brian T. Atkinson*

ing beer and shooting pool. If you get lucky they'll listen to you. A lot of times it's pretty rowdy. You have to get above the roar of the crowd, and we've always been pretty good at that.

Kent's opened the door for a lot of guys like us. He's given them residencies and gigs, and probably not a lot of people would even listen to the demo tape. It's guys like him that helped invent this scene where basically anybody with a guitar and enough work ethic can go out and make a living. We've actually done a bunch of shows with William Clark Green lately, and he's really good. He's got a couple songs that are really taking off on the charts, and he's a perfect example of a young guy that Kent's helped out. Kent's been such a good friend to the music scene in Texas.[1]

[1] Willy Braun, interview with Brian T. Atkinson, June 5, 2014. For more on Willy Braun and Reckless Kelly, see Dan Harr, "Reckless Kelly's Willy Braun Opens up with Q&A," *Music News Nashville*, September 30, 2011, www.musicnewsnashville.com/reckless-kellys-willy-braun-opens-up-with-qa (accessed January 30, 2015).

I bought *Adam Carroll: Live at Cheatham Street* when I was in eighth grade or freshman year in high school. It's a fantastic record. In the intro, Kent Finlay's like, "Welcome to Cheatham Street Warehouse. This is an exciting night. It's always exciting when Adam Carroll's at Cheatham Street Warehouse." I always loved his voice and that nostalgia. There definitely are venues that cater to songwriters, but there's never been a place like Cheatham Street or a person like Kent. I've never seen anything like it, and we never will again. It's a damn shame, but it's the truth. I've never seen anyone sit on a stool and listen to every song played in a building. Cheatham Street's absolutely a legendary place, in my mind.

I first met Kent at a benefit when we were just hanging out. I think it was the annual Cheatham Street Music Foundation benefit called Big-Fest. We were in town that Sunday, and I got introduced to him. I think we played one Saturday night after, and I kept playing Cheatham Street more and more, and we warmed up to each other, and the friendship grew and grew, and now he's pretty much like my dad. I ask for his advice all the time. He's always calm and has something beneficial to say, and he always has a one-liner, advice that carries through.

He's mentored me, for sure. He's always interested, and he's interested in talking about songwriting the most. Every time I talk to him, he asks, "How's your writing going? Have you written a song?" I've never met anybody in my life who listens to more original songs than Kent, and he genuinely listens. We went out to dinner a couple months ago when the cancer started coming back, and I wanted to talk to him about that, but he wanted to talk about songwriting. So that's what we talked about: songwriting. I've never met anybody who's like him or even comes close.

I was going through a writer's block that lasted ten months, and I told him that I could not write. Everything I was intending to write was

William Clark
Green and Kent
Finlay, Texas
Music Theater,
San Marcos,
April 27, 2014.
Photo by Brian T.
Atkinson

complete bullshit, and I told Kent I wasn't even attempting to write. It's
hard to remember exact quotes because half the time I talk to Kent I'm
hammered at Cheatham Street, but he said something along the lines
of, "If you don't write anything than nothing good will come of it."

"Hangin' Around" was our first cowrite together. I showed up and
pretty much just had this chord progression, and we went to the Wood-
shed across the street from Cheatham Street. The thing about writing
with Kent is he almost guides you in the direction that you need to go.
He doesn't force it. Some songwriters are very blunt like I am: "No, that's

bullshit." "No, that sucks." Kent will guide you where he feels a song needs to go. We wrote the song about how everybody in a small town stays in a small town and never gets out and experiences life. It was easy to write, one of the quickest cowrites I've ever had. We probably knocked out the song in an hour and a half. I was nervous he wasn't gonna like what we did with the production, but he loved it. It's actually our radio single right now.

I couldn't even tell you who wrote which line. When you write with someone, it doesn't matter if they write a line or a word. A cowrite's fifty-fifty anyway. Kent was a very, very big contributor to the song, and I enjoyed the guidance that he gave. We fed off each other. I'm fairly sure I came up with the name "Mary Ann," but, when I did, he loved it. I remember him very much liking that line ["I sure will miss Mary Ann but I won't miss her new boyfriend.]" When I said that out loud, he just smiled and went, "Yeah. That's a good line." It's almost like fate. [Finlay's unreleased song "The Beer Joints Have All Closed" includes the line, "Mary Ann's happy with her new man, I suppose."]

We wrote another song that's going on my next record too, called "Still Think about You," in Steamboat, Colorado [during the annual MusicFest gathering]. It's definitely an angry, blunt tune, and I think it means something to both of us. I was talking to Kent and my producer yesterday, and I think we're definitely gonna try to put it on the next record. Kent's exceptionally good at telling a great story. I don't know if I'm good at that or not, and I don't think we've written that amazing story song just yet. We're gonna get together and write together here in a week or so, and maybe that's something we can do: come up with the epic story.[1]

[1] William Clark Green, interview with Brian T. Atkinson, April 28, 2014. For more on William Clark Green, see Caroline Corrigan, "William Clark Green Interview," YouTube, www.youtube.com/watch?v=5INfYMTPhCs, November 10, 2013 (accessed January 30, 2015); "William Clark Green Interview," You Tube, www.youtube.com/watch?v=j7ymRUKpULk, October 27, 2012 (accessed January 30, 2015).

# 53 | Hayes Carll

I was playing covers in bars, totally unaware of the whole songwriter scene, but then I started seeing kids in bars wearing Pat Green and Cory Morrow T-shirts and saw this young Texas country scene going on. From what I'd heard, it was cool, but it wasn't hitting me on a really deep level. Then I remember finding Adam Carroll on this tape a friend had given me, and I was blown away. Back then everyone I was listening to was either dead or had already established themselves, so finding new music was really exciting. He was doing what I wanted to do, and he was really gifted. So I started stalking him a little bit. I went to a show in Houston at the Mucky Duck, and then, when he would come through town, I started skipping my own shows. I would kill off a family member and say my grandfather passed away or something as an excuse to cancel my gig so I could go watch Adam play at Anderson Fair or Mucky Duck or wherever he was.

Adam had this unique combination of being funny and poignant and really descriptive. There's that song about going hunting with his dad and the mud and he ran out of Schlitz ["Errol's Song"]. I had never been hunting with my dad, but I could taste it and feel it. I knew what it was like. It's a unique thing to be able to do that. He's also a really unique and killer guitar and harmonica player. I like his voice, the way he played, the looseness to it. It was almost like he was making it up as he went, which I have seen him do. He had such lyrical detail and everyman storytelling, and it was funny. Not many people can pull off funny and poignant, and I was drawn to that. He has this East Texas John Prine vibe that really resonated with me.

The really memorable nights I've had at Cheatham have been song swaps. There was one that I did with Adam and Walt Wilkins. I had never drawn a crowd at Cheatham Street more than twenty people, and that

Hayes Carll, Austin City Limits Music Festival, Austin, September 19,
2011. Photo by Brian T. Atkinson

night it was packed. We had a great time, and I remember thinking, *This is different. This is a lot cooler with people.* I know that night I played "Arkansas Blues" because Adam called me at one in the morning on his drive home, and he said, "Hayes, I was just imagining what it'd be like if Christopher Walken sang 'Arkansas Blues.'" Then he proceeds to do it as Christopher Walken, so it's Adam Carroll singing Hayes Carll as Christopher Walken: "I hide behind my guitar like a sparrow in the night." It was fucking hilarious. That's when I realized that the things going on in Adam's head are not necessarily what happen in everybody else's.

I had heard about Kent through Todd Snider, who used to talk about him during the shows, and I'd heard Randy Rogers do one of Kent's songs. So I'd picked up that he was this influential guy to a lot of song-writers that I appreciated, like Adam, but I always viewed Kent as a more serious version of Wrecks Bell from [Galveston's] the Old Quarter, in that he was mentoring songwriters. I had that figure in Wrecks, my father-figure guy who would give me a place to play and encourage me. I viewed Kent in that way that he'd been that for a lot of guys on a more intensive level as far as the songwriting.

Kent and Wrecks are both in party towns where that might not be ap-preciated. [Their clubs] were an oasis for songwriters, a place where you could go and not only get up and play your song but were encouraged to do so. It was not the right room to play "Free Bird" or "Brown-Eyed Girl," and every room that I was hitting at the time would much rather hear those types of songs. So it was people like Wrecks and Kent who really kept me from going crazy or being depressed about the whole idea of being a performer. You could work on your craft and go in and show what you've done and find like-minded people who you could talk to about being a songwriter. Plus, they could tell you stories about other people who made it out of cover song purgatory. That was huge.[1]

---

[1] Hayes Carll, interview with Brian T. Atkinson, October 6, 2014. For more on Hayes Carll, see Brian T. Atkinson, *I'll Be Here in the Morning: The Songwriting Legacy of Townes Van Zandt* (College Station: Texas A&M University Press, 2012), xv–xix; Brian T. Atkinson, "Townes Van Zandt's Sixth Annual Wake, Old Quarter (Galveston, TX)," *No Depression*, March/April 2003, http://nodepression.com/ (accessed June 2, 2015); "Brian T. Atkinson, "Hayes Carll at the Continen-tal Club, Austin, TX, May 12," *Maverick Country* (UK), August/September 2006, 25–26; Brian T. Atkinson, "4 to Watch For," *Paste*, December/January 2004, 70; Brian T. Atkinson, "Hayes Carll: Little Rock," *American Songwriter*, March/April 2005, 61; Brian T. Atkinson, "Hayes Carll Q&A, *Texas Music*, Spring 2008, 22, 25–27; Brian T. Atkinson, "Everything Is Relative in Holiday Song," *Austin American-Statesman*, December 27, 2009; Brian T. Atkinson, "Hayes Carll: KMAG YOYO," *Lone Star Music*, January/February 2011, 45. For more on Rex "Wrecks" Bell, see Atkinson, *I'll Be Here in the Morning*, xv–xvii.

As a young songwriter when I was coming up in Houston, I was furious constantly. You can't really beat people over the head with rock and roll if you're just a guy and a guitar, so I'd be trying to play solo acoustic. It's really discouraging when people aren't listening to that, and there was no place in Houston that had rules and respect like Cheatham. I moved to San Marcos for a while, and I had a friend who was, like, "You have to go to Cheatham and check out the songwriter thing." We lived about fifteen minutes outside town, and that was the only excuse I had to leave the house. It's a college town, and my wife and I didn't really go to the "bro" bars, but Cheatham Street was always a cool place to go hear music or try out songs and kind of a refuge from the college scene there.

I've never played my own gig at Cheatham, only songwriter night. I'd go try a new song. Wednesday night, songwriter night, was the cool thing. When somebody's up there by themselves on songwriter night, there's such a level of respect paid. You don't get a bunch of bullshit and people talking over you. There's not any place like that that's so decidedly for listening. Otherwise, nobody listens to you until somebody says, "Listen to this guy." I still have shows all the time where people are just there for the social aspect and don't give a shit about the music.

I just went to songwriter night three weeks ago, and I played a brand new song and a couple old ones. When I was writing the tunes for [2014's *The Lights from the Chemical Plant*] I played them at Cheatham Street before I really played them anywhere else. Whether it's something good or somebody just getting in front of people to figure their shit out, Kent's always been very supportive and nice in a huge way. What's so cool about that night is at the beginning he gets up and basically says, "Everybody be quiet and respectful and listen." Everybody sticks to that. He'll definitely bitch people out if things get out of hand when somebody's trying to go up there to play their song.

Robert Ellis, Cheatham Street Warehouse, May 2015. Photo by Halley Anna Finlay

The support and community that comes with a safe haven like song-writer night is phenomenal. He kicks it off with "I'll Sing You a Story," the song about songwriting and getting everyone in the mood to listen to lyrics. On the basic level, he's fostering and supporting and getting the people in San Marcos off their asses. I know people who wouldn't even think about playing songs, but they went to Cheatham and they found out about that night, and then they're, like, "I can put this together." It gives them edification and feedback, something to work on and focus on. Having a judgment-free zone like that is invaluable. You would imagine the repercussions from that would be pretty far-reaching. I wish I had come to Cheatham Street a little earlier.[1]

[1] Robert Ellis, interview with Brian T. Atkinson, June 6, 2014. For more on Robert Ellis, see Chris Mugan, "Lone Star: Robert Ellis Interview," *Independent* (UK), www.independent.co.uk/ arts-entertainment/music/features/lone-star-robert-ellis-interview-9174328.html, March 8, 2014 (accessed January 30, 2015); www.robertellismusic.com/.

# 55 | Joe Pug

I think, increasingly, Americana music is being played to urbane city types, like NPR-listening-type people, which is fine. You can make a living that way, and I'm glad they listen to the music, but playing down at Kent's place you're definitely struck by the fact that these are folks who are not working in an office and who have grown up with country music in an authentic and genuine way. You just really have the feeling that if you get them into your music then it's a real achievement. Cheatham Street's old school, and it seems without fail during the most dramatic part of your song the damn train goes by, especially if you're playing quiet music like I do.

Songwriter night's critical and can't be replaced by chat rooms or any digital equivalent. There's something about being in your early twenties and being really nervous to play the new song you just wrote in your bedroom in front of other songwriters. Also, hearing other songwriters play who are much better than you and really throw down the gauntlet is [important]. I guess that that could happen to a certain degree over the Internet, but I don't think it would get your blood flowing in the same way. You know exactly how many people are there ahead of you before you have to go up. You're counting it down and get really nervous, and then, after, there's the sense of relief and accomplishment.

I played one in Chicago at a place called Lilly's. You work all day at your job, and you're thinking all day that you're heading to the open mike, and you won't know anybody there. Then you get off work, you have some dinner, and you sit in your car. You just wait outside the venue with your guitar. You go in and sign up. You know exactly what spot you are on the list. It's really harrowing, but it really made you get your shit together songwriting-wise because you were so nervous that you wanted to play a song that was absolutely unassailable.

Joe Pug, Catfish Concerts, Austin, May 11, 2014. Photo by Brian T. Atkinson

Those are definitely disappearing. Kent's is the platonic ideal of a songwriters' night. His would be more intimidating to play and not just because of the reputation, which stretches far and wide across the country. I mean, I tour all the time, and there's this network of musicians who play this kind of music, and everybody, even if they haven't played there, know[s] of Cheatham Street and they know of Kent. It's something people talk about. So you have that, and then you have the fact that Kent himself doesn't miss one. He's sitting there in his button-up shirt and his black hat at the corner of the bar and watching you play. I mean, this is a guy who's seen George Strait and Todd Snider play in a folding chair in front of him. You want his opinion. So, yeah, I'm sure it's really fucking nerve-wracking.[1]

[1] Joe Pug, interview with Brian T. Atkinson, June 4, 2014. For more on Joe Pug, see Aidin Vaziri, "Introducing Singer-Songwriter Joe Pug," SFGate, www.sfgate.com/music/article/Introducing-singer-songwriter-Joe-Pug-6046263.php, January 29, 2015 (accessed January 30, 2015); Dave Mistich, "The Great Despiser Gets Inspired: An Interview with Joe Pug," Pop Matters, www.pop-matters.com/feature/161576-the-great-despiser-gets-inspired-an-interview-with-joe-pug, August 29, 2012 (accessed January 30, 2015).

I have this long, illustrious love affair with Texas and especially Austin. It started years ago when I was on the road opening for Bob Schneider when he came out with the record called *Lonelyland* [in 2000]. I met his merch[handise] girl, Sandy, and she said, "You need to come play Austin." So I came, and I played at the Saxon Pub. [Austin-based artist manager] Roggie [Baer] sees me and says, "I want to book you." I was with a big booking agent, and I left them and went with Roggie. She said, "You should play this room called Cheatham Street Warehouse in San Marcos, Texas." "All right. What is it?" She said, "Oh, everybody plays there. It's legendary." That's all I had to hear.

So I went down and played a show. I met HalleyAnna there and Kent, and everybody was so nice. They were already fans of my [1998] record *One Left Shoe*. I remember talking to Kent about my song "Silver Lining." He really liked the overall vibe and that I mentioned hot dogs in the song. We had a discussion about hot dogs, and he liked the hook, a cool little drop-D guitar riff. He also liked that his daughter liked it and they were sharing it. We were talking about the recording of that song because I had a huge budget. Jim Keltner [Bob Dylan, John Lennon] played drums. Dean Parks [Paul Simon, Crosby, Stills and Nash] played the other guitar. The other thing about Kent is that he knows all the names of the session guys, the guys on the periphery.

I wrote "Silver Lining" with Jewel. We had already written "You Were Meant for Me," and we were just on this roll writing songs together. It seems we could do no wrong for a while. We'd get together, and song after song would come out. It was such an innocent stage of our lives. I was more of a sage rocker traveling the country, and she was a newbie down from Homer, Alaska. When we wrote "Silver Lining," I remember telling Kent, that we were looking for a word to rhyme with "buck," "stuck," and "luck." I came up with "John Kruk."

Steve Poltz, Hotel San Jose, Austin, February 8, 2014. Photo by Brian T. Atkinson

I used to play at Cheatham Street with Beaver Nelson and Adam Carroll and Scrappy Jud Newcomb. The first time I talked to James McMurtry was when I opened for him at Cheatham. I played the song that Barbra Streisand did, "The Way We Were." I remember James walked up and said, "I like the fact that you did that song, 'The Way We Were,' because I think it pissed off my fans. Anyone who pisses off my fans is a friend of mine. It took a lot of balls to sing." I wasn't even doing it to be ironic. I think it's a great song.

Every time I've been in there, it's almost like going to a college for songwriters, an institution of higher learning. All you have to do is ask, "What should I be listening to?" Kent's gonna know something good about some record. Also, I remember when he would sing his song about the blow-up doll, and I would harmonize on it. I love the fact that he just really cares about the song. That's really all that guy cares about. He lives for the song. He lives for songwriters.

Adam Carroll seemed like he was a natural for Cheatham Street. He's one of the few guys that actually has a draw there. Only certain people seemed to draw: James McMurtry, Todd Snider, Adam Carroll. I never drew a crowd, but Adam Carroll's songs are just such a part of Texas. He has a real eye for detail and seeing things, the way John Prine does. He has that great song, "Errol's Song." "When we're out of Schlitz, we're out of beer."

The thing is, we'd get in the van, and I couldn't even sit next to Adam. I can't even look at him. I don't know why, but I start giggling. They'd always separate us. I look at Adam, and he looks down, and we start laughing uncontrollably for the whole ride, and there's nothing being said. We drove all the way from Texas to California, and I swear Beaver would go, "Do not sit those guys together." We'd get in the back of the van, and I'd be crying, with tears coming out of my eyes. Scrappy and Beaver would say, "What are you guys laughing at?" "We don't know." There's just something that happens.[1]

[1] Steve Poltz, interview with Brian T. Atkinson, July 29, 2014. For more on Steve Poltz, see Frank Goodman, "Puremusic Interview with Steve Poltz," *Puremusic*, www.puremusic.com/84sp.html (accessed January 30, 2015); Steve Poltz, "21 Questions with Steve Poltz," *Nervous Breakdown*, April 2, 2011, www.thenervousbreakdown.com/spoltz/2011/04/21-questions-with-steve-poltz (accessed January 30, 2015). For more on Beaver Nelson, see www.beavernelson.com/. For more on Scrappy Jud Newcomb, see Melanie Haupt, "Scrappy Jud Newcomb," *Austin Chronicle*, www .austinchronicle.com/gyrobase/AMDB/Profile?oid=oid:398974 (accessed January 30, 2015).

# 57 | Scott H. Biram

Kent and I sat down one time in Cheatham Street in the middle of the day. He told me about how he liked to write songs in the morning before he talked to anybody else. I took that to heart. I feel like the best songs have come to me in the middle of the night. I wake up and just write that stuff down or in the morning. It was really good advice that's done a lot for my songwriting. I have a song called "Long Fingernail" that I wrote at five in the morning. I wrote "Lost Case of Being Found" right when I woke up. I saw my hands playing it when I woke up, and I wrote it down real fast. I've written so many songs in the morning. I'm laying there half awake and half asleep, thinking about words, and some little phrase will get stuck in my head that doesn't necessarily make sense, but it sounds cool. That's something else Kent mentioned that day: you're still in that dream state and in touch with something a little different than regular waking life.

Terri Hendrix and I used to play together a lot. I used to open up for her at the Triple Crown a bunch of times when I was first starting out. I haven't spoken to her for about fifteen years, but she wrote me an e-mail a couple years ago because I did this song "Ain't It a Shame," which is an old cover of a dude doing a harmonica-only song, a guy named E. R. Wilson. She asked would it be okay if she covered it. I was still doing a lot of covers when I started. I was doing a lot of Townes Van Zandt and Bob Dylan and Leadbelly and Woody Guthrie, and I had a few of my own. I used to do so many Townes songs: "Flyin' Shoes," "Lungs," "Our Mother the Mountain." I did pretty much every one of them off [Van Zandt's 1993 live album] *Rear View Mirror*. I still play them by myself at home, but I can't fit them into my repertoire for my live show. I try to play as many originals as I can.

I told Kent I wanted to play Triple Crown and Cheatham Street at the

Scott Biram, Triple Crown, San Marcos, Texas, July 2015. Photo by Christopher Paul Cardoza

same time, and he said, "Oh, that doesn't work. We tried that in the seventies with George Strait and the Cheyenne Social Club." He said the crowd got split when George tried to do both at the same time. He was always very adamant about not having bands playing other places in town. You had to be full-on Cheatham Street.

Then I played songwriter night one time with Randy Rogers and an older guy up there. This was like fifteen years ago, right when Randy was starting to gig. Someone asked me to come up there and sit in. That was the only gig I got to play there because Kent was all about mixing the crowds between the clubs. Being the first person to ever play at the Triple Crown, I couldn't really be like, "I'm never playing the Triple Crown." When I did that song circle thing with Randy, Kent came up to me after, and he goes, "Well, I guess you found a way to get in here."[1]

[1] Scott H. Biram, interview with Brian T. Atkinson, May 2, 2014. For more on Scott H. Biram, see Evan Schlansky, "Scott H. Biram," *American Songwriter*, March 23, 2014, www.americansongwriter.com/2014/03/scott-biram (accessed January 30, 2015); Austin Powell, "Blood, Sweat & Murder: The Gospel According to Scott H. Biram," *Austin Chronicle*, October 21, 2011, www.austinchronicle.com/music/2011–10–21/blood-sweat-and-murder (accessed January 30, 2015).

I went to Southwest [Texas State University] when it was still called Southwest with Randy Rogers. He still went by "Randall." He comes up to a group of us in class and goes, "Hey, I'm Randall, I've got a gig tonight. Wanna come?" I was, like, "Sure." That was before I was doing any music at all, but I was working at Lone Star Music for my internship. We walked in, and I was, like, "Whoa, this place is kick ass. So amazing." When I started doing music, I really wanted to play there because of the history.

I played my first gig at Cheatham Street in 2006. One time I was playing "Folsom Prison Blues," and a train goes by right at the end. It was perfect timing. We did a huge show opening for Randy there in 2009 when we were out with them for three weeks. They were pranking me starting the first night. I was, like, "Oh, no. You are not gonna prank me and not get retaliated on." My bass player and their merch[andise] guy and me dressed up in these huge chicken and gorilla suits and went flying across the stage during one of their songs. It was hilarious.

Kent and I obviously talked about songwriting, but most of the stuff I know about him is from Randy. Randy puts Kent on a pedestal, and he should. Kent's amazing. I remember hearing "Hill Country" and I was, like, "Dude, that's so cool." Randy was like, "Well, that's Kent's song." Kent and I talked about songwriting, and having someone like that, who writes such great songs, tell me he likes my songs is extremely validating.

I was starting to write a ton back then. I would have been playing "Ten Years Pass" and "Heartbreakers Hall of Fame" and "Slow Swinging Western Tunes" off my first record [2006's *Heartbreakers Hall of Fame*]. I remember one time I went to one of those jams, and I was kind of nervous. I had never done anything in front of a crowd playing guitar, and I knew a lot of people in there, so I at least felt comfortable trying a song. I went up and did "Ten Years Pass," which is about my hometown. After

Sunny Sweeney,
Waterloo
Records, Austin,
August 6, 2014.
Photo by Brian T.
Atkinson

I played "Ten Years Pass," Kent told me he liked it. He was really sweet. Kent said, "Everybody can relate to that song."

I saw everybody at Cheatham: Randy Rogers, Bruce Robison, Hayes Carll, Todd Snider, pretty much all the Texas guys. I saw Wade Bowen and Randy and somebody else. It was super. You know when you go to songwriter nights and you're, like, "Ugh." People are talking and they're just there to drink. Wade sings so good, and nobody was talking. I was like, "Yes, this is awesome." A lot of people have been introduced to Kent through Randy, a whole different group. That's really neat. Their relationship's so cool. Randy might as well be my brother. He's gotten pretty deep about Kent before. He loves him.

Kent is the nicest person on the planet. Everything he's done in life revolves around music, and he's so supportive. When I worked for Lone Star Music, Susan Gibson and I were talking about him, and she was, like, "There are some people who are supportive of women, and some are not. He's supportive of women as . . . artist[s]." That made me feel great. There are bars that won't let you play there because you're a girl. Kent was, like, "If you have the songs and the band, you can play."[1]

[1] Sunny Sweeney, interview with Brian T. Atkinson, May 22, 2014. For more on Sunny Sweeney, see Brian T. Atkinson, "Sunny Sweeney Causes a Stir with *Provoked*," CMT *Edge*, August 5, 2014, www.cmtedge.com/2014/08/05/sunny-sweeney-causes-a-stir-with-provoked, (accessed January 30, 2015); "CountryMusicRocks Interview with Sunny Sweeney," YouTube, https://www.youtube.com/watch?v=nGIgRGvOje4, August 23, 2011 (accessed January 30, 2015).

# 59 | Brennen Leigh

I used to play guitar for Sunny Sweeney when she didn't have anybody. I love Sunny's songwriting. She and I have a similar mind-set, and we're really good friends. It was easy for us to get together and sit down and write. She's very honest, maybe honest to a fault, in her writing. That makes what she writes extremely relatable. If it something's fluffy and fabricated and not based in reality, people might like the song, but deep down inside they'll feel like something [is] missing. There's none of that with Sunny. She writes real country songs.

I always felt like Kent's writing is really honest too, in and of itself. I love "Hill Country." That's a classic, classic song. It's much bigger than our little enclave of writers and musicians in Central Texas. That song could be about anywhere. It is about a specific region, but I think

Brennen Leigh and Noel McKay, Catfish Concerts, Austin, April 11, 2013. Photo by Brian T. Atkinson

that anybody who loves a place and sees that place being bought up by corporations can relate to that song. His song "Yesterday's Oatmeal" is so simply stated, and the language in it is like the way people speak in real life. That's a real gift, to be able to place casual, common language into a song and make it sound beautiful.

I think above all Kent's a philanthropist of art, someone who spreads and encourages and cultivates art. This world in the music business can be really thankless. There's not a lot of encouragement, especially when you're starting out. It's really good to have someone like Kent, and that's what makes him such a diamond in the rough. It's not like he'd just tell you your song's great no matter what. It's not just flattery. It's creating a positive environment that makes it free for creativity to exist.[1]

[1] Brennen Leigh, interview with Brian T. Atkinson, June 11, 2014. For more on Brennen Leigh and Noel McKay, see Brian T. Atkinson, "Brennen Leigh and Noel McKay Take on the World," CMT Edge, September 16, 2013, www.cmtedge.com/2013/09/16/brennen-leigh-and-noel-mckay-take-on-the-world (accessed February 6, 2015); Chrissie Dickinson, "New Style, Old School for Co-ed Country Duo," Chicago Tribune, September 27, 2013, http://articles.chicagotribune.com/ (accessed February 6, 2015).

"Yesterday's Oatmeal" is an extremely complicated song that's disguised as a simple song, and those are my favorites. It's a very vivid take on a relationship that's falling to pieces, clever and sad, and it makes you laugh at the same time. I think it's probably pretty easy to make someone sad, but it's making up for it by making light of the situation in a way. That's what makes it listenable. If it's just sad it doesn't work because nobody wants to be summarily brought down. Making you laugh is the thing that allows Kent to be unflinching.

Kent was really famous as we got in that circle of people who wrote songs in the vein that [my brother and I did in the McKay Brothers]. His songwriter night was the thing you wanted to go to and meet up with people doing the same thing. He was the linchpin of that community of people who were there for each other's moral support and wanted to hear each other's songs. Cheatham Street was the place, almost like a secret club. There weren't a lot of people sometimes, but everyone was glad to see each other. We all had the same goal: to be better writers.[1]

[1] Noel McKay, interview with Brian T. Atkinson, June 11, 2014.

Left to right: HalleyAnna Finlay, Jenni Finlay, Brennen Leigh, Noel McKay, and Rod Picott, Catfish Concerts, Austin, March 25, 2013. Photo by Brian T. Atkinson

# 61 | Jamie Wilson
## (The Trishas)

Even after I was married and moved away an hour south, I would still come up and do those songwriter nights whenever I could. One thing I learned from those Wednesday nights is that not all songs are good and that no matter how much you think they're good or not, you're playing them for the listener. It depends on how it affects the people listening to you. Kent was always really honest about which ones and which parts he liked. The ones he liked had imagery, and it's something I've tried to do more. It's like painting a picture with words and not wasting words, not just saying words just to have them there. If you don't need them there, just don't say anything. He always commented on images, so I try really hard to have an image in my mind and paint that for the listener and hope that it comes across. Those are always the ones that end up becoming favorites. He's right.

I think his mentoring is priceless, really. The mentor and venue owner and all [of] that [go] together, because Kent's gives anybody a gig whenever he thinks they're ready for a gig. He's looking out for you. He looks to see when he has folks coming in who'll have a big crowd, and he makes sure to hand-pick which of the younger kids he should give a shot. He'll give you a show on a Monday or a Tuesday night when he feels you're ready, and you have a forty-five-minute set. That's part of mentoring: making someone feel like they're worth it. There's nothing harder than getting gigs when you're first starting out, and there's nothing that drags you down more than people saying, "No, you can't have a gig because you don't have a crowd. We need a bigger name in here."

Kent gives shots. He doesn't care what your name is. As soon as he thinks you're ready, you're in. That's how you cut your teeth and figure

Jamie Wilson, Cheatham Street Warehouse, San Marcos, February 10, 2015. Photo by Brian T. Atkinson

out how you're doing and what your stage banter is and what works and what doesn't. You play empty shows at Cheatham Street all the time, and that's great, perfect for someone starting out to go play a room where there are only ten people. They're really great music fans, and they like Kent Finlay, and they go listen to whatever nineteen-year-old kid he's letting come play. It gives people confidence and chops. Then you work your way up to Thursday, Friday, Saturday nights. All of a sudden, you have a crowd. It's all because Kent gave you a chance. That's why people still come back and play his venue even after they're long gone from San Marcos. He did that for everybody. That's a big, big, huge thing. Every town should have one of those.[1]

[1] Jamie Wilson, interview with Brian T. Atkinson, April 25, 2014.

I had just moved to Wimberley in 2003 and had a lot of intense things happen that led me to songwriting. I was over thirty, so it was pretty intimidating to start that late, and also my brothers were at the top of their game. My brother Bruce [Robison] told me about songwriter night, and he really encouraged me to do it because of his own experience getting up onstage. So I took a similar path . . . because he was my touchstone as far as trying to figure out my way. I really wanted to get rid of the stage fright and let it all out of my system and see if anything stuck as a songwriter but do it anonymously.

I got up onstage for the first time, and I didn't even have a stage-ready guitar. Bruce lent me his old Guild that had a little pick-up in it. I get up and play one of the first songs I ever wrote, and Kent was sitting at the bar like he always does. I get off stage, and he says, "I want to talk to you. What's your name?" I told him my married name because I wanted to do this thing on my own merit. "I've never seen you before. I love your singing." He was so fatherly like he is when he talks to you. He gave me such beautiful, kind words about my material and said I had to keep coming back. That prompted me to continue. I basically promised him and myself that I'd stick to it.

Songwriter night is like a family. You see a lot of the same people every week. It's a community, and we support each other. You can get up on this stage, and everybody here will listen and interact with one another. You don't feel like you're in competition, and that makes it less frightening, for one thing. Kent gets up, and he's already established this rapport with everybody in the crowd by introducing himself and saying what songwriting meant to him. He did it differently every time, so you knew it was from the bottom of his heart.

The second or third night I got offstage, and he gave me this pen because he used to hand out pens to budding songwriters who he felt a

*Robyn Ludwick and Bill Chambers, Catfish Concerts, Austin, July 13, 2014. Photo by Brian T. Atkinson*

connection to or thought they were really promising in their craft. That meant a lot to me. So I kept going and made sure I was there every week, and I started writing more and getting more confident every time, and Kent was always there. Never missed a night. One night we just started talking, and I was like, *All right. This is it. I'm gonna tell him who I am.* You know, he liked me for who I am. I said, "Hey, Kent, my brother said to tell you hi." He looked at me and said, "Who's your brother?" I said, "Oh, Bruce Robison." He stood there in disbelief. Then he said, "Well, no wonder you're such a good writer."[1]

[1] Robyn Ludwick, interview with Brian T. Atkinson, October 28, 2014. For more on Robyn Ludwick, see Mando Lines, "Robyn Ludwick: *Little Rain*," *No Depression*, June 28, 2014, http://nodepression.com/album-review/robyn-ludwick---little-rain (accessed May 16, 2015); "Robyn Ludwick w/ Bill Chambers," Catfish Concerts," http://catfishconcerts.com/robyn-ludwick-w-bill-chambers (accessed January 30, 2015).

# 63 | Owen Temple

I was starting to play around more and was pretty lucky to get booked at Cheatham Street before I met Kent. I had heard about Cheatham Street, but the first time I showed up, I'm embarrassed to say, I was treating it just like another venue. Sure enough, there's Kent Finlay, and I start talking to him and realize that this is not a typical venue, and this was not your usual venue owner. There was a light in his eyes, and he took interest in the songs and stories. I thought, *Wait, there's more to this.* In the last fifteen years, I've gotten to know the rest. Kent listens. He responds to what you said, and it's not just hitting play on a tape recorder. It's a reflection or a great question about what you said, or he gives another angle. I'd say as far as listening and conversation, he's one of the best people for sharing and trading ideas and talking about what I was trying to do playing clubs and writing songs and what he was trying to do with his room and what he has done for so many years.

There was a period in my career where I played fewer shows, and I wasn't certain that songwriting was my future. I went to grad school and got a master's in psychology at the University of Wisconsin, and I was thinking about maybe teaching and research, but I came back and decided to be a full-time professional songwriter. It became 100 percent of my focus. After I went through that period and I had committed myself fully to the road and developing, . . . then we became closer. I guess it was when I'd taken on the full burden of the craft that our conversations and our friendship got deeper. Kent sensed the seriousness and the gravity and that I was trying to improve and write better songs.

Adam Carroll and Jordan Minor and me were having a conversation with Kent one time. Everybody who's been to one of the Cheatham Street potlucks knows that Kent nails pinto beans and black-eyed peas. We pointed that out, and he said, "You know, I'd just as soon eat cornbread

Owen Temple, International Folk Alliance, Kansas City, Missouri, February 23, 2014. Photo by Brian T. Atkinson

and beans as steak or caviar." We all thought that was true too. It's almost like, "Yeah, you got all you need with cornbread and beans. It's as satisfying as any other meal." You're wealthy if you just open your eyes. We just imagined a character who would fit in well at Cheatham Street and would have the gratitude that Kent's statement had when we wrote "Cornbread and Beans."

Usually, it's just one: songwriter. [Or] mentor. Curator. Teacher. Historian. He's all those. Kent has encouraged and participated in and helped create the best of what Texas music has been and is. In a lot of ways, Kent gave me a second chance after I backed off from music. A lot of venue owners would say, "No, no, you backed off. Sorry, I don't have time for you." He gave me the second chance, and we started building songs and nights and a friendship at Cheatham Street together. One of my dreams is that we will get to write a song together someday.[1]

[1] Owen Temple, interview with Brian T. Atkinson, March 26, 2014. For more on Owen Temple, see Brian T. Atkinson, "Owen Temple Opens Wide in *Stories They Tell*," CMT *Edge*, November 18, 2013, www.cmtedge.com/2013/11/18/owen-temple-opens-wide-in-stories-they-tell (accessed January 30, 2015); Brian T. Atkinson, "Five Highlights from Folk Alliance 2014," CMT *Edge*, February 26, 2014, www.cmtedge.com/2014/02/26/five-highlights-from-folk-alliance-2014 (accessed January 30, 2015).

# 64 | Jack Ingram

My first gig at Cheatham Street was sitting in with Todd Snider around 1996. We played for half an hour or forty-five minutes, and then Kent got up and played some songs. I don't think Kent really dug me that much. I didn't dig me that much, either. At some level, though, I think he knew the dedication I had to learning the craft. I had a career going, and people liked my songs, but I wasn't satisfied with what I was doing. I mean, I'm still not satisfied wholly, but at least I know [that] I know what I'm doing now. Back then I was just trying to put the pieces together. So Kent might not have been a fan of my songs, but I feel secure that he knew I cared as much as I should.

I knew of Todd in 1994 or when *Songs of the Daily Planet* came out. Somebody played me the record and said I'd like it. I did. At that point, we had the same booking agent, and in '96 they gave me three weeks of dates with Todd on the East Coast. That's where we formed a friendship. When I started to get to know Todd and figure out his whole deal I started to understand how important San Marcos was to his story and Kent was to him. I heard a lot about Kent on the road with Todd, and I learned more about him through watching Todd onstage talking about San Marcos and those stories down there and this guy named Kent Finlay, this mythical figure, Todd's godfather of songwriting. I said, "Hey, man, I've gotta go check this place out."

I love Kent's reverent and steadfast approach to songwriting. He just has such great respect for what it means to people. There are people who try their best to hold up traditions, and I think those people are important. They don't bend in their commitment to their one piece of the whole pie. Songwriting and storytelling are very important pieces down here in Texas. They manifest on the radio and in the shows you see, but, man, a guy like Kent understands songwriting and how to get

Jack Ingram, Austin City Limits
Music Festival, Austin, September
19, 2011. Photo by Brian T.
Atkinson

it and keep it and figure it out [and] take care of it in his own way. I have great respect for that lifelong commitment.

That first night Todd asked me to come sit in with him we were sitting in that green room drinking wine. [Darrell Staedtler] had written "Rewrite, Rewrite, Rewrite" on the wall. I remember reading that and thinking, I understand what he's saying there. I understand that editing yourself is important in songwriting, but it seemed like a message of being afraid. One of the most important things to me about songwriting is to quiet the inner voice telling you that you're not good enough and that you should shut up and that you shouldn't write about things that are truthful because they might hurt or be embarrassing. My answer to that was, "No, man, if you're at Cheatham Street, there's a pretty good chance you're in college or you're just starting out. I think the main thing to do is just write first. Don't edit yourself. Speak the truth in your song. If it's too wordy, then you go back and shorten it up. You need to write. Don't be afraid. Just write." So I wrote on the wall, "Bull shit. Write."

I used to stay with this guy named Tom Littlefield, who lived out off of

Fesslers Lane out by the airport in Nashville. On the way to his house was this shitty little motel called the Airways Motel. I was always intrigued by it, a tiny little place with like four or five rooms, with little barbecue pits beside it and free cable. In between tours with Todd, I hooked up with him and we sat down and started talking about this Airways Motel. I was just married at the time, so we talked about that, and I started laughing about this Airways Motel, and somewhere or another it turned into a song about tough marriage can be, how tough figuring yourself out can be. I think it was the first song that Todd and I wrote together.

Kent comes into the story with Todd's ability to create characters. I love them. They seem like characters even though they're coming from somewhere in him. You don't feel like you're always staring down the barrel of his . . . gun. . . . You feel like these are crazy characters, fun people to hang out with. It's hard to write stories from inside yourself. I have a hard time creating something that's not me, and I feel like Todd brings that element to things that we write. He takes the truth and blows it up and makes a great story.

Somebody told me that "Barbie Doll" was very closely tied to Kent because of his song "Plastic Girl." I think Todd and I were just sitting around talking about girls from Dallas. If I remember right, we were out at his place on Highway 100, and we were talking about shows. I think I said something about girls from Dallas being Barbie dolls, but I'm sure he came up with the title "Barbie Doll," the entitled girl. Todd came up with most of that song, which has always been fairly obvious to me. My contribution to that song was more the details of the girl I see every night. I've always been grateful to Todd for bringing that kind of energy, that thing that seems so unreal but real at the same time.

One of the fun things about this style of music is how closely things are related, how close the bloodline is: Kent to Todd, Todd to me. I've always loved that about this whole thing. I used to sit and read the credits to Jerry Jeff and Willie Nelson and Waylon Jennings records. Everybody's name would show up on everybody else's credits. It seemed like some eternal hang, and Cheatham Street was just part of the fabric.

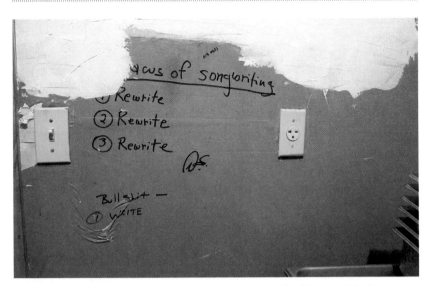

Darrell Staedtler and Jack Ingram's inscriptions on the wall of the Woodshed
Recording Studio, San Marcos. Photo by Brian T. Atkinson

Kent's a curator. He knows and practices the craft and has figured out
songwriting, and he's tried to show other people and send them on their
way with the tools they need to get better. He's just a gentle soul who
cares about what he's doing. Maybe other people know Kent's motiva-
tion for the club, but for me his whole thing revolves around the song
and making sure people knows what that skill is. I love that he took in
Todd and Randy Rogers, two people who had charm and charisma to
carve out a place in the world as an entertainer. By Kent teaching them
the respect he has for songwriting, they go do their thing with varying
degrees of success, and they're teaching others skills that Kent taught
them. I don't know how that's remembered, but when I think of Kent,
I can just see him in the club, the guy who says, "This is important. We
need to learn this stuff." Talking about songwriting. Smiling.[1]

[1] Jack Ingram, interview with Brian T. Atkinson, June 5, 2014. For more on Jack Ingram, see Brian
T. Atkinson, I'll Be Here in the Morning: The Songwriting Legacy of Townes Van Zandt (College Station:
Texas A&M University Press, 2012), 198–204; Rich Koster, Texas Music (New York: St. Martin's
Press, 1998), 73; "Jack Ingram Interviews & Exclusives," CMT Artists, www.cmt.com/artists/jack-
ingram/video-interviews (accessed January 30, 2015)

# Afterword

Kent Finlay sat up straight later that afternoon. He nodded us over. Smiled bittersweetly. His inner circle—immediate family, close friends, songwriters—gathered tightly around him. "The hills of Cow Gap," he whispered. Then the spark returned behind his eyes, and two dozen redbirds gathered in the backyard. He cleared his throat and started: "The hills of Cow Gap stood rugged and awesome / But you have to have fill dirt when you're building a road." We helped through the verses and all joined for the choruses. "They call it the Hill Country / I call it beautiful," we sang and swayed as he conducted. "I'd call it progress if it could be saved."

Kent knew this would be the last he ever sung. After we finished, he took a deep breath and told us directly: "I love my songwriters. I love Texas. I love the Hill Country. I love Cheatham Street. I love my children. I love this house. I love you all. I've had such a great life." He closed his eyes.

You simply couldn't write a better coda.

Kent Finlay (center) with the Texas Playboys. Photo by Don Anders; courtesy Finlay family archives

James Kent Finlay—man and mentor, father to three and father figure to hundreds, songwriter and song finder—passed away overnight at his home in Martindale, Texas, on Texas Independence Day 2015. He was seventy-seven. Legions immediately felt the silence. "Country music—and just music in general, really—lost a great friend," George Strait said in a statement the next day. "His legend will live forever in Texas. We'll never forget our friend Kent Finlay."[1] The last song we know he heard was Adam Carroll's "Highway Prayer."

He left us just days before we submitted this book's manuscript to the publisher. We are thankful that we were able to share passages from the book with him during his final weeks. He was so proud. All these songwriters paying homage. "Wow," he'd say, "that's really something." The words ring true. If we kept going on about how much we learned about living life fully as we wrote *Kent Finlay, Dreamer*, we'd go on and on forever. Instead, we'll say this: Kent, we love you. Thank you for all the memories. We're sure the state of Texas would agree: you were one of a kind.

—Brian and Jenni
March 5, 2015

[1] Billy Dukes, "George Strait Mourns Loss of Clubowner, Friend and Early Believer Kent Finlay," Taste of Country, March 2, 2015; www.tasteofcountry.com/ (accessed March 6, 2015)

## "Highway Prayer"

For those who the road is all that matters
For them who have lived on borrowed time
For those who the seeds of life have scattered
For them who are too far down the line

For those who have lived on next to nothing
Playing in a bar in Jacksonville
With nothing but the songs that they are singing
With nothing but the spaces left to fill

*Here's a highway prayer*
*Here's a highway song*
*Don't stay too late*
*Don't cry too long*

You're coming home
Home again
You can tell them all
Where you've been

I used to think the road was all that mattered
I used to like to live on borrowed time
I used to like to live on next to nothing
But I'm still out here living line by line

Living in some old torch singer's memory
Out here on the road to Tennessee
The place where all our songs and prayers go sailing
I'll say one for you if you'll sing one for me

*Here's a highway prayer*
*Here's a highway song*
*I won't stay too late*
*I won't cry too long*

I'm coming home
Home again
I'll tell them all
Where I've been

—Adam Carroll
*Old Town Rock and Roll*, 2008. Art Mob Music (BMI)

# Postscript

*If he were doing it for money | He'd be doing something else | All he wants from life | Is a chance to give himself | To some future generation | Who'll be touched when they've heard | His rhymes and his rhythms | And the wisdom of his words.*
　—Kent Finlay, "The Songwriter," 1968

"The Songwriter" embodies what he gave to the community. I think anybody who writes songs should listen to that song. Kent laid out this template that said, "Hey, it's not wrong to want to spend all your time in a notebook with a guitar in your hand. In fact, there might be some value in that." That song really hit me. There's a lot that's vulnerable: this could be me. I'm this guy who's out there living line to line and being okay with it although I have a tumultuous life. It's saying it's okay for you too, if that's your inclination. Do you want to write songs? Do you really? "The Songwriter" says what that Charles Bukowski poem ["As Crazy as I Ever Was"] says: if you don't wake up at 3:00 a.m. and have the urge and necessity to go to the typewriter, then you're not really a writer.
　—Matt Harlan[1]

[1] Matt Harlan, interview with Brian T. Atkinson, May 19, 2014.

*Matt Harlan, Catfish Concerts, Austin, May 19, 2013. Photo by Brian T. Atkinson*

```
┌─────────────────────────────────────────────┐
│                                             │
│                                             │
│                                             │
│                 Kent Finlay                 │
│                  Dreamer                    │
│                                             │
│         512-357-6237                        │
│         512-787-4432                        │
│         papernapkin@cheathamstreet.com      │
│                                             │
└─────────────────────────────────────────────┘
```

*Kent Finlay's business card*


## The Players: Biographies

**Marcia Ball**, born March 20, 1949, in Orange, Texas, but raised in Vinton, Louisiana, has won several Grammy Awards for her blues albums, including *Presumed Innocent* (2002) and *So Many Rivers* (2004). The current Austin resident, a legendary pianist whose style frequently moves between blues and country and jazz, was inducted into the Austin Music Hall of Fame in 1990. (www.marciaball.com)

**Scott H. Biram**, born April 4, 1974, in Lockhart, Texas, has released eight studio albums from his lo-fi debut *This Is Kingsbury?* (2000) through *Nothin' but Blood* (2014) for Bloodshot Records. Biram's unique one-man band approach matches folk against fright as he combines influences including Doc Watson and Lightnin' Hopkins with punk rock attitude. (www.scottbiram.com)

**Willy Braun**, born March 5, 1978, in Challis, Idaho, has fronted Reckless Kelly for nearly two decades. The buoyant live act has released eight albums, from their debut *Millican* (1998) through *Good Luck & True Love* (2011) and *Long Night Moon* (2013), which won a Grammy Award for Best Album Package. The band was formed in Bend, Oregon, but has lived in Austin, Texas, for years. (www.recklesskelly.com)

Cody Canada, born May 25, 1976, in Pampa, Texas, was the lead singer for Texas Red Dirt music pioneers Cross Canadian Ragweed for more than fifteen years. The band found significant commercial success with their albums *Soul Gravy* (2004), *Garage* (2005), and *Mission California* (2007), among others. In 2011, Canada left Cross Canadian Ragweed and formed Cody Canada and the Departed. (www.thedepartedmusic.com)

Hayes Carll shot his career from a cannon with *Trouble in Mind* (2008). The Woodlands, Texas, native's third album, a vibrant vortex backing machetes ("Faulkner Street") with memories ("Knockin' over Whiskeys"), catapulted him from rising talent into an established tunesmith. The current Austin resident, born January 9, 1976, achieved even wider spread success with *KMAG YOYO* (2011). (www.hayescarll.com)

Joe "King" Carrasco entered public consciousness with his buoyant *Party Weekend* (MCA Records, 1983). Carrasco, born in December 6, 1953, in Dumas, Texas, furthered his reputation as a good-time Tex-Mex rock and roller with albums such as *Bordertown* (1985), *Hot Sun* (1999), and *Que Wow* (2012). Carrasco splits his time between Central Texas and Puerto Vallarta, Mexico. (www.joeking.com)

Adam Carroll, born March 19, 1975, in Angleton, Texas, sketches vibrant vignettes capturing the bustling Gulf Coast region ("Bernadine," "Rough Side Accordion"). Indelible landscapes frequently frame the journey ("Errol's Song"). "There are only a couple songwriters who consistently catch my ear," Slaid Cleaves says. "Adam shows the gold in life's little details." (www.adamcarroll.com)

Slaid Cleaves's *Still Fighting the War* (2013) spotlights an artist in peak form two decades into his career. Cleaves's seamless collection elegantly delivers vivid snapshots as wildly cinematic ("Rust Belt Fields") as they are carefully chiseled ("Voice of Midnight"). Cleaves, born June 9, 1964, in Washington, DC, but raised in Berwick, Maine, currently lives in Austin. (www.slaidcleaves.com)

Ernie Durawa, born December 4, 1942, in San Antonio, Texas, grew up with legendary Tex-Mex rocker Doug Sahm. He joined Sahm's super-group Texas Tornadoes, also featuring iconic accordionist Flaco Jimenez and keyboardist Augie Meyers, in 1989. The band's eponymous debut (1990) earned a Grammy Award for Best Mexican-American Album. (www.erniedurawadrums.com)

Omar Dykes, born in McComb, Mississippi, formed Omar and the Howl-ers in Hattiesburg, Mississippi, before relocating to Austin, Texas, in the mid-1970s. In 1987, Dykes signed with Columbia records and released the band's most commercially successful album, *Hard Times in the Land of Plenty*. Dykes's gritty vocals shine as brightly on the recent *Runnin' with the Wolf* (2013). (www.omarandthehowlers.com)

Robert Ellis's diverse commercial debut *Photographs* (2013) accents time-less folk ("Friends Like Those") with buoyant country ("Comin' Home") and smooth soul ("What's In It for Me?"). The current Nashville, Ten-nessee, resident, born in Houston, followed with the critically acclaimed *The Lights from the Chemical Plant* (2014). (www.robertellismusic.com)

Joe Ely, born February 9, 1947, in Amarillo, Texas, has worked with punk pioneers the Clash through alt-country progenitors Uncle Tupelo and seemingly everyone between. He's frequently worked with Guy Clark, John Hiatt, and Lyle Lovett on acoustic song-swap tours. Ely has released two dozen records, from *Honky Tonk Masquerade* (1978) through *Satisfied at Last* (2011). He lives in Austin. (www.ely.com)

Radney Foster, born July 20, 1959, in Del Rio, Texas, first found success with his duo Foster and Lloyd ("Crazy Over You," "Texas in 1880"). Foster launched his solo career with the popular *Del Rio, TX 1959* (1992) and has thrived as both a producer and songwriter for the past two decades, with collaborations with the likes of the Randy Rogers Band and mainstream country star Keith Urban. (www.radneyfoster.com)

Jon Dee Graham's finest songs find healing within heartbreak ("Codeine," "Beautifully Broken"). The longtime Austin resident, who wrote and played guitar in the groundbreaking bands True Believers and the Skunks, has held a Wednesday-night residency with James McMurtry at the capital city's Continental Club for two decades. He was born February 28, 1959, in Eagle Pass, Texas. (www.jondeegraham.com)

William Clark Green, born in May 1986, in Tyler, Texas, began writing songs while attending Texas Tech University in Lubbock. Green's early albums such as *Dangerous Man* (2008) and *Misunderstood* (2010) showed the young artist rapidly rising in the Texas Red Dirt scent. Green hit his stride with *Rose Queen* (2013), which features "Hangin' Around," a cowrite with Kent Finlay that topped the Texas music radio chart. (www.williamclarkgreen.com)

Cleve Hattersley served as primary songwriter for Greezy Wheels, a pioneering cosmic cowboy band during the movement's seventies heyday. He went on to become booking agent for New York City's legendary Lone Star Cafe before reforming Greezy Wheels around millennium's turn after a nearly quarter century hiatus. (www.cleveandsweetmary.com)

Diana Finlay Hendricks, born December 28, 1957, has chronicled Texas culture for both daily newspapers (*San Marcos Daily Record*) and national magazines (*Chili Monthly* magazine). Hendricks, a lifelong resident of San Marcos, co-owned Cheatham Street Warehouse for more than ten years. Her children with Kent Finlay are Jenni, Sterling, and HalleyAnna Finlay. (www.dianahendricks.com)

Terri Hendrix, born February 13, 1968, in San Antonio, Texas, particularly showcases her vast musical diversity on *Cry Till You Laugh* (2010). Bluesman Sonny Terry ("Hula Mary"), Rodney Crowell ("Slow Down"), and jazz icon Ella Fitzgerald all haunt her ninth studio album, which she calls the "yin and yang of life." Hendrix recorded *Live in San Marcos* (2001) at Cheatham Street Warehouse. (www.terrihendrix.com)

Ray Wylie Hubbard, born November 13, 1946, in Soper, Oklahoma, initially gained widespread recognition as the songwriter behind the Jerry Jeff Walker hit "Up against the Wall, Redneck Mother" (1973). Hubbard escaped that albatross by enlivening later albums such as *Snake Farm* (2006) and *Grifter's Hymnal* (2012) with his mystical Hill Country blues and literate songwriting. (www.raywylie.com)

Jack Ingram, born November 15, 1970, in The Woodlands, Texas, was a popular regional singer-songwriter for more than a decade before skyrocketing his single "Wherever You Are" to number one on the Billboard country charts. He's since charted six songs in the top forty, including "Love You," "Measure of a Man," and "Barefoot and Crazy." Ingram currently lives in the Austin area. (www.jackingram.net)

Eric Johnson, born August 17, 1954, in Austin, Texas, achieved mainstream notoriety with his platinum third album *Ah Via Musicom* (1990) and the record's Grammy-winning single "Cliffs of Dover" (Best Rock Instrumental Performance). Johnson's seven studio records spotlight his fluid movement between rock and country and blues and jazz guitar. (www.ericjohnson.com)

Hal Ketchum scored early with his major-label debut *Past the Point of Rescue* (Curb Records, 1991) and the top-ten songs "Small Town Saturday Night," "Hearts Are Gonna Roll," and the title track. For his eleventh studio record, *I'm the Troubadour* (2014), he moved to Austin's Music Road Records. Ketchum, born April 9, 1953, in Greenwich, New York, lives in the Texas Hill Country. (www.halketchum.com)

Brennen Leigh and Noel McKay craft story songs with equal measures heart ("Great Big Oldsmobile") and humor ("Let's Go to Lubbock on Vacation"). Clearest evidence: the Austin-based songwriters' debut duo collection *Before the World Was Made* (2013). "These are modern-day duets a la George Jones and Melba Montgomery," producer Gurf Morlix says, "but with sophisticated songwriting." (www.brennenleighand-noelmckay.com)

Robyn Ludwick, born September 15, 1972, in Kerrville, Texas, followed her brother Bruce Robison's footsteps by cutting her teeth at Cheatham Street Warehouse's songwriters' night. She went on to release the critically acclaimed albums *For So Long* (2005), *Too Much Desire* (2008), *Out of These Blues* (2011), and *Little Rain* (2014). "Robyn is one of the bravest writers I know," Walt Wilkins says. (www.robynludwick.com)

john Arthur martinez, born June 10, 1961, in Austin, Texas, made his mainstream mark by finishing second place on the first season of television talent show *Nashville Star* in 2003. He has released six studio albums, including *Spinning Our Wheels* (1998), *Long Starry Night* (2004), and *Purgatory Road* (2009), which features the title track cowritten with Kent Finlay. (www.johnarthurmartinez.net)

James McMurtry, born March 18, 1962, in Fort Worth, Texas, spins stories with a poet's pen ("Ruby and Carlos") and a painter's precision ("Choctaw Bingo"). His latest album *Complicated Game* (2015) echoes high-water marks such as *Just Us Kids* (2008) and *Childish Things* (2005) with literate storytelling ("Long Island Sound") and sharp narratives ("South Dakota"). (www.jamesmcmurtry.com)

Monte Montgomery's "When Will I" became a regional anthem in the late 1990s. Additionally, he wrote the theme song for the popular television show *Last Man Standing*. Montgomery, born August 11, 1966, in Birmingham, Alabama, but raised in Central Texas, arguably best displays his range as a guitarist on his bending and stretching live interpretation of the Dire Straits song "Romeo and Juliet." (www.montemontgomery.net)

Steve Poltz, born February 19, 1960, in Halifax, Nova Scotia, earned early success as a founding member of indie rock band the Rugburns. However, he might be best known through his collaborations with pop-folk singer Jewel, most notably cowriting her smash hit "You Were Meant for Me" and appearing in its video. The San Diego resident tours heavily on the folk circuit. (www.poltz.com)

Joe Pug, born Joseph Pugliese on April 20, 1984, in Greenbelt, Maryland, earned his first significant break opening for legendary outlaw country figure Steve Earle as Earle toured behind his album *Townes* (2009). The current Austin resident's debut *Messenger* (2010) and the following *The Great Despiser* (2012) connect the dots between. (www.joepugmusic.com)

Bruce Robison, born June 11, 1966, in Bandera, Texas, has notched several country hits with his songs, most notably the three number ones: "Angry All the Time" (Tim McGraw and Faith Hill, 2001), "Travelin' Soldier" (Dixie Chicks, 2003), and "Wrapped" (George Strait, 2006). Robison and his wife Kelly Willis have released two albums of duets (2013's *Cheaters Game* and 2014's *Our Year*). (www.bruceandkellyshow.com)

Randy Rogers, born August 23, 1979, in Cleburne, Texas, cut his teeth at Cheatham Street Warehouse before releasing his debut album *Live at Cheatham Street Warehouse* (2000) and going on to become a highly successful country artist. Indeed, the Randy Rogers Band has charted more than a half-dozen singles, including "Tonight's Not the Night (For Goodbye)" (2005) and "One More Sad Song" (2012). (www.randyrogersband.com)

Will Sexton, born in 1970, in San Antonio, Texas, and his brother Charlie both learned guitar from the "Godfather of Austin Blues" W. C. Clark while still in their teens. They began opening for Stevie Ray Vaughan around the same time at Cheatham Street. Will Sexton has collaborated with Waylon Jennings, Stephen Stills, and Joe Ely, with whom he cowrote the popular "All Just to Get to You." (www.willsexton.com)

Todd Snider, born October 11, 1966, in Portland, Oregon, admits to being the "natural bullshitter in the neighborhood." Peak early collections such as *Live from the Daily Planet* (1994) through the excellent *East Nashville Skyline* (2004) back the claim. The longtime Nashville resident currently balances his longtime solo career with the supergroup side project Hard Working Americans. (www.toddsnider.net)

Darrell Staedtler, born December 27, 1940, in Llano, Texas, lived in Nashville for a decade from the mid-sixties before returning to Texas. He wrote hit songs for George Strait ("Blame It on Mexico"), Lefty Frizzell ("Honky-Tonk Stardust Cowboy"), and the Willburn Brothers ("It's Another World"). The City of Llano declared June 10, 2010, Darrell Staedtler Day.

George Strait, born May 18, 1952, in Poteet, Texas, launched his star at Cheatham Street Warehouse before Kent Finlay drove him to Nashville for his first recording session. Strait later became one of the most popular singers in country music history, earning the nickname King of Country. Strait's first hit "Unwound" in 1981 began a career including an unprecedented sixty number one country music singles. (www.georgestrait.com)

Jesse Sublett, born May 15, 1954, in Johnson City, Texas, made greatest waves in music as a songwriter and bassist in punk band the Skunks. Sublett turned toward more literary pursuits in the 1980s. He has written a memoir (2004's *Never the Same Again: A Rock and Roll Gothic*) as well as pulp fiction books such as *Rock Critic Murders* (1990) and *Tough Baby* (1990). (www.jessesublett.com)

Sunny Sweeney immediately turned heads with her debut *Heartbreakers Hall of Fame* (2006) and its keen storytelling ("Ten Years Pass") and stunning vocals ("Here Lately"). Sweeney, born December 7, 1976, in Longview, Texas, followed with the more polished *Concrete* (2011), which notched her first top-ten single ("From a Table Away"). She garnered significant critical acclaim three years later with *Provoked* (2014). (www.sunnysweeney.com)

**Owen Temple**, born September 4, 1976, in Kerrville, Texas, released six strong albums—from his debut *General Store* (1997) through *Mountain Home* (2011)—before his early-career high-water mark *Stories They Tell* (2013). The Austin resident's latest collection spotlights a singular songwriter in peak form. Accordingly, Temple has been a Kerrville Folk Festival New Folk Songwriting Competition finalist twice (2007 and 2011). (www.owentemple.com)

Texas native **Travis Warren** became the lead singer of the alternative rock band Blind Melon ("No Rain," "Change") ten years after bandleader Shannon Hoon passed away in 1995. The band's only album during his tenure, *For My Friends* (2008), closes with Warren's "Cheetum Street," a real-life acoustic lament framing his childhood split between parents in Texas. (www.blindmelon.com)

**Walt Wilkins**'s songs—particularly resonant on *Fire, Honey and Angels* (1999) and *Plenty* (2012)—move both cerebrally and spiritually. Wilkins, born December 29, 1960, in San Antonio, Texas, earned a wider reputation when Pam Tillis recorded his high-water mark "Someone Somewhere Tonight" on her album *Rhinestoned* (2007). He cowrote "Blanco River Meditation #2" with Kent Finlay.

**Jamie Wilson**, born August 10, 1981, in Houston, Texas, broke into the Texas country scene as a lead singer in the Sidehill Gougers before embarking on a solo career. Her *Dirty Blonde Hair* EP (2010) displayed Wilson's significant songwriting chops, which carried her into work with the Trishas, an all-female singer-songwriter band with Kellie McKwee, Liz Foster, and Savannah Welch. (www.jamielinwilson.com)

## Selected Songs by Kent Finlay

| Song Title | BMI Song Number |
| --- | --- |
| "Between You and Me" | 14545292 |
| "Blanco River Meditation #2" | 14545293 |
| "Boys with Guitars" | 1454294 |
| "Buffalo Gal" | 157830 |
| "Bull Rider's Mother" | 5308047 |
| "Christmastime in Luckenbach" | 212698 |
| "Close Enough to You" | 6000289 |
| "Counting the Days Till Christmas" | 249667 |
| "Denied Dreams" | 5308046 |
| "Dividing the Estate (A Heart at a Time)" | 9976561 |
| "Don't Tell Me" | 3907836 |
| "Double Load Blues" | 11752405 |
| "Fadin' Out Fadin' In" | 7780830 |
| "Get You off My Mind" | 13015767 |
| "Girl Named Texas" | 6716657 |
| "Gone Again" | 5308048 |
| "Hangin' Around" | 14746323 |
| "Here Come the Heartaches Again" | 9228162 |
| "Honky Tonk Memory" | 18159710 |
| "House" | 17938343 |
| "I Don't Want to Talk It Over" | 620473 |
| "I Got a Good Woman" | 9228166 |
| "I Got the Dog and He Got You" | 9228158 |
| "I'm Going Coastal" | 9199245 |
| "I've Never Been in Jail" | 686553 |
| "Lost" | 5771952 |
| "Midland on My Mind" | 6024243 |
| "Mud Daubers Are a Comin'" | 1022152 |
| "Paying My Dues" | 1159460 |
| "Plastic Girl" | 1178669 |
| "Purgatory Road" | 10783805 |

| | |
|---|---|
| "Reaganomic Blues" | 1232569 |
| "Rosalinda Where Are You Tonight?" | 14698137 |
| "Santa Claus Is Coming Christmas Night" | 1288920 |
| "Saturday Night in a Redneck Town" | 14553455 |
| "She Knows My Weaknesses and Loves Me Anyway" | 5798187 |
| "Soda Pop" | 1367452 |
| "Somebody Took My Sunshine Away" | 9228165 |
| "Spinning Our Wheels" | 6716673 |
| "Statistician's Blues" | 6000301 |
| "Sweet on You" | 14553456 |
| "Tennessee Whiskey and Texas Swing" | 5798189 |
| "There's a New Girl in My Life" | 1489044 |
| "They Call It Hill Country" | 14553457 |
| "They Call It the Hill Country" | 1493531 |
| "24 Hours a Day" | 3719203 |
| "We're Going Home for Christmas" | 1618308 |
| "What Makes Texas Swing" | 1635642 |
| "What Might've Been" | 2124494 |
| "When I Come Back to Farming" | 14937492 |
| "Who Says It's Lonely at the Top" | 5798179 |
| "Wisdom Wall" | 14937491 |
| "Workin' Man" | 14553458 |
| "You Could've Left Me" | 8178950 |

## Authors' Websites

Brian T. Atkinson: www.briantatkinson.com
Jenni Finlay: www.jennifinlaypromotions.com
Eight 30 Records: www.eight30records.com
Squeaky String Productions: www.squeakystring.com

# Index